CONRAD, LANGUAGE, AND NARRATIVE

In this re-evaluation of the writings of Joseph Conrad, Michael Greaney places language and narrative at the heart of his literary achievement. A trilingual Polish expatriate, Conrad brought a formidable linguistic self-consciousness to the English novel; tensions between speech and writing are the defining obsessions of his career. He sought very early on to develop a 'writing of the voice' based on oral or communal modes of storytelling. Greaney argues that the 'yarns' of his nautical raconteur Marlow are the most challenging expression of this voice-centred aesthetic. But Conrad's suspicion that words are fundamentally untrustworthy is present in everything he wrote. The political novels of his middle period represent a breakthrough from traditional storytelling into the writerly aesthetic of high modernism. Greaney offers an examination of a wide range of Conrad's work which combines recent critical approaches to language in poststructuralism with an impressive command of linguistic theory.

MICHAEL GREANEY is Lecturer in English Literature at Lancaster University. This is his first book.

CONRAD, LANGUAGE, AND NARRATIVE

MICHAEL GREANEY

Lecturer in English Literature,
Lancaster University

CAMBRIDGE
UNIVERSITY PRESS

PUBLISHED BY THE PRESS SYNDICATE OF THE UNIVERSITY OF CAMBRIDGE
The Pitt Building, Trumpington Street, Cambridge, United Kingdom

CAMBRIDGE UNIVERSITY PRESS
The Edinburgh Building, Cambridge CB2 2RU, UK
40 West 20th Street, New York, NY 10011–4211, USA
10 Stamford Road, Oakleigh, VIC 3166, Australia
Ruiz de Alarcón 13, 28014 Madrid, Spain
Dock House, The Waterfront, Cape Town 8001, South Africa

http://www.cambridge.org

First published 2002

Printed in the United Kingdom at the University Press, Cambridge

Typeface Baskerville Monotype 11/12.5 pt.   *System* LaTeX 2$_\varepsilon$ [TB]

A catalogue record for this book is available from the British Library.

Library of Congress Cataloguing in Publication data
Greaney, Michael.
Conrad, language, and narrative / Michael Greaney.
p.   cm.
Includes bibliographical references and index.
ISBN 0 521 80754 9 hardback
1. Conrad, Joseph, 1857–1924 – Language.   2. Conrad, Joseph, 1857–1924 – Technique.
3. Fiction – Technique.   4. Narration (Rhetoric)   I. Title.
PR6005.04 Z7355   2001
823'.912 – dc21   2001035601

ISBN 0 521 80754 9 hardback

To my parents

Contents

vii

Acknowledgements

In writing this book I have benefited from the advice and support of many colleagues and friends. My special thanks are to David and Jan Ashbridge, Neil Bennison, David Carroll, Robert Hampson, Tony Pinkney, Tony Sharpe, Anne Sweeney, the late Tony Tanner, and Andrew Tate. The Department of English at Lancaster University provided the stimulating and supportive context in which this book was written; I have also benefited from the assistance of the Joseph Conrad Society (UK).

Introduction

In 1907, when he already had some of the greatest novels in English to his name, Joseph Conrad confessed to Marguerite Poradowska that 'l'Anglais m'est toujours une langue etrangère'.[1] Like so many of the major modernist authors whose work has been assimilated into the canon of English literature, Conrad was an 'outsider', a foreigner on whom posterity has conferred the status of honorary Englishman, but who probably belongs with that later group of twentieth-century writers described by George Steiner as 'extraterritorials'.[2] Born in the Czarist-ruled Polish Ukraine in 1857, Conrad joined the French navy in 1874 before obtaining a berth on a British vessel in 1878. Seventeen years later he published his first novel, *Almayer's Folly*, the beginning of a career that produced some of the most venturesome fiction in the literature of what was his third language. The transformation of Józef Teodor Konrad Korzeniowski into Joseph Conrad was a prodigious feat of literary self-fashioning; but Conrad took profound exception to being paraded in the literary journalism of his day as 'a sort of freak, an amazing bloody foreigner writing in English'.[3] It is very easy – and rather misleading – to assume that the English language was an obstacle between Conrad and creative expression; one could argue with equal justification that Conrad's sense of estrangement from his adoptive tongue was the very enabling condition of his fiction. We would do well to consider the possibility that Conrad wrote his masterpieces *because* rather than *in spite* of the English language.[4] Not, I should hasten to add, because English is in any sense superior to Polish or French, although this idea strongly appeals to F. R. Leavis, who maintains that 'Conrad's themes and interests demanded the concreteness and action – the dramatic energy – of English.'[5] It might be truer to say that the English language is, from the very start, one of the central 'themes and interests' of this trilingual Polish expatriate. Conrad found in his acute feeling for the slipperiness of words the resources to reinvent the language of English fiction. His formidable

I

self-consciousness over the possibilities of language and narrative is the central focus of this study.

One of the defining idiosyncrasies of Conrad's literary career was his powerful distrust – even, at times, hatred – of writing. His letters treat the act of writing as a form of exquisite mental torture producing an excruciatingly slow trickle of words. 'Sisyphus was better off',[6] he declared, in a mood of extravagant self-pity that is entirely characteristic of these dispatches from the purgatory of literary composition. Nowhere is Conrad's writerly ordeal more graphically rendered than in the famous lament to his French translator Henry-Durand Davray: 'La solitude me gagne: elle m'absorbe. Je ne vois rien, je ne lis rien. C'est comme une espèce de tombe, qui serait en même temps un enfer, ou il faut écrire, écrire, écrire.'[7] Less melodramatically, Conrad's friend and sometime collaborator Ford Madox Ford confirms that 'Conrad hated writing more than he hated the sea . . . *Le vrai métier de chien.*'[8]

No less hateful for Conrad than the business of writing is its textual product. His fiction is mesmerized by the spoken word – the charismatic oratory of Mr Kurtz, the sibylline counsel of Stein, the richly enigmatic storytelling of Charlie Marlow – but deeply inimical to its own medium. Mutilated texts are scattered across the landscapes of his fiction: Kaspar Almayer makes a bonfire of the account books and musty documents strewn around his office; the first print-run of Don José Avellanos's history of Costaguana is dismembered in the Monterist insurrection; the evening newspaper that reports the Greenwich explosion is ripped in two by Winnie Verloc.[9] Not content with visiting punitive violence on every species of writing within the novels, Conrad's fiction endeavours to negate its own writtenness, usually by ventriloquizing a raconteur – Marlow or one of his many counterparts – behind whose garrulous personal presence the text silently effaces itself.

Throughout his literary career Conrad sought to overcome – or circumvent – the perceived limitations placed on his creative enterprise by the rebarbative impersonality of 'cold, silent, colourless print'.[10] His fiction is haunted by the dream of a community of speakers sharing a language of transparent referentiality and self-present meaning, such as an intimate circle of storytellers or the close-knit crew of a merchant vessel. Raymond Williams describes the ship in Conrad as a 'knowable community of a transparent kind',[11] a sort of waterborne *Gemeinschaft* whose values and traditions are preserved in the anecdotal wisdom of generations of sailors. Conrad's ships and storytelling cliques are his versions of what one scholar, in another context, has termed 'linguistic utopia'.[12]

Idealized speech communities of this sort locate authentic language in some distant, pre-Gutenberg era when the living voice enjoyed a kind of discursive monopoly on human communication.

Conrad's nostalgia for a lost era of authentic storytelling finds expression in the very structures of his fiction. He famously masquerades as a 'vocalizing' narrator or raconteur in the Marlow tales, 'Youth', 'Heart of Darkness', *Lord Jim*, and *Chance*; many of his short stories – including 'Karain: A Memory', 'Lagoon', 'Amy Foster', 'Falk: A Reminiscence', 'Gaspar Ruiz', 'The Informer', 'The Brute', 'The Partner', 'Because of the Dollars', 'The Warrior's Soul', 'Prince Roman', and 'The Tale' – are also narrated by 'word of mouth'. Edward Said has written on Conrad's fondness for the 'tale-within-a-tale' device as follows:

the dramatic protocol of much of Conrad's fiction is the swapped yarn, the historical report, the mutually exchanged legend, the musing recollection. This protocol implies (although often they are explicitly there) a speaker and a hearer and . . . sometimes a specific enabling occasion. If we go through Conrad's major work we will find, with the notable exception of *Under Western Eyes*, that the narrative is presented as transmitted orally. Thus hearing and telling are the ground of the story, the tale's most stable sensory activities and the measure of its duration; in marked contrast, seeing is always a precarious achievement and a much less stable business.[13]

As Said remarks, Conrad's writings do not always aspire to the condition of speech: as well as *Under Western Eyes*, there is *The Arrow of Gold*, whose 'source' is a 'pile of manuscript', and 'The Inn of the Two Witches', whose 'source' is a 'dull-faced MS.' found by its narrator in a box of second-hand books.[14] But Conrad prefers on the whole to let it appear that his writings originate in informal conversation or oral tradition. Of 'Karain', for example, he claims that 'there's not a single action of my man (and good many of his expressions) that can not be backed by a traveller's tale'.[15] The first hint for *Nostromo* was a 'vagrant anecdote' (p. vii); the subject of *The Secret Agent* was suggested in a 'casual conversation' with a friend, who 'may have gathered those illuminating facts at second or third hand' (pp. ix–x). Even such tales as 'The Idiots', 'An Anarchist', and 'Il Conde', which don't formally deploy the tale-within-a-tale convention, purport to be the most recent links in a chain of *spoken* narratives.

Conrad clearly believed he had much to gain by emphasizing the structural and idiomatic continuity between the written word and the living voice; most of his fiction takes the form of what Jacques Derrida would call a 'writing of the voice'.[16] In Derridean terms, Conrad's use of the storytelling proxy is a classically 'phonocentric' gesture, one that

reproduces an age-old privileging of speech over writing. In his critique
of the cult of the voce, Derrida takes up the structuralist model of language as an impersonal system of signs – which he chooses to call *écriture*,
or 'writing-in-general'. His most notorious formulation of his sense of
speech as a function of writing is given in his discussion of Rousseau.
In the course of unmasking the logic of supplementarity in Rousseau –
the sense that writing always already inhabits the speech upon which it
is supposedly parasitic – Derrida has cause to reflect on his own critical
methodology. It would be tempting, he suggests, to believe that having demystified Rousseau's philosophy of language we have arrived at a
transparent understanding of the man and his thoughts. But he accepts
that his own discourse is subject to the same compromising textuality
that it detects in Rousseau. In the light of this caveat, Derrida issues a
caution that has become the master-slogan of deconstructive criticism:
'il n'y a pas de hors-texte'.[17]

Similar questions of language, truth, and textuality are broached in
'Outside Literature', Conrad's tribute to the scrupulous exactness of
expression that characterizes the language of 'Notices to Mariners'.[18]
Conrad differentiates confidently in this article between literary and non-
literary language, between 'imaginative literature', where metaphorical
language proliferates freely, and sailors' discourse, which is free from any
trace of indeterminacy. However, the nagging possibility that there may
well be nowhere 'outside' literature, or nothing outside text, is never
far from the surface of Conrad's fiction. Conrad had plenty of reasons
for wanting to get outside literature: he wanted to appeal to a mass
readership; he wanted the spoken voice to override the dead letter; above
all, he wanted to escape *literariness*, the duplicity and figurality of language.
In a moment of wishful thinking, Conrad once styled himself 'the most
unliterary of writers';[19] but the impossibility of getting 'outside literature'
into some utopian realm of mathematical plainness or pure orality is one
of the constant revelations of his fiction.

Conrad's fiction is not unwavering in its commitment to the living
voice; the antithesis between the spoken word and 'cold, silent, colourless print' gradually develops into a more complex opposition between
authentic and inauthentic language – where the latter comprehends any
spoken or written discourse that flaunts its own uprootedness, figurality
or ambiguity. He displays a particular and sustained fascination with
gossip, a 'speech genre'[20] – to borrow Mikhail Bakhtin's useful term –
that constantly threatens to pervert authentic storytelling. Conrad's nautical raconteur, Charlie Marlow, is deeply exercised by the problem of

raising his narrative discourse above the level of mere gossip. Conrad's heroes, including Kaspar Almayer, Tom Lingard, Mr Kurtz, Lord Jim, Nostromo, Razumov, Flora de Barral, Axel Heyst, and Doña Rita, all learn what it means to be subjected to invasive narrative curiosity. The storytelling on which the Conrad speech community thrives degenerates all too easily into gossip, hearsay, or rumour, discourses that are degraded and emptied of authority by thoughtless repetition.

An important corollary of Conrad's suspicion of language is his ambivalent conception of silence.[21] Though his conspicuously talkative characters like Schomberg and Kurtz are markedly less sympathetic than laconic men of action like Falk, MacWhirr, and Singleton, Conrad never allows any simple antithesis between degraded speech and ideal silence. The predicament of painfully inarticulate figures like the title-hero of *Lord Jim* or Stevie in *The Secret Agent* might remind us that voicelessness has little to recommend it. The reticent intellectual does not fare much better in Conrad than the tongue-tied Everyman: Razumov can't turn his back on the subversive whispers of his fellow students; nor can Axel Heyst escape the world of degraded public language into wordless isolation. Language soon pours into any discursive gap left by silence: consider, in this regard, the following description of Peyrol in *The Rover*: 'His reticence about his past was of the kind that starts a lot of mysterious stories about a man.'[22] The ideal speech community in Conrad always seems on the point of becoming its opposite – an echo chamber of free-floating rumours, irresponsible gossip, and disembodied voices.

If problems of voice, textuality, and silence bear significantly on Conrad's speech communities, then so too do broader ideological issues of gender and nationality. For example, there appears to be no place for women in his storytelling cliques; a representative illustration of this exclusion is 'Falk', where a group of men, 'all more or less connected with the sea', swap yarns in a Thames hostelry whose dilapidated condition

brought forcibly to one's mind the night of ages when the primeval man, evolving the first rudiments of cookery from his dim consciousness, scorched lumps of flesh at a fire of sticks in the company of other good fellows; then, gorged and happy, sat him back among the gnawed bones to tell his artless tales of experience – the tales of hunger and hunt – and of women, perhaps![23]

This diverting sketch of Neolithic raconteurs reveals one of the unspoken norms of Conrad's speech communities: storytelling is an exclusively male occupation. There are plenty of female voices in Conrad, but there is no female equivalent of Charlie Marlow; indeed, Conrad's privileging

of the voices of Marlow and his counterparts is problematically dependent on his repression of non-male storytelling.

Also marginalized in Conrad's fiction are non-European voices.
Notoriously, in 'Heart of Darkness', African voices are audible only as
formless jabbering or menacing shrieks, as riotously incomprehensible
as the wilderness from which they emanate. These voices are excluded
from the tale's narratorial ensemble, emptied of semantic content and absorbed into the jungle's sinister acoustic. Conrad's sense of the limitations
of face-to-face storytelling becomes increasingly visible in the political
fiction, where he can't seem to extend his speech communities beyond
the horizons of European experience. By the time of *Nostromo*, there is a
profound tension between the intimate experience of storytelling and the
vast compass of Conrad's political vision. Whether charting the impact
of Anglo-American imperialism on a turbulent Latin American republic,
evoking a London infested with eastern European dissidents, or imag-
ining democratic Geneva as an outpost of Russian autocracy, Conrad's
political fiction exhibits a breathtaking geographical scope which belies
his reputation as the novelist of isolation and inwardness. Incipient in
Nostromo, and more fully realized in *The Secret Agent* and *Under Western Eyes*,
is a transformation of the community of speakers into a conspiracy whose
members are linked by what they *don't* know about one another. In *The
Secret Agent* and *Under Western Eyes* the central criminal plot – Vladimir's
projected attack on Greenwich, the assassination of Mr de P– – becomes
a metaphor not only for modern society in the deadlock of permanent
conspiracy but also for the secretive, duplicitous text of modernism.

The shape of the present study reflects my sense that Conrad's mount-
ing suspicion of language, together with his diminishing faith in utopian
dreams of oral or communal modes of storytelling, culminates with
Under Western Eyes. This book falls into three parts: the first examines
changing ideas about speech and writing in the nautical prose and early
Malay fiction, in 'Falk' and *Victory*, and in *The Arrow of Gold*; the second
devotes three chapters to the role of Charlie Marlow, whose problematic
'yarns' – 'Youth', 'Heart of Darkness', *Lord Jim*, and *Chance* – are the
products of an intricate confrontation between traditional storytelling
and modernist reflexivity; the third considers how, in Conrad's great sequence of political fiction – *Nostromo*, *The Secret Agent*, and *Under Western
Eyes* – his linguistic nostalgia finally yields to the rebarbative textuality
of modernism.

My critical method has necessarily been influenced by the debates
that have transformed literary studies in recent years; no serious student

of Conrad can afford to ignore the impact of feminist, postcolonialist, Marxist, and poststructuralist reinterpretations of his work.[24] My own predisposition is towards those schools of thought that focus our attention on matters of language, form, and structure. This preference for a formalist approach takes its cue from Edward Said, whose provocative contention that Conrad's 'working reality, his practical and even theoretical competence as a writer, was far in advance of what he was saying'[25] might be seen as the jumping-off point for the present study. Though not theoretical in any systematic sense, this study draws on elements of deconstruction, narratology, and Bakhtinian dialogics whenever they seem to clarify and enliven our understanding of the texts in question. One possible objection to my critical method of 'close reading', with its detailed and sustained attention to matters of textual detail, might be that it encloses itself in a linguistic utopia where words refer only to other words, with politics and history conveniently ignored. The celebrated Conrad scholar Eloise Knapp Hay was memorably dismissive of those who approach his work armed with nothing more than 'verbal ingenuity and the Oxford English Dictionary'.[26] Implicitly a defence of 'close reading' from the charge of historical myopia, this study is written in the belief that one can analyse the dense linguistic textures of Conrad's narrative without sacrificing a proper awareness of its potent political themes.

PART I

Speech communities

CHAPTER ONE

'The realm of living speech': Conrad and oral community

This chapter will examine the speech communities of Conrad's nautical writings and early Malay fiction, and consider the emergence in his short stories of a model of storytelling that would find its most sophisticated expression in the Marlow narratives. I want to suggest that, whatever affiliations Conrad has to premodern linguistic communities, his engagement with the powerful tensions between speech and writing, telling and listening, leads him not backwards into traditional storytelling but forwards into a precocious modernism.

Conrad's memoir, *The Mirror of the Sea*, can be read as an introduction for the lay reader to the lexicon of the sea, full of praise for the exemplary clarity of 'sea-talk' and disdain for 'lubberly book-jargon'.[1] Sloppy imitations of 'sea-talk' in the popular press incur Conrad's special displeasure: the bogus romanticization of second-hand versions of nautical life is doubly obnoxious to this sailor-turned-writer. There is a certain territorial pride in Conrad's scornful critique of those ignorant landlubbers who toy carelessly with the sailor's linguistic tools. Conrad sees nautical language as a precision instrument earmarked for a specific purpose and not to be tampered with by amateurs. He lingers on particular words and phrases with affection – and perhaps a touch of envy towards sailors, who, unlike professional writers, experience no trouble in finding *le mot juste*:

He [the chief-mate] is the man who watches the growth of the cable – a sailor's phrase which has all the force, precision, and imagery of technical language that, created by simple men with keen eyes for the real aspect of the things they see in their trade, achieves the just expression seizing upon the essential, which is the ambition of the artist in words. (20–1)

As Conrad indicates in 'Outside Literature', journalists who ransack the sailor's lexicon for picturesque phraseology are likely to distort it in ways that would, at sea, be not merely careless but dangerous. His quarrel with journalism is part of a wider suspicion of metaphoricity, ludicity, rhetoric – any form of language in which words are displaced from their primary context and deployed elsewhere as mere ornament.

Conrad was powerfully attracted by the idea of the sea as the place where language is in good order; but his maritime fiction tends to focus on the idea of 'sea-talk' in crisis. Jacques Berthoud has argued that a certain tension between figurative and technical vocabularies is a defining characteristic of the language of Conrad's nautical fiction.[2] In 'Typhoon', Captain MacWhirr's obdurate level-headedness is seen in his suspicion of metaphor, his blank incomprehension of 'images in speech'.[3] But the narrator is not himself constrained by MacWhirr's embargo on metaphor. Indeed, the whole tale, ostensibly a celebration of the invincible stolidity of MacWhirr, is constructed around the metaphorical association of the elemental chaos of the typhoon with the below-decks mayhem caused by the rioting 'coolies'.[4] A similar discursive division between technical and imaginative language is evident in *The Nigger of the 'Narcissus'*. The 'official' languages of the *Narcissus* are the raucous banter of the sailors and technical 'sea-talk' of the kind celebrated in *The Mirror of the Sea*. The stability of this linguistic community is challenged by the voices of the shifty agitator, Donkin, and the mortally ill hypochondriac, James Wait. 'His picturesque and filthy loquacity' – the narrator scornfully reports of Donkin – 'flowed like a troubled stream from a poisoned source'.[5] Donkin's scrawny physique is taken as evidence of his moral inferiority to his burly taciturn shipmates who are nevertheless gullible enough to swallow his complaints: 'inspired by Donkin's hopeful doctrines they dreamed enthusiastically of the time when every lonely ship would travel over a serene sea, manned by a wealthy and well-fed crew of satisfied skippers' (p. 103). If Donkin stokes up political discontent, James Wait connects with the crew at a more disturbing level: his charismatic voice has many of the sailors cringing with dread when their minds ought to be on the job in hand. These mutinous voices precipitate a breakdown of order that is marked by linguistic confusion: 'squabbling uproar', 'execration', 'confused shouts', 'deafening hubbub'. When Captain Allistoun re-asserts his authority, the language of the ship once more displays terse efficiency as the gruff staccato interchange of orders given and received replaces the cacophony unleashed by Wait and Donkin. The novella's 'victory' over linguistic disorder is sealed when, at the threshold of death, James Wait writhes in 'a frantic dumb show of speech' (p. 151) – the loss of his fine baritone is the novel's 'vengeance' on the subversive charms of rhetoric. The danger for the crew of the *Narcissus* is narcissism: a self-regarding pride in their own achievements or a self-serving concern for their own comfort. The linguistic equivalent of narcissism would be the infatuation of a text with its own medium: this, for Conrad, would be a decadent betrayal of the proper instrumental and referential functions of language. Yet the famous valedictory sentences of this novella, where Conrad conjures up 'a shadowy ship manned by a crew of Shades' (p. 173), show just how ready he was to transform the vivid seascape into a world of symbols.

It would be naïve to expect Conrad's sea fiction – or any of his writings – to abound in images of perfect speech communities. But in *An Outcast of the Islands* Conrad presents a sketch of the Rajah Lakamba's retinue which might stand as his image of an ideal oral community:

Small groups squatted round the little fires, and the monotonous undertone of talk filled the enclosure; the talk of barbarians, persistent, steady, repeating itself in the soft syllables, in musical tones of the never-ending discourses of those men of the forests and the sea, who can talk most of the day and all the night; who never exhaust a subject, never seem able to thresh a matter out; to whom that talk is poetry and painting and music, all art, all history; their only accomplishment, their only superiority, their only amusement. The talk of camp fires, which speaks of bravery and cunning, of strange events and of far countries, of the news of yesterday and the news of tomorrow. The talk about the dead and the living – about those who fought and those who loved.[6]

This community of storytellers is remarkable above all for its lack of divisions. It is not subdivided into tellers and listeners; nor has experience been hived off into the institutional subdivisions of poetry, painting, and so forth. There is no strict division between imaginative and informational narrative – or even between the living and the dead. That the voices of the dead are audible is a given for the Malay characters in this novel; they retain a vital organic connection with an ancestral past from which the Europeans have cut themselves off. The Malay raconteurs who gather in Lakamba's courtyard inhabit a 'community of speech' of the sort nostalgically evoked, according to Derrida, in the writings of Jean-Jacques Rousseau and Claude Lévi-Strauss. Prior to the advent of writing there was, according to the phonocentric tradition, a 'community immediately present to itself, without difference, a community of speech where all the members are within earshot'. The determinants of 'social authenticity' detected by Derrida in phonocentric thought are '[s]elf-presence, transparent proximity in the face-to-face of countenances and the immediate range of the voice'. Writing, meanwhile, is stigmatized by Rousseau and Lévi-Strauss as the precondition of 'social *distance*'. After the invention of writing, people are held 'so far apart as to be incapable of feeling themselves together in the space of one and the same speech, one and the same persuasive exchange'.[7]

Tensions between speech and writing figure significantly in Conrad's Malay trilogy, which charts the commercial and political rivalries between indigenous peoples, Arab traders, and European expatriates in the south-east Asian Archipelago. The trilogy is much concerned with the emergence of a new bureaucratic order that produces such paltry specimens as Kaspar Almayer and Peter Willems to carry on the work begun by the pioneers of empire. Marooned in what is for them a God-forsaken tropical backwater, these expatriate derelicts are playing out the closing stages of miserably unsuccessful careers. Almayer, in particular, seems mesmerized by the spectacle of his own failure: he views life through a narcotic haze, dreaming of the bonanza of upriver gold deposits that will secure his future in Europe. Much of the ignominious pathos of Almayer's demise derives from the steady revelation of his helplessly peripheral position in a complex speech community teeming with rumours and intrigue. As the sole white man in the region, Almayer is not privileged but 'ruined and helpless under the close-meshed net of their intrigues' (*Almayer's Folly*, p. 27) – intrigues masterminded by his nemesis Babalatchi. A smokescreen of secrecy lies over the Pantai power-struggles: the illicit gunpowder trade, Lingard's navigational secrets, the mineral deposits of fabulous value in Dyak territory, and the mystery of Dain's 'death' remain all but invisible to Almayer.[8] Blissfully ignorant of his rivals' plots and the nocturnal liaisons of his wife and Babalatchi – themselves staple subjects of fireside gossip in the settlement – he ends up comprehensively routed by his commercial rivals, cuckolded by his wife, badly let down by his mentor and foster-father, and abandoned by his daughter.

The accent in these novels is on the power of speech. Writing, deployed as an instrument of cultural dominance by Europeans, is largely ineffectual. The decrees and statutes of the Dutch authorities, the maps and guide-books wielded by European tourists, and the ledgers and account-books of Almayer and Willems, collectively attest to a strain of cultural imperialism that enshrines authority in the written word. The commitment of Almayer, the 'empty-headed quill-driver', to 'conscientious book-keeping' (*An Outcast*, p. 300), conjoins a reference to his failed career as a trader with his broader affiliation to print culture. Almayer's arrival in Sambir, armed with bureaucratic paraphernalia and 'books of magic' (*An Outcast*, p. 299), causes a sensation; but 'he could not guide Patalolo, control the irrepressible old Sahamin, or restrain the youthful vagaries of the fierce Bahassoen with pen, ink, and paper. He found no successful magic in the blank pages of his ledgers' (p. 300). The contents of his neglected office, which seems like the 'temple of an exploded superstition', are musty relics of print culture. The trilogy charts the skirmishes between speech and writing in a community where the spoken word reigns. The novels contain an anatomy of oral culture: the tales, recitals, and prayers that define a sense of belonging; the formal parleys and illicit eavesdropping, elaborate flattery, and tendentious rumours that express friction between rival factions. In this word-of-mouth culture information and opinion are manipulated with a subtlety that defies the authority of the written word. The plot of *Almayer's Folly* hinges on the identity of a disfigured corpse which Babalatchi persuades everyone is that of Dain Waris. Both Almayer and the Dutch authorities are hoodwinked by Babalatchi: the impromptu inquest of the Dutch search-party can only acquiesce in the popular rumours about Dain's death. Not for the last time in Conrad, popular opinion wins out over forensic inquiry as an arbiter of identity. If the locals do not possess the firepower to reclaim territory, they do manage the climate of opinion more adroitly than the Dutch. It is appropriate that Almayer should ultimately use his record books, the appurtenances of his pretence of cultural superiority, to light the fire that consumes his house: it is the final capitulation of writing to speech.

Conrad's literary career might be seen as a determined but deeply problematic bid to negate writing, to found a writerly aesthetic on the principles of oral or communal storytelling. Some of his earliest tales, such as 'The Lagoon' and 'Karain: A Memory', set a pattern that would be reproduced in a dozen or so short stories as well as in the Marlow narratives: the narrator (usually anonymous) reports and frames the oral performance of a storyteller. 'Karain', in which a Malay chief narrates to British sailors, is a valuable opportunity for Conrad to stage his own peculiar relationship with his British readership – the Polish exile becomes a British author by masquerading as a travelling storyteller. The storytelling situation provides a reassuring context for the negotiation of multiple frontiers: between the homely and the exotic, speech and writing, past and present, colonist and colonized.[9] A sketch of the ideal dialogic encounter is given in the preamble to Karain's confession:

There are those who say that a native will not speak to a white man. Error. No man will speak to his master; but to a wanderer and a friend, to him who does not come to teach or to rule, to him who asks for nothing and accepts all things, words are spoken by the camp-fires, in the shared solitude of the sea, in riverside villages, in resting-places surrounded by forests – words are spoken that take no account of race or colour. One heart speaks – another one listens.[10]

Storytelling is idealized as dialogue between equals that transcends all cultural boundaries in an intimate communion of souls. Except that, in Conrad's version, the modern decline of storytelling might well be traced to the fatal moment when tellers were differentiated from listeners, or specialist storytellers set apart from passive auditors. One might even argue that the fundamental division in Conrad's characters is that between his often long-winded or aggressive vocalizers – Kurtz, Marlow, Schomberg, Willems, Captain Mitchell, Adolf Verloc, as well as various anonymous storytellers – and those unsung heroes of his fiction, the listeners, like Heyst, Razumov, Jim, and Stevie. If anything characterizes the relationship between speaker and listener in Conrad, it is a sense of imbalance; the relationship tends to be a power-struggle rather than a partnership.

Linguistic partnership is at the centre of a story from *Within the Tides* that deserves to be more widely known if only because it presents with diagrammatic clarity the curiously self-divided nature of Conrad's fiction. 'The Partner' is the story of an encounter in a coastal hostelry between the narrator (a writer of fiction for periodical magazines) and a gruff stevedore who also proves to be something of a raconteur. The stevedore's narrative – the tale of two joint owners of a ship, one of whom instigates a nautical insurance swindle – is preceded by a discussion on the art of storytelling in which the ruffian accuses professional writers of fabricating narratives and tampering with the truth for the sake of artistic effect. No artistic pretensions disfigure his own story, which is simply a bid to dispel the canard that Captain Henry Dunbar committed suicide on the *Sagamore* – the stevedore leaves artistry to the effete purveyors of magazine fiction. Aggressively unceremonious, he plunges headlong into his tale without bothering to establish a context; he jumps between different segments with no regard for smooth transitions or descriptive interludes; and he continually rebuffs his interlocutor's polite expressions of curiosity and understanding. Considerably bemused by the stevedore's forthright anecdote, the narrator decides that leaving it unadorned would be the next best thing to *viva voce* delivery:

This story to be acceptable should have been transposed to somewhere in the South Seas. But it would have been too much trouble to cook it for the consumption of magazine readers. So here it is raw, so to speak – just as it was told to me – but unfortunately robbed of the striking effect of the narrator.[11]

These concluding words put into play a set of conceptual oppositions (raw/cooked, speech/writing, nature/culture) which serve as the axes against which we must plot Conrad's own decentred position as would-be storyteller and reluctant novelist. The tale's narrative technique is, then, a structural analogy to its content. The partnership between bluff honesty (the ruffian) and ingratiating fraudulence (the writer) reflects the collaboration between the honest partner (George Dunbar) and the fraudulent partner (Cloete, himself a veteran of the advertising trade and therefore no stranger to linguistic deception). Ultimately, the sense of creative rivalry expressed in the story is indicative of the division in Conrad's own artistic identity between traditional storyteller and professional author. The tale scores a satirical point at the expense of the stevedore's naïveté, his puritanical equation of fiction with fraudulence, but it registers a deeper uneasiness at its own status as an artistic commodity. Not only is the storyteller closer to experience than the novelist, but he also enjoys a more intimate rapport with his audience; the professional author is condemned to write in isolation for a readership with whom he has a solely economic relationship.

As numerous critics have remarked, the best introduction to this aspect of Conrad's art is Walter Benjamin's essay 'The Storyteller: Reflections on the Works of Nikolai Leskov'.[12] That Benjamin makes no reference to Conrad is immaterial, so richly suggestive of Conrad is his elegy for traditional storytelling. Benjamin weaves around his short critical biography of Leskov a series of profound reflections on the demise of 'communicable experience' in the modern age, a demise of which the disappearance of the storyteller is the primary symptom. Benjamin's 'storyteller' is a composite figure. On the one hand he is the archetypal raconteur of some bygone, but recognizably medieval age; on the other, 'storyteller' is an honorific title for members of that dying breed of writers whose fiction most *resembles* the ancient oral forms. 'Less and less frequently', writes Benjamin, 'do we encounter people with the ability to tell a tale properly'.[13] For Benjamin the authenticity of discourse decreases as a function of its distance from real human speech. This decline, Benjamin contends, coincides with the ascendancy of print culture – and, in particular, with the rise of the story's most formidable rival genre: the novel. Alone among literary genres, the novel subsists independently of oral tradition:

The storyteller takes what he tells from experience – his own or that reported by others. And he in turn makes it the experience of those who are listening to his tale. The novelist has isolated himself. The birthplace of the novel is the solitary individual, who is no longer able to express himself by giving examples of his most important concerns, is himself uncounseled, and cannot counsel others.[14]

Benjamin reserves special praise for those writers – as well as Leskov he cites Stevenson, Poe, and Kipling – whose work goes some way to healing the rift between the living voice and the spoken word.

It would be easy to caricature Benjamin's argument as an exercise in naïve phonocentrism that gestures vaguely to some Golden Age when everyone displayed an innate flair for storytelling that has somehow been amputated by post-Gutenberg technology. In fact, Benjamin issues a stern reproof to such glib nostalgia for the good old days of fireside yarns:

The art of storytelling is reaching its end because the epic side of truth, wisdom, is dying out. This, however, is a process which has been going on for a long time. And nothing would be more fatuous than to want to see in it merely a 'symptom of decay', let alone a 'modern' symptom. It is, rather, only a concomitant symptom of the secular productive forces of history, a concomitant that has quite gradually removed narrative from the realm of living speech and at the same time is making it possible to see a new beauty in what is vanishing.[15]

Rather than lamenting the demise of storytelling, we should savour its poignant afterlife in the works of those latter-day storytellers whose writings honour the primacy of the living voice. However, Benjamin is notably unspecific on the question of *when* 'written' storytelling supplanted its oral predecessor. Perceptible in his essay is what Raymond Williams, in his survey of literary representations of 'organic community', terms the 'escalator'-effect: as soon as one tries to affix the label to a specific historical period, it begins to recede over the horizon of myth.[16] The same is true of Benjamin's narrative: is he evoking a pre-1914, pre-1800 or pre-Gutenberg utopia? His use of overlapping historical frames is part of a strategic synthesis of myth and history in the service of an adversarial diagnosis of modernity. Conroy terms Benjamin 'the storyteller of the storyteller', and his essay is indeed less a scholarly article than a meta-story. Poised ambiguously between myth and history, Benjamin's storyteller is a protean construct whose ghostly afterlife in Leskov is a reproach to modernity's slow dehumanization of language.

The evacuation of narrative from the 'realm of living speech' entails the loss of that discursive space for intersubjective contact in which the living voice once flourished. The fragmentation of the realm of living speech has left individuals incarcerated in their own subjectivity, like the shell-shocked Great War veterans who returned from the front 'not richer, but poorer in communicable experience'.[17] For Benjamin, the ravaged battlefields of the War are a scar on history itself, marking the decisive watershed between traditional storytelling and modern print culture. Nowhere is the decrease in the communicability of experience better exemplified than in the words of modernism's archetypal neurotic speaker, J. Alfred Prufrock, who is locked in perpetual mental rehearsal of possible conversations where language fails woefully to convey intent: 'It is impossible to say just what I mean!'

A further obstacle to open communication in Conrad is the language barrier. A considerable number of his speech communities are multilingual environments – a (non-exhaustive) survey of his fiction would reveal that Dutch, Malay, Arabic, and Chinese are spoken in *Almayer's Folly* and *An Outcast of the Islands*; French and a number of unidentified African languages are spoken in 'Heart of Darkness'; French and German are spoken in *Lord Jim*; Spanish and Italian are spoken in *Nostromo*; Russian, French, and German are spoken in *Under Western Eyes*. Although it is not always made obvious, considerable quantities of Conrad's dialogue are to be understood as having been 'translated' from a non-English source language. It is sensible to assume, for example, that French was the day-to-day business language for European traders and sailors on the Belgian Congo in 'Heart of Darkness'; equally, we can reasonably suppose that Italian is the common language of the Viola household in *Nostromo*. Whilst these linguistic differences are often unobtrusively noted by Conrad's narrators, they are rarely made the centre of attention, and only a handful of Conrad critics have given them more than a cursory glance.[18] At times in Conrad the language barrier is solid and visible – 'Amy Foster' is his most poignant depiction of non-communication between speakers of different languages – but elsewhere it seems rather conveniently to evaporate: Karain's narrative, for example, seems to present no problem to his Anglophone auditors, whilst in *Lord Jim* Marlow gathers information in Patusan without recourse to a phrase-book. It occasionally seems as though Conrad regarded English as the *lingua franca* of every corner of the earth; and even when English is not spoken, other languages are readily translatable into English. Problems of translation do occasionally surface – in 'Heart of Darkness', for example, where Marlow fails to understand various African languages; in *Lord Jim*, a novel which in two key scenes (Marlow's interviews with the French Lieutenant and Stein) effectively becomes bilingual; and in *Under Western Eyes*, a text narrated by a professional translator obsessed with cultural miscommunication. In these texts the privileged status of English as the *lingua franca* or master-discourse of Conrad's fictional worlds does not go unchallenged; indeed, one of Conrad's greatest achievements as a writer is his use of an imperfectly Anglicized fictional discourse that bears the traces of many different speech communities. In the light of the various challenges to traditional storytelling and open self-expression in Conrad's fiction – the sense of imminent failure of communication and communicability in a fragmented, polyglot world – his motif of 'secret sharing' seems an increasingly remote ideal; but as Conrad's linguistic scepticism intensifies, the possibility of striking up an intimate rapport with a near-stranger in which 'one heart speaks – another one listens' becomes all the more precious to him.

'"Listening"', says Councillor Mikulin in *Under Western Eyes*, '"is a great art."'[19] If this observation is true, he has discerned an intriguing gap in our knowledge of aesthetics. Evidently, listening is an art that has achieved greatness without having its governing aesthetic principles subjected to the same kind of intellectual scrutiny that is commonly applied to, say, oratory or literary composition. 'Perhaps', Jan B. Gordon remarks, 'we will understand the way in which speech is preserved in texts when we develop a hermeneutics of listening (an audiology?) to match our post-modern fascination with grammatology.'[20] On the face of it, the inauguration of such an 'audiology' would be an unconscionably ambitious undertaking, raising on the one hand the problem of methodological limits – philosophy, psychology, and linguistics would all have a contribution to make; and, on the other, the problem of resistance to theory – it is not easy to let go of the notion that hearing is as natural and spontaneous as breathing, and in as little need of theoretical explication.[21] Still, given his trilingualism, his decentred position in the polyglot culture of modernism, and his encounters with the African and Asian outposts of empire, Conrad's fiction contains plenty of stimulating material for the would-be audiologist.[22]

Conrad's famous description of the purpose of his art – 'by the power of the written word to make you hear, to make you feel . . . before all, to make you *see*' – is more often remembered for its rousing crescendo than its perceptual sequence: the shift from hearing through feeling to vision is one that the fiction itself struggles to perform. For Aaron Fogel, the claims of Conrad's aesthetic manifesto confirm the patterns of his fiction, where listening and hearing are the primary senses: 'Some *over*hearing, some intense aural idea or obsession, comes first – hearsay, legends, the image of talk, frightening information – and tempts the character into a seemingly compulsive participation.'[23] No small part of this 'compulsive participation' is the effort to *see* the source of all this fascinating discourse, to clap eyes on the Axel Heyst or Lord Jim or Mr Kurtz about whom we hear so much and of whom we are permitted to see so little. Probably the most sustained instance of '*over*hearing' in Conrad's writings is the following passage in *A Personal Record*, which recalls his first encounter with the reputation of 'Kaspar Almayer':

I had heard of him at Singapore; I had heard of him on board; I had heard of him early in the morning and late at night; I had heard of him at tiffin and at dinner; I had heard of him in a place called Pulo Laut from a half-caste gentleman there, who described himself as the manager of a coal-mine; which sounded civilised and progressive till you heard that the mine could not be worked at present because it was haunted by some particularly atrocious ghosts. I had heard of him in a place called Dongola, in the Island of Celebes, when the Rajah of that little-known sea-port (you can get no anchorage there in less than fifteen fathom, which is extremely inconvenient) came on board in a friendly way with only two attendants, and drank bottle after bottle of soda-water on the after-skylight with my good friend and commander Captain C–. At least I heard his name distinctly pronounced several times in a lot of talk in Malay language. Oh, yes, I heard it quite distinctly – Almayer, Almayer – and saw Captain C– smile while the fat, dingy Rajah laughed audibly. To hear a Malay Rajah laugh outright is a rare experience, I can assure you. And I overheard more of Almayer's name amongst our deck passengers (mostly wandering traders of good repute) as they sat all over the ship – each man fenced round with bundles and boxes – on mats, on pillows, on quilts, on billets of wood, conversing of Island affairs. Upon my word, I heard the mutter of Almayer's name faintly at midnight, while making my way aft from the bridge to look at the patent taffrail-log tinkling its quarter-miles in the great silence of the sea. I don't mean to say that our passengers dreamed aloud of Almayer, but it is indubitable that two of them at least, who could not sleep apparently and were trying to charm away the trouble of insomnia by a little whispered talk at that ghostly hour were referring in some way or other to Almayer. It was really impossible on board that ship to get away definitely from Almayer . . . (pp. 75–6)

This remarkable passage might be read as an attempt to map the oral hinterland of *Almayer's Folly*, the polyphony of gossiping voices without which the novel itself would never have been written. Like Conrad's evocation of Malay storytelling in *An Outcast of the Islands*, this passage responds with fascination to the 'never-ending' discourses of an oral community; but in this instance there is something strangely oppressive about the incessant murmur of talk that captures the narrator's attention. For example, these constant whispers communicate nothing about Almayer beyond his name, which has become nothing more than a

pretext for the more vivid anecdotes of the haunted coal mine at Pulo
Laut and the laughing Rajah with an appetite for soda-water. Repetitive
gossip transforms Almayer into 'Almayer'; he becomes a kind of verbal ghost, haunting every minute of Conrad's day. The act of listening
has become an involuntary obsession ('I had heard...I had heard...I
had heard...I had heard...I had heard...I had heard...I heard...I
heard...I overheard...I heard'), and those inescapable words 'Almayer,
Almayer' have become a mantra that Conrad is incapable of not
hearing.

Conrad's fiction is as deeply exercised by the problem of authentic
listening as it is by that of authentic storytelling. Gazing at the portrait of
Kurtz's Intended, Marlow remarks: '"She seemed ready to listen without
mental reservation, without suspicion, without a thought for herself."'[24]
Conrad's storyteller seems here to be fantasizing about his perfect audience, but Kurtz's fiancée fails to measure up to Marlow's idealistic
speculations; indeed, it would be difficult to find anyone in Conrad's
fiction who listens with the unprejudiced selflessness Marlow imputes to
'the girl'. Certainly Marlow's passive and obtuse listeners tend to confirm the suspicion of the narrator of *An Outcast of the Islands* that our ears
are 'rebellious to strange sounds' (p. 198). The ideal listener in Conrad
would be someone whose presence permits his or her interlocutor to
think aloud without the fear that anything he or she says may be taken
down and used in evidence. Qualities of this sort appear to be displayed
by Dr Kennedy in 'Amy Foster': 'He had the talent of making people talk
to him freely, and an inexhaustible patience in listening to their tales.'[25]
But on the whole Conrad's fiction can't seem to realize the dialogic ideal
in which 'one heart speaks – another one listens'. According to Fogel,
'The End of the Tether' and 'Heart of Darkness' represent 'a transition
from preoccupation with the egotistical speakers [such as Peter Willems
or Captain Mitchell] whose desire is *to make the other listen* to a preoccupation with the egotistical listeners who desire *to make the other speak*.'[26]
Councillor Mikulin in *Under Western Eyes* takes pride of place in the latter category: with his tentative, delicately truncated sentences and air of
quietly thoughtful sympathy he elicits a flood of compromising words
from Razumov. This shift in the balance of power from speakers to listeners does not, however, imply that Conrad's listeners are automatically
privileged – his most perceptive listeners are often traumatized by what
they hear.

Conrad's scenes of overhearing are interpreted by Aaron Fogel as
defining moments of 'aural trauma':

Marlow, Razumov, Stevie, Winnie, Heyst, Hirsch – among others – overhear
the world involuntarily, amplifying, hearing one-sidedly and distortedly, so that
moments in which they are 'made to hear' define them and obligate them against
their will; an overhearing is one of the determining and catastrophic events in
their lives.[27]

Fogel takes overhearing to indicate traumatically excessive hearing (a
notable omission from his list of traumatized listeners is Flora de Barral,
the victim of vituperative personal attack from her governess in *Chance*);
but overhearing also denotes the wilful interpretative ingenuity in Fogel's
discovery of puns and 'chimes' in Conrad's lexicon, such as the 'off-
rhymes' of 'silver' and 'silence', 'Gould' and 'gold' in *Nostromo*. Fogel's
Conrad is an '*over*hearer' of the English language whose fiction in turn
requires its readers to *over*hear unidiomatic nuances and inflections in
Conrad's prose. I would like to amplify this notion of amplification beyond its apparent limits in Fogel's scheme of things. The two forms
of overhearing (as trauma and over-interpretation) are more intimately
linked than Fogel suggests. Conrad's work cautions against the perils of
over-interpretation: his 'overhearers' are traumatized by precisely the
kind of overhearing, the releasing of a hidden semantic surplus, that
Fogel performs.

Consider in this regard Conrad's presentation of the act of listening in
'The Brute'. This story opens with the narrator ducking into a London
tavern where our storyteller, a 'talkative stranger', is already holding
forth to the assembled company on an unspecified but apparently shocking subject: '"That fellow Wilmot fairly dashed her brains out"',[28] he
says. '"It made me sick to think of her going about the world murdering people"' (p. 107). 'She', in this instance, is not a woman but a
ship: the *Apse Family*, a huge, clumsy merchant vessel with a notorious
safety record. The joke here is based on the narrator's temporary misunderstanding of the anthropomorphic pronouns of maritime slang. His
presence as a marginal auditor makes possible a brief scene of linguistic defamiliarization, a mildly shocking rediscovery of the metaphorical
power of words.

Such moments of aural defamiliarization are common in Conrad. In
The Nigger of the 'Narcissus' James Wait calls out his surname as he joins the
crew with the roll-call already in progress. The chief-mate, Mr Baker,
incorrectly assumes that someone has impudently demanded him to
'wait!', a simple misunderstanding which underscores the symbolic significance of the new crewman's name. The journey of the *Narcissus* will be
plagued by delays: its crew will be forced to wait patiently for the weather

to change and for the hero to die. Baker's mistake is felicitous – he involuntarily articulates the quasi-allegorical level of meaning in Wait's name, anticipating the delays that will plague the journey. What Baker 'overhears' is in effect the novella's symbolic idiom, which emerges fleetingly prior to the reassertion of a univocal idiom. So the play on words is more than merely a joke – the insubordination sensed by Baker is actually a part of the equivocality of language that nautical discourse strives to suppress. It is an equivocality Baker himself reveals through his slip of the ear, thus implicating himself in a small linguistic mutiny that foreshadows the more serious shipboard unrest fomented by the malcontent Donkin.

There are many such 'slips of the ear' in Conrad. In these moments of creative misinterpretation, overhearing restores to language a polysemy that official discourse strives to suppress. Conrad's fiction could usefully be contrasted with what Derrida calls the '*discourse of the ear*'.[29] In the preface to *Margins of Philosophy*, Derrida meditates on the function of hearing in western philosophy, with particular regard to what he terms *s'entendre-parler*, or the structure of 'hearing-oneself-speak'. Since *entendre* in French signifies both to hear and to understand, this expression reinforces the perfectly natural assumption than in hearing ourselves speak we simultaneously grasp the full meaning of our utterances. This logic is part of the pretensions of philosophy to 'univocal rigidity' and 'regulated polysemia'. Derrida dwells on the ear's anatomical structure, on the intricate involutions, cavities, and canals of this 'differentiated, articulated organ' which can, on closer inspection, scarcely represent a sharp demarcation between mental experience and the 'outside' of the spoken word. Derrida's discourse of the ear focuses on the 'play of limit and passage', the sense that the oblique membrane of the tympan is both the boundary between language and subjective interiority, and an open thoroughfare between the two. Derrida insists on the *play* of limit and passage because neither image is adequate on its own. If we regard the ear as a limit, then we accept a clear ontological difference between the spoken word and subjective interiority, with the 'inside' as prediscursive consciousness. Alternatively, to regard the ear as a *passage* suggests a seamless continuity between the spoken word and mental experience. For Derrida, the ear is a zone of porous liminality, the site of the problematic interanimation of language and subjectivity. In hearing-oneself-speak, preverbal meaning, once voiced, is immediately heard and grasped in a tight loop of intentionality. But Derrida's investigations suggest that the speaker is neither origin nor arbiter of his or her own meanings;

he questions the immediate reappropriation of language to thought. Conrad's fiction raises similar questions over the relationship between voice, listening, and intention. Frequently in his fiction the hearer ascribes 'incorrect' meanings to discourse: hearing becomes a pre-emptive counter-interpretation, forestalling or deferring the 'intended' meaning of the utterance. Accidents of spatial relations permit the discovery in the most casual utterances of meanings that exceed both the preverbal intent of the speaker and the interpretative designs of the listener. The logic of *s'entendre-parler*, of comprehending (understanding *and* enclosing) one's own meaning, is continually violated by Conrad's logic of overhearing, which subverts 'univocal rigidity' and 'regulated polysemia', and throws language open to unregulated duplicity.

If we want to understand more about the particular dramatic circumstances in which Conrad subverts the 'discourse of the ear', then we might consider Mikhail Bakhtin's brief but suggestive comments on the subject of overhearing in his discussion of the 'History of Laughter'. According to Bakhtin, in the 'grotesque realism' of the seventeenth century the author is presented as eavesdropping on the coarse gossip of women or servants. Later, however

the frank talk of the marketplace and the banquet hall were transformed into the novel of private manners of modern times . . . Seventeenth-century literature with its dialogue was a preparation to the 'alcove realism' of private life, a realism of eavesdropping and peeping which reached its climax in the nineteenth century.[30]

For Bakhtin, the alcove is metonymic of an entire way of life: nineteenth-century middle-class culture, into whose private spaces the novelist discreetly peeps. In place of Bakhtin's 'alcove realism', Conrad creates what might be called 'veranda modernism'. The veranda occupies a special place in the imaginative architecture of Conrad's fiction. The opening scene of his first novel finds Almayer dreaming of gold on his veranda; Kayerts and Carlier chase one another around their veranda in 'An Outpost of Progress'; Freya Nielsen plays the piano on the veranda of her father's house in 'Freya of the Seven Isles'; Schomberg holds court on his veranda in *Victory*; the narrator of *The Shadow-Line* learns of his job opportunity through a convoluted scene of overhearing on a veranda; it is on the courthouse veranda that Marlow has his first brush with Jim – a character whose life-story he narrates on yet another veranda. The veranda is a place of privilege, a place where the leisured expatriate or unemployed sailor can while away his listless postprandial hours with a hand of cards or a cool drink served by silent nameless Asian servants. The veranda is also the customary venue for European talk, for long evenings occupied by gossip, yarn-spinning, and cigars. Given that many scenes of overhearing in Conrad take place on the veranda, one might – taking some inspiration from the architectural conceits of Derrida's 'Tympan' – term the veranda the 'ear' of the building: like the ear, the veranda is both limit and passage. It is the venue for overhearing, tales of hearsay, and is the structural equivalent of the ear, neither inside nor outside its parent-structure. It is a supplementary space, both extending and completing the building. The veranda is the venue for storytelling but also the site of overhearing where inside and outside, culture and nature, overlap. If we need a visual shorthand for the transition in storytelling in Conrad's fiction, we may say that narrative has been relocated from the camp-fire to the veranda, the zone of cultural privilege but linguistic instability – and nowhere is this transition better illustrated than in the gossip that flourishes on the veranda of Schomberg's hotel in 'Falk' and *Victory*.

CHAPTER TWO

'Murder by language': 'Falk' and Victory

In his book on gossip in nineteenth-century fiction, Jan B. Gordon discerns, on the margins of a society where value is vested in the written word (marriage contracts in Jane Austen, legal documents in *Bleak House*, the erudite tomes under composition in *Middlemarch*), an 'oral community' whose discursive share in informational transfer is consistently negated by authority as mere 'idle talk'.[1] Orality in these fictions, as in Conrad, can simultaneously be grasped both as 'metaphysical Origin' (the Voice as temporally and ontologically prior to writing) and as a subversive interruption of *written* master-narratives. I have already argued that Conrad's fiction subscribes to the former conception of the Voice, that the pseudo-orality of much of his fiction betrays an allegiance to the 'phonocentric' tradition of western thought. But in 'Falk' and *Victory*, texts that anathematize the subversive babble of gossip, Conrad might appear to have repudiated the naïve myth that meaning is immanent in the spoken word. On closer examination, however, gossip in Conrad bears many of the defects traditionally ascribed to writing: it is a dangerous supplement to authentic language, a groundless, parasitic discourse, propagating itself freely in the absence of an originating Voice. In its use of 'rootless' gossip as a foil for its own claims to linguistic authenticity, Conrad's fiction closely echoes Martin Heidegger's philosophical denunciation of 'idle talk':

[B]ecause this discoursing has lost its primary relationship-of-Being towards the entity talked about, or else has never achieved such a relationship, it does not communicate in such a way as to let this entity be appropriated in a primordial manner, but communicates rather by following the route of *gossiping* and *passing the word along*. What is said-in-the-talk as such, spreads in wider circles and takes on an authoritative character. Things are so because one says so. Idle talk [*Gerede*] is constituted by just such gossiping and passing the word along – a process by which its initial lack of grounds to stand on becomes aggravated to complete groundlessness.[2]

As theorized by Heidegger and given imaginative representation by Conrad, gossip partakes of a kind of 'oral textuality', flaunting the onto-logical groundlessness that is the very condition of its dissemination.

Conrad's denunciation of gossip contrasts intriguingly with its upward valuation by scholars in recent years. Gordon's book represents the culmi-nation of a steady revival in the fortunes of gossip as the object of scholarly investigation, which began in the 1960s with the debate between the an-thropologists Max Gluckman and Robert Paine and continued with the publication of Patricia Meyer Spacks's *Gossip*.[3] According to Gluckman, gossip is an insular parlance developed in a given social group to con-solidate a communal version of experience against the eccentricities of individual members or the threatening novelty of the parvenu. Gossip is a 'hallmark of membership',[4] a code the stranger must crack if he or she is to gain access to the group, and it has a supervisory function, creating a vigilant neighbourhood of potential narrators on the watch for the slightest impropriety that might threaten the stability of the 'us'-group.[5] What Gluckman's study neglects, as the title of Paine's rejoinder suggests, is the content of gossip. For Paine, gossip is a means of boosting one's own prestige by denigrating others in their absence. The values of the community are continually evoked in lieu of corroboration, but only to underwrite the gossiper's personal agenda: 'It is the individual and not the community that gossips. What he gossips about are his own and others' aspirations, and only indirectly the values of the community.'[6] The disagreement between Gluckman and Paine is ultimately superfi-cial, for it rests on the kind of rigid antithesis between self and group that gossip continually undermines – as is abundantly evidenced in the speech communities of Conrad's fiction.

Scholars in this area invariably run up against the problem that gossip is the most fugitive of speech genres: anthropologists who seek to gather empirical evidence have to gain access to a close-knit speech community from which they must also maintain a scholarly distance – a problem not dissimilar to that faced by the narrator of *Victory*, or by the narra-tor of any novel: how can his or her privileged, pristine metalanguage report gossip without itself *becoming* gossip? In George Meredith's *Amaz-ing Marriage* (1895) the narrative is shared out between an anonymous narrator, and 'Dame Gossip', whose garrulous intrusions divulge confi-dential information in a manner that would be beneath the dignity of the (male) narrator.[7] Dame Gossip's opposite number in Conrad's fic-tion is the German hotelier Wilhelm Schomberg, who wields language to recklessly damaging effect in 'Falk' and *Victory*. Like Charlie Marlow,

Schomberg is one of Conrad's stock of 'transtextual'[8] characters. He makes a cameo appearance in *Lord Jim*, imparting '"an adorned version of the story to any guest who cared to imbibe knowledge along with the more costly liquors"',[9] but enjoys a much more significant – if never quite central – role in 'Falk' and *Victory*. These tales need to be read as Conrad's vexed negotiations with a verbal medium whose immense expressive and creative powers harbour alarming destructive potentialities. On the evidence of 'Falk' and *Victory*, Conrad would seem to concur with Roland Barthes's definition of gossip as a form of 'meurtre par le langage'.[10]

Conrad's literary agent J. B. Pinker failed to place 'Falk' for serial publication: the tale's frank treatment of an episode of cannibalism at sea was deemed unsuitable for popular magazine fiction. As Conrad recalled, '["Falk"] stank in the nostrils of all magazine editors.'[11] Those squeamish editors, anxious to protect their readers from Conrad's noxious writing, are oddly reminiscent of a number of excessively fastidious characters in the tale itself: *Schiff-führer* Hermann, whose abnormally pristine vessel attests to a phobia of contamination; Falk, a man of action who exhibits an acute fear of words; Schomberg, with his fear of *fracas* and confrontation; and Falk's crewmates, who jettison the *Borgmester Dahl*'s stock of rotting beef – a sensible enough precautionary measure with dire unforeseen consequences. Narrated over the remnants of a largely inedible dinner, 'Falk' reflects subversively on the boundaries of good taste in matters of food and language; indeed, the word 'squeamish' is the subject of a minor semantic controversy between the tale's narrator and Hermann. Chided by the narrator for being '"too squeamish"' in his response to Falk's confession, Hermann is initially unrepentant: '"He seemed to think it was eminently proper to be squeamish if the word meant disgust at Falk's conduct"' (p. 222). Subsequently inquiring as to the precise meaning of that '"very funny word"', Hermann is offered the following definition: '"you exaggerate things – to yourself. Without inquiry, and so on"' (pp. 236–7). The repetition of the word, and the discussion over its precise meaning accords it a privileged position in the lexicon of 'Falk'. The tale emphasizes that squeamishness, superficially a mere nervous reflex of disgust, is symptomatic of deeper anxieties at the breakdown of ontological boundaries, which Tony Tanner has described as the crisis of 'decategorization' in 'Falk'.[12] Squeamishness is a form of psychological censorship whereby people take refuge in ignorance or, like Schomberg, in pre-emptive fictionalizations that fend off a direct encounter with experience. The narrator's useful distinction between 'inquiry' and 'exaggeration' points to a dichotomy in his own discourse between the quest for truth – for hard facts about Falk's past – incumbent upon any responsible narrator, and the imaginative freedom to which all storytellers are entitled.

'Falk"'s narrator exhibits a double squeamishness: on the one hand, Falk's cannibalism represents a naked confrontation with raw actuality, disclosing a comfortless Darwinian vision of internecine struggle for survival in which all the regulating fictions of culture have collapsed. The tale approaches this core of unmediated actuality with a certain reluctant obliqueness; its pursuit of linguistic transparency and authenticity – the model of which is Falk's harrowing confession – is compromised by the vociferous interruptions of Schomberg, who devotes himself to manufacturing scurrilous substitutes for first-hand experience. Schomberg's gossip occasions metafictional reflections about the power and perils of narrative that pre-empt any naked confrontation with reality. But language too holds its own subtle terrors: indeed, Falk's cannibalism is in one sense a mere metaphor for Schomberg's discursive cannibalism; so the tale's core of 'absolute truth' is assimilated as yet another metafictional motif.

In many respects, Schomberg is the precise antithesis of Falk. If Schomberg is addicted to words, Falk – as far as is humanly possible – consciously spurns them. Just as Schomberg functions as a cautionary personification of the destructive potential of compulsive storytelling, so Falk represents the debilitating effects of an excessive reluctance to speak. So successful is Schomberg's petty gossip in taking advantage of Falk's monolithic silence that Falk's ' "only sign of weakness" ' is his aversion to the hotelier:

'He had for Schomberg a repulsion resembling that sort of physical fear some people experience at the sight of a toad. Perhaps to a man so essentially and silently concentrated upon himself (though he could talk well enough, as I was to find out presently) the other's irrepressible loquacity, embracing every human being within range of the tongue, might have appeared unnatural, disgusting, and monstrous.' (p. 197)

Falk's Achilles heel is his squeamishness about Schomberg's presence, a phobia described, intriguingly enough, in the very language of histrionic disgust ('unnatural', 'disgusting', 'monstrous') that the revelation of his own cannibalism will elicit from Hermann: 'He choked, gasped, swallowed, and managed to shriek out the one word, "Beast!" ' (p. 218). It is a tribute to the power of gossip that the tale's most domineering figure, in so many respects a law unto himself, ' "quailed before Schomberg's tongue" '

(p. 201). With the example of Schomberg in mind, it could seem that *all* spoken language leaves a nasty taste in the mouth, and that Falk's exemplary silence – broken only to impart his confession – is the appropriate (non-)response to a world of corrupt garrulity.

The narrator's own narrative is very carefully placed between the extremes of irresponsible garrulity and vulnerable reticence represented by Falk and Schomberg. If confession is the ostensible model of our captain-narrator's tale, gossip is its parasitic supplement. After all, the narrator has been sworn to secrecy by Falk, and even after twenty-five years – a decent enough interval, if not quite the half-century moratorium once recommended by Søren Kierkegaard as an appropriate gap between events and their discussion in gossip[13] – there is a lingering anxiety that telling stories about Falk in a Thames hostelry is not all that different from gossiping about him in a Bangkok hotel. The narrator is at pains to distance himself from Schomberg's gossip, which he represents as small talk in more than one sense – a pusillanimous attempt to *belittle* Falk. Whilst Schomberg is determined to drag Falk down to the level of local eccentric, the narrator's rhetoric lends Falk (and Hermann's niece) a grand elemental dignity. Drawing on mythological parallels to persuade us of their larger-than-life dimensions (Hermann's niece resembles a pagan deity, Falk a centaur or Hercules), the narrator's positive exaggerations, his use of timeless, archetypal parallels, self-consciously elevate Falk and the niece above the insidious pettiness of Schomberg's narrative.

If Falk's dark secret – that he consumed the flesh of a dead crewmate on a broken-down steamer drifting among the ice-floes of Antarctica – is more shocking that Schomberg could ever imagine, the hotelier's appetite for narrative nevertheless resembles Falk's gastronomic transgression: gossip is the real staple of his *table-d'hôte*, where he serves up and consumes with gusto scraps of other people's private lives. Schomberg's gossip is cannibalistic in the sense that it treats people as just so much fodder for its all-consuming narratives. It is an especially choice irony that a purveyor of hospitality should be so virulently parasitic on other people's private business. Professional host and narratological parasite, Schomberg's ambiguous structural position is analogous to that of the deconstructionist critic as discussed in the well-known debate between M. H. Abrams and J. Hillis Miller.[14] Abrams closes his paper by anticipating the intellectual manoeuvres Miller will perform and pre-emptively accommodating them to the principle of liberal pluralism that finds its expression in the very consensual 'dialogue' that Miller's linguistic nihilism might seem to undermine. Miller's reply is predictably uncompromising. Addressing the charge (originally made by Wayne C. Booth) that the deconstructive reading of a given work is 'parasitical' on 'the obvious or univocal reading', Miller performs an etymological inquiry into the word 'parasite' (and its cognate terms in 'para'), teasing out the latent traces of meaning that enable it to signify at once 'proximity and distance, similarity and difference, interiority and exteriority, something at once inside a domestic economy and outside it'. What Miller calls the 'osmotic mixing' of host and guest, host and parasite, undermines those ancient binarisms around which hospitality – and hermeneutics – organize themselves, just as Schomberg's own institutional hospitality is strangely indissociable from his parasitical language.

Falk's confession is presented as the norm of truth against which Schomberg's egregious lies are exposed. It is invested by the narrator with '"the absolute truth of primitive passion"' (p. 223): thus it becomes the bench-mark of authenticity against which other narratives are measured, the master-narrative on which small talk is parasitic. The confession delivers up the kind of raw, unmediated experience about which most of us are so squeamish:

'Remembering the things one reads of it was difficult to realise the true meaning of his answers. I ought to have seen at once – but I did not; so difficult is it for our minds, remembering so much, instructed so much, informed of so much, to get in touch with the real actuality at our elbow. And with my head full of preconceived notions as to how a case of "Cannibalism and suffering at sea" should be managed I said – "You were then so lucky in the drawing of lots?"
'"Drawing of lots?" he said. "What lots?"' (p. 226)

Falk's experience belies the preconceptions fostered by book-learning: it cannot be contained by those rigid cognitive templates constructed by formal education or popular myth. In a tale where experience is so often pre-empted by discourse, Falk's recollections defy all expectation and shatter cliché-ridden modes of thought, to take a primal grasp on reality in all its appalling immediacy.

The strange atmosphere of this story is evoked in part through Conrad's skilful juxtaposition of Falk's tragic ordeal with the darkly comic one experienced by the captain-narrator. 'Falk' belongs to a distinctive Conradian subgenre that also includes 'The Secret Sharer' and 'The Shadow-Line': the confessional retrospect on the initiatory ordeal of a newly promoted captain. No sooner have Conrad's novice captains acceded to the highest professional rank than they become prey to the kind of self-doubt and existential isolation for which no formal qualification can prepare. In 'Falk', as in 'The Shadow-Line', the hero is a novice skipper against whom circumstances conspire with seemingly malevolent intent, leaving him strangely marginalized and helpless at a time when he should be enjoying unprecedented power. The predecessor of 'Falk''s captain-narrator left the ship's finances in a mess; his fellow officers are suspicious and unfriendly; the crew is struck down with fever; the replacement steward makes off with his savings; the one tug-boat operator on the river takes unaccountable exception to him; and his private life is the subject of scurrilous rumours circulated by Schomberg. As Tanner has noticed, in many respects his predicament is a milder version of Falk's on the *Borgmester Dahl*. '"[F]athoms deep in discontent"' (p. 173), the captain-narrator passes through a phase of depression, reaching the point of capitulation to gossip – in part because Schomberg's innuendo is closer to the truth than the narrator would care to admit: '"It was no use fighting against this false fate. I don't know even if I was sure myself where the truth of the matter began"' (p. 195). The narrator even confesses to a superstitious fear of language: '"It was as if Schomberg's baseless gossip had the power to bring about the thing itself"' (p. 214). No small part of his education is occupied by dealing with linguistic problems. The former captain has left a legacy of texts scarcely worth the paper they're written on – '"some suspiciously unreceipted bills, a few dry-dock estimates hinting at bribery, and a quantity of vouchers for three years' extravagant expenditure"' – together with a large account-book filled with '"page after page of rhymed doggerel of a jovial and improper character"' (p. 153); whilst Falk's tariff of charges is a '"brutally inconsiderate document"' (p. 161). These official documents are no less problematic than the spoken words that conspire to undermine the captain's authority. The local authorities are comparably powerless in the face of gossip. The vignettes of expatriate bureaucracy in 'Falk' – the sketches of 'the Siegers gang' and the staff of the British Consulate – depict officialdom as complacently susceptible to whatever gossip is doing the rounds: it seems that even the Consul-General will presently hear and believe Schomberg's gossip. Chaotic paperwork and complacent bureaucrats offer no more than token resistance to the swift dissemination of unsubstantiated rumour. Gossip constructs the secret history of which it is ostensibly a mere disclosure – leaving the narrator, who fondly imagined himself to be the author of his own destiny, fighting a rearguard action against popular opinion.

Conrad's paralysed novice captains are near relations of his tentative storytellers, struggling to take command of recalcitrant material.

The young captain faces a predicament surely analogous to Conrad's: that of the artist plagued by doubts over his uncertain mastery of his medium – doubts that are presented in a more extreme form in Falk's aversion to language. How can Falk possibly begin to speak openly of his past when the likelihood is that a candid avowal of his transgression will lead to permanent exclusion from human contact? Struggling to move beyond his painfully limited repertoire of grunts and anguished gestures into genuine reciprocal communication, agonizing on the threshold of speech, Falk suffers a kind of speaker's block: his pained body language is the visible symptom of the inner anguish that he cannot force into words. For Falk, as for the storyteller, language is a necessary evil. Frequently for Conrad's storytellers, however, this very squeamish reluctance to speak enables narrative to get off the ground. For a complex of reasons, Conrad's narrators find it strategically useful to pass off narrative authority as alienated passivity – narrative becomes something overheard, that originates elsewhere, emerging in spite of their own discretion.

A spatial representation of the relation of gossip to official narratives is given when the narrator embarks with the constable – reluctantly extracted from his berth in the consulate offices – on a quest for the pilot Johnson. This manhunt takes them through the impoverished, dilapidated districts of Bangkok: '"an infinity of infamous grog shops, gambling dens, opium dens"' (p. 190), inhabited by what seems to Conrad's heroes like mere human detritus. This is a whistle-stop tour of a community that the white colony is not accustomed to seeing: a forgotten community of speakers who have no voice in the coffee-room gossip of the harbour – the former ship's captain gone to seed, the nameless locals, the decaying buildings, roads strewn with rubbish, an environment where alcohol, narcotics, gambling, and crime flourish. Small wonder that the constable is anxious to return to his lovingly tended garden: for him, horticultural order is evidently preferable to the spectacle of cultural 'decategorization' in riverside Bangkok. The constable interviews Maltese, Chinamen, Klings, confers with an obese Italian murderer, obtains information from a 'shrivelled old hag' and from groups of native women smoking outside hovels. Johnson's home is ultimately located behind a '"mound of garbage crowned with the dead body of a dog"' (p. 191), but it seems that Johnson has already been bought off by Falk. The object of gossip is, it seems, always the last person to hear it.

Described by the narrator as '"a slide of rubbish"' (p. 173), and dismissed by Hermann as '"trash"' (p. 184), gossip is insistently likened to the garbage that litters 'Falk'. Gossip is language that has passed from private ownership back into the public domain, where it is collectively (dis)owned – the foul linguistic surplus to be discarded and forgotten by respectable citizens. The expression '*Schomberg's* gossip' is repeated insistently as the tale strains to make Schomberg and gossip synonymous: gossip belongs to, originates in, is perpetrated by no one but the hotelier. Gossip, of course, can never be unilateral: any listener becomes an accessory, all the more so when he or she feels the need to repeat gossip in order to deny it. However, apart from his accusation that Falk is a miser – which might more accurately be levelled at Hermann, whose squeamishness about expenditure ultimately overcomes his disgust at Falk – nothing of what Schomberg has said is in fact irrelevant. Schomberg has marshalled all the relevant information (thus conveniently relieving our narrator of performing the same chore). His gossip – or, rather, the gossip ascribed to him – is the disreputable *sjuzhet* to the 'authentic' *fabula* of Falk's confession. If Schomberg is 'the black *alter*-image of the valuable narrator',[15] he is also a displaced self-portrait of the storyteller; or, at least, a portrait of kinds of storytelling he feels squeamish about. What better occasion for responsible talk could there be than gratuitous talk?

Where 'Falk' differs from 'The Secret Sharer' and *The Shadow-Line* is in its tone: it is, in spite of its grisly cannibalistic theme, a comic tale – a comedy of errors, one might say, in which the captain's ordeal involves correcting the errors that have been broadcast about him. Fluctuating between sheer textuality and raw experience, the tale struggles to affirm the primacy of the latter even as it ultimately concedes the triumph of the former. Schomberg's victory is sealed in the concluding paragraph where the narrator finds himself and Falk immortalized in a new tale that testifies to the irrepressibility of gossip: 'there was some vague tale still going about the town of a certain Falk, owner of a tug, who had won his wife at cards from the captain of an English ship' (p. 240).

A remarkable tale in its own right, 'Falk' might also usefully be regarded as a tragicomic 'first draft' of the novel in which Schomberg's gossip will assume much more destructive powers: *Victory*. While critics tend to disagree about the value of this novel – published in 1917, it hovers on the threshold of Conrad's later 'decline' – there seems to be little fundamental disagreement over its meaning. According to the canonical interpretation, *Victory* is an anti-philosophical novel, a repudiation of the life-denying scepticism of late-nineteenth-century philosophy and a vindication of life, love and action.[16] The tragic career of Axel Heyst, the reclusive Swede paralysed by the dead hand of his father's

Schopenhauerian scepticism, is commonly thought to be Conrad's dramatic refutation of intellectual detachment. Heyst's philosophy of sceptical detachment from human contact is compromised when he twice offers help to people in distress – interventions that seem all the more quixotic in the light of his prior stance of detachment – thereby forming fatal 'ties' with the world he sought to renounce. This lesson of human interdependence is scarcely original – it goes back at least as far as John Donne's dictum that no man is an island – and neither does it seem to offer the basis for a substantial 400-page novel. Even readers like William W. Bonney, who have sought to complicate matters, succeed merely in standing the traditional interpretation of *Victory* on its head: 'The tragedy of *Victory*', Bonney contends, 'is not that Axel Heyst cannot commit himself, but rather that Axel Heyst cannot preserve his pose of detachment.'[17]

What I think this prevailing view of *Victory* lacks is a sense of the way the novel's narrative and linguistic complexities cut against the grain of its ostensible 'message'. If Heyst's life-denying scepticism, his bid to make his life 'a masterpiece of aloofness',[18] is a legitimate target for dramatic refutation, the violence of that refutation is scarcely commensurate with Heyst's transgressions. Heyst's nemesis – an unholy trinity of desperadoes acting on a tip-off from Schomberg who invade his island paradise on the scent of his (non-existent) cache of 'minted gold' – constitutes a devastating return of the repressed. *Victory* needs to be understood as a double allegory in which the existential drama, the repudiation of Heyst's scepticism, consorts problematically with its textual allegory in which Heyst is the blameless prey of Schomberg's murderous gossip. In the light of this paradoxical doubleness, the narrative methods of *Victory* – which have hitherto been interpreted in inadequate psychological terms – become less puzzling than they have long appeared, and the novel itself perhaps not quite so childishly straightforward as some readers have made it out to be.[19] *Victory* is the most crystalline version of the pattern of ordeal by language to be found in several of Conrad's novels. There is an almost diagrammatic simplicity to the novel that can usefully prepare us for the more intricate variations on similar themes in the Marlow narratives and political fiction. Heyst is Conrad's archetypal fugitive from language; his flight from Schomberg's gossip presents in its most abstract form a drama that is also enacted in the Marlow tales, in *Under Western Eyes*, and in *The Secret Agent*. As Lord Jim and Razumov will discover, the autonomous, extra-linguistic human subject is an endangered species in Conrad's fiction, constantly vulnerable to the predations of gossip or the violence of textuality, always in search of some extra-textual utopia, whether that utopia is found in habitual silence (Stevie and Razumov), or in the exotic sanctuaries of Patusan or Samburan (Jim and Heyst).

Like the Great de Barral in *Chance*, and Charles Gould's father in *Nostromo*, Heyst *père* is an absent father who leaves his offspring a debilitating legacy. A polymath and prolific writer, his intellectual legacy is enshrined in the volumes that line the walls of his son's Samburan bungalow. Given the widespread devaluation of language in *Victory*, the elder Heyst's suspicion of language might seem eminently sensible:

'I suppose he began like other people; took fine words for good, ringing coin and noble ideals for valuable banknotes. He was a great master of both, himself, by the way. Later he discovered – how am I to explain it to you? Suppose the world were a factory and all mankind workmen in it. Well, he discovered that the wages were not good enough. That they were paid in counterfeit money.' (pp. 195–6)

'"Look on – make no sound"' (p. 175): in his deathbed exhortation Heyst's father urges his son to abstain from language, to maintain a spectatorial detachment from life. But the ultimate consequence of this is to leave Axel Heyst grievously vulnerable to the discourse of others. The novel combines a profound suspicion of the 'emptiness' of words with an almost superstitious conception of the power of language magically or maliciously to transform reality. Empty words, like counterfeit money, have a force quite independent of their semantic content, just as Heyst's illusory bags of 'minted gold' present a quarry irresistible to Ricardo's predatory instincts.

The slurred verdict of the old soak McNab, that Heyst is a '"ut-uto-utopist"' (p. 8), aptly describes the motives behind Heyst's retreat to Samburan: almost a stranger to human speech, the island is his utopian refuge from language. Heyst is fastidiously reluctant to contest other versions of reality; it is a measure of his self-absorbed temperament that he should be so surprised to figure in other people's words:

The idea of being talked about was always novel to Heyst's simplified conception of himself. For a moment he was as much surprised as if he had believed himself to be a mere gliding shadow among men. Besides, he had in him a half-unconscious notion that he was above the level of island gossip. (p. 206)

Heyst cannot remain an insubstantial *tabula rasa* for long. The dilapidated coaling station, with its overgrown road, rickety wharf and broken fences, is being slowly consumed by vegetation: culture is yielding to nature, just as surely as Heyst's civilized bookishness will succumb to

Schomberg's brutish voice. Recommending avoidance of all affective 'ties' – ' "I only know that he who forms a tie is lost. The germ of corruption has entered into his soul" ' (pp. 199–200) – Heyst's decision to 'bind himself to silence' (p. 19) turns out to be the most damaging tie of all.

The pivotal role of gossip in *Victory* has been succinctly described by Tony Tanner:

'[G]ossip' . . . effectively destroys Heyst, his 'courtesy' being powerless against, and annihilated by, the gratuitous 'calumny' of others, mainly emanating from our old friend, or rather Conrad's old *bête noire*, Schomberg. The gentleman, and speech – these were considered two of the 'highest' products of evolution. And in their degraded, perverted, or 'scandalously' travestied forms – Mr Jones and Schomberg's gossip – they can destroy the higher, 'authentic' forms . . . [Heyst] succumbs to the slanderous and malicious mal-naming of him by Schomberg's gossip, a kind of verbal 'mud' which sticks to him and drags him back to the old earth of our common origin, from which he can only finally and fully escape by the purifying, terminating fire.[20]

Unsurprisingly, perhaps, Tanner lays emphasis on Schomberg at the expense of the dozens of anonymous gossips in the novel. Schomberg's *hotel* is the true seedbed of gossip in the novel. Heyst's incongruously urbane manner, unpredictable comings and goings, and unlikely business transactions, establish him as a local eccentric whose antics fascinate the community of expatriate sailors and traders who patronize the hotel. It is the venue for an incessant buzz of gossip, the discursive life-blood of the speech community – the 'hail-fellow-well-met crowd' (p. 29) – from which Heyst absconds. *Victory*, like 'Falk', strives to exonerate the wider speech community – as well as its own narrative discourse – from participation in gossip, which is ascribed firmly to Schomberg. But one need only consider Morrison's reputation to recognize that Schomberg is simply the most conspicuous member of a community of gossips:

Some men grumbled at him. He was spoiling the trade. Well, perhaps to a certain extent; not much. Most of the places he traded with were unknown not only to geography but also to the traders' special lore which is transmitted by word of mouth, without ostentation, and forms the stock of mysterious local knowledge. It was hinted also that Morrison had a wife in each and every one of them, but the majority of us repulsed these innuendoes with indignation. (p. 11)

Morrison's philanthropy – he is too feckless to obtain payments for his shipments of rice to 'God-forsaken villages' – poses a threat to local trading practices in the same way that the Tropical Belt Coal Company, with its anonymous European shareholders and modern industrial techniques, spells the end for lone adventurers and entrepreneurs. The prurient allegations of polygamy levelled at Morrison typify gossip's tendency to regard gaps in its own knowledge as guilty secrets in the lives of others. Traders' gossip is a species of oral cartography in which there can be no *terra incognita*. Gossip makes gaps and silences testify incriminatingly against the likes of Morrison and Heyst by interpolating the most damaging inferences it can dream up, rewriting detachment as misanthropy and chivalry as self-interest. As ever, responsibility for originating such scandalous assertions is promptly disavowed by the narrator. The principle of deniability, the luxury of instant retraction, ensures that the gossip-figure never has to answer for his mistakes. The local speculation over Heyst's relationship with Morrison similarly distances the narrator from the cynical extremes of gossip: 'we all concluded that Heyst was boarding with the good-natured – some said: sponging on the imbecile – Morrison' (p. 19). Innocent, face-value assumptions are qualified, as in the parenthetical counter-claim in this sentence, by suspicious counter-interpretations in which generous co-operation is read by an anonymous subsection of the 'us'-group as parasitism.

Schomberg's hysterical diatribes against Heyst, which amount to an extended conversation with himself, are another instance of narratological parasitism disguising itself as vigorous condemnation of its moral equivalent:

'I won't say anything of his spying – well, he used to say himself he was looking for out-of-the-way facts, and what is that if not spying? He was spying into everybody's business. He got hold of Captain Morrison, squeezed him dry, like you would an orange, and scared him off to Europe to die there. Everybody knows that Captain Morrison had a weak chest. Robbed first and murdered afterward! I don't mince words – not I. Next he gets up that swindle of the Belt Coal. You all know about it. And now, after lining his pockets with other people's money, he kidnaps a white girl belonging to an orchestra which is performing in my public room for the benefit of my patrons, and goes off to live like a prince on that island, where nobody can get at him.' (p. 61)

Espionage, robbery, murder, fraud, kidnapping – it is an extraordinary charge-sheet; but Heyst's original, and in Schomberg's eyes most heinous, crime is that he does not stay at the German's hotel. As a visible non-guest, Heyst, like Falk before him, incurs all the intemperate spleen Schomberg can muster. Tanner has noted the 'theme of the uninvited guest' in *Victory*: Jones's sojourn on Samburan is 'a black parody of "hospitality" – with parasitic scavengers trying to act as "gentlemen" guests'.[21] Schomberg's allegations paint Heyst as literal exponent of the murderous parasitism of gossip. 'A rumour sprang out' – a rumour traced inevitably back to

Schomberg – 'that Heyst, having obtained some mysterious hold on Morrison, had fastened himself on him and was sucking him dry' (p. 20). For those who decline to have him as their host, Schomberg becomes a parasite: 'Human beings, for him, were either the objects of scandalous gossip or else the recipients of narrow strips of paper, with proper bill-heads stating the name of his hotel. – "W. Schomberg, proprietor; accounts settled weekly"' (p. 98). Schomberg endeavours to make Heyst 'accountable' – for the collapse of the T.B.C.C., the death of Morrison, for his own sexual inadequacy – in the sense of 'narratable'; and it is this subordination of autonomous individuality to collective language that Barthes likens to murder.

In *A Lover's Discourse* Barthes describes gossip (*le potin*) as the verbal nullification of presence:

Gossip reduces the other to *he/she*, and this reduction is intolerable to me. For me the other is neither *he* nor *she*; the other has only a name of his own, and her own name. The third-person pronoun is a wicked pronoun: it is the pronoun of the non-person, it absents, it annuls. When I realize that common discourse takes possession of my other and restores that other to me in the bloodless form of a universal substitute, applied to all the things which are not here, it is as if I saw my other dead, reduced, shelved in an urn upon the wall of the great mausoleum of language. For me, the other cannot be a *referent*: you are never anything but you, I do not want the Other to speak of you.[22]

This is the last of three meditations under the epigraph/summary: 'Pain suffered by the amorous subject when he finds that the loved being is the subject of "gossip" and hears that being discussed promiscuously.'[23] For Barthes (in the amorous persona adopted here), gossip depersonalizes the human subject by translating the proper name – the token of autonomous individuality – into an anonymous pronoun, a process of de-naming that is analogous to murder. Barthes's dismay at this substitution of discursive absence for physical presence represents the nostalgic obverse of the deconstruction of human subjectivity performed with such iconoclastic verve in his other theoretical writings. He denounces gossip because 'it absents, it annuls'; but *Victory* shows the reverse to be true. 'Whenever three people came together in his hotel, he [Schomberg] took care that Heyst should be with them.' This Biblical allusion – which is echoed in references to the obsessive talk of Napoleon Bonaparte in *Suspense*[24] – suggests that there is something not merely malicious but sacrilegious about Schomberg's gossip.[25] The hotelier's gossip is a concerted campaign against Heyst's perverse attempt to live his entire life *in absentia*.

In the aftermath of Heyst's 'abduction' of Lena, Schomberg's wounded pride, his risible histrionics, become a 'recognised entertainment' (p. 95), rivalling the ladies' orchestra, whose grotesque cacophony is described as 'murdering silence with a vulgar, ferocious energy' (p. 68) – which is precisely what Schomberg's gossip does: 'The hotel-keeper multiplied words, as if to keep as many of them as possible between himself and the murderous aspect of his purpose' (p. 167). Twice the narrator remarks of Heyst that the music 'pursued him' (p. 66) – so much so that he attends one of the concerts. This is a comic foreshadowing of the ferocity with which Schomberg's implacable gossip 'pursues' Heyst to Samburan, attempting to repatriate him to the speech community that convenes at his hotel. The itinerant ladies' orchestra is clearly a metaphor for gossip – Conrad's equivalent of the speech community of shrill, censorious gossiping women scathingly depicted by George Eliot in *The Mill on the Floss* (Part 7, ch. 2), where Eliot assures us that public opinion is 'always of the feminine gender'. Given that there is already a question mark over Schomberg's masculinity, a suspicion that behind the pantomime machismo of his 'officer-of-the-reserve manner' lurks a 'confounded old woman of a hotel-keeper',[26] Schomberg's addiction to gossip is presented as further evidence of his lack of authentic manliness.

The bogus masculinity of Schomberg parallels the failed masculinity of Heyst, whose scandalous liaison with Lena leaves him 'mixed up with petticoats' (p. 59), suggesting the absence of any tenable model of masculinity for him to adopt. Through the figure of Heyst, Conrad is testing to destruction models of masculinity derived from metropolitan modernism (the *flâneur*) and popular adventure literature (the desert island hero). Heyst is, with *Nostromo*'s Martin Decoud, one of Conrad's colonial *flâneurs*,[27] viewing himself as 'an indifferent stroller going through the world's bustle' (p. 199). The colonial *flâneur* has been transplanted from the droll spectacle of city life to the outposts of empire, where urbane detachment is impossible to sustain. Like Decoud, Heyst finds no responsive audience for his playful repartee; and like Decoud he commits suicide on an island – the spatial equivalent of the linguistic isolation that both endure. The *flâneur* as a model of subjectivity is sustainable only in the context of a metropolitan modernism of which Conrad was a sceptical exponent, posing it constantly in tension with its colonial other. A moving target in his native cityscape, the *flâneur* cannot endure a sedentary island existence; but the other option available, that of adventure hero, is already a discredited anachronism in Conrad's fiction.

Throughout *Victory* mobile subjectivity is brought under the jurisdiction of language. Just as Heyst, an atheist, is the miraculous answer to the prayers of Morrison, so Schomberg's gossip conjures up Mr Jones and his confederates – Jones was directed to Schomberg by a fellow card-player in the Hotel Castille in Manila, about whom Schomberg had once 'set a lot of scandal going' (p. 101) – and the same gossip subsequently dispatches them to Samburan. The trio parasitically exploit Schomberg's hospitality – note too that they intimidate the hysterically talkative Schomberg with anecdotes about their criminal past – until he persuades them that a still more inviting host awaits them on Samburan. The readiness of Jones and his partners-in-crime to believe Schomberg's gossip has been deemed by some critics to be a lapse in psychological plausibility ('surely in reality Jones and Ricardo would not allow themselves to be used by Schomberg'[28]); but the point surely is that the trio are to be understood in narratological rather than psychological terms, as agents or extensions of the power of gossip, rather than as rounded, autonomous 'characters'.

In the final crisis, when Heyst cannot find the conviction to defend himself and Lena, the novel's credentials as an abortive adventure tale are sealed when its hero capitulates to language:

'It ["the world"] would say, Lena, that I – that Swede – after luring my friend and partner to his death from mere greed of money, have murdered these unoffending ship-wrecked strangers from sheer funk. That would be the story whispered – perhaps shouted – certainly spread out, and believed – and *believed*, my dear Lena!' (pp. 361–2)

Acquiescing in the inevitability of Schomberg's victory, Heyst finds definitive confirmation of his father's linguistic pessimism. His sceptical philosophy can prove itself only through its own failure, when the island of selfhood succumbs to the predations of language.

Heyst's tragedy has a curious impact on the structure of this text. A four-part novel, *Victory* has a very conspicuous break between the restricted first-person narrative of Part I, and the impersonal omniscience of the remainder of the novel. Part I is something in the nature of an interim report on the character of Axel Heyst – a patchy composite of anecdotes drawn from his 'early days' in the tropics, to 'now', when he is 'becomingly bald on the top' (p. 7). Snatches of conversation about Heyst are reported from a Malacca bank manager, the head of a trading-house, as well as one 'old McNab', and, of course, Schomberg himself. These are supplemented with vague accounts of a hazardous excursion to

New Guinea and a spell travelling in Tesman's schooner. The desultory, anecdotal structure of Part I, appropriately enough, reflects Heyst's own 'mooning' disposition. He resists absorption into the undifferentiated 'us'-group because his life is *discontinuous* – his origins are obscure, he has no family or close friends, no home or permanent job. A series of escapades rather than a continuous narrative, Heyst's career in the tropics is conducted in defiance of routine or pattern.

From the beginning of Part II onwards, the remainder of the novel is narrated omnisciently. Interpretations of this 'break' between anecdotal and omniscient narrative have commonly ascribed it to the psychology of the protagonist. Robert Hampson and Daphna Erdinast-Vulcan have both offered interpretations along these lines.[29] By presenting the novel's divided form as an extrapolation of its hero's divided psyche, such psychological readings discount what seems to me to be a far more compelling reason for the novel's transition to omniscience. This transition, which coincides with a dangerous escalation in the intensity of Schomberg's gossip, is an act of detachment that curiously replicates on a formal level the very existential detachment sought by Heyst. Previously the narrator had been happy to present himself as one of Schomberg's many interlocutors, rubbing shoulders with the 'hail-fellow-well-met crowd', but from Part II onwards, the novel purges itself of any resemblance to gossip. The narrator withdraws to a position of splendid extra-diegetic isolation to enjoy the detachment denied to Heyst; and from this perspective of non-intrusive omniscience the transcendent narrator of Parts II–IV can indeed 'look on – make no sound'. This policy of non-intervention protects the narrator from the effects of the same strategy as imperfectly implemented by Heyst. By incarnating gossip in the person of Schomberg, the narrator disclaims any responsibility for the punitive discursive violence inflicted on Heyst. By staging the 'victory' of speech over writing (the destruction of the mild-mannered bibliophile Heyst by the voice of Schomberg), *Victory* deflects the worst excesses of language from its own discursive textures. Heyst ends by torching his bungalow: the written texts that were the basis of his life become the fuel of the fire to which he consigns himself. As so often in Conrad, writing is destroyed or mutilated, but whereas in later works – especially *Nostromo* and *The Secret Agent* – that violence extends into the text's own formal structures, in *Victory*, the transcendent author seems to enjoy the very immunity from language that was denied his hero.

CHAPTER THREE

'Drawing-room voices': language and space
in The Arrow of Gold

The Arrow of Gold (1919) belongs with *The Rover* (1923) and the unfinished *Suspense* (1925) as part of the 'trilogy' of Mediterranean adventure stories written during the final years of Conrad's literary career. None of these novels enjoys a sparkling critical reputation, but *The Arrow of Gold* has been singled out by no less an authority than Zdzisław Najder as 'Conrad's weakest novel'.[1] As Conrad's best biographer, Najder is better qualified than anyone to assess whether the supposedly autobiographical elements of this novel – the Carlist gun-running, the passionate love affair, the duel – have any real basis in the facts of Józef Korzeniowski's life; but his verdict on the artistic qualities of *The Arrow of Gold* is too peremptory. Recent critics, including Robert Hampson, Susan Jones, and Andrew Michael Roberts, have rediscovered *The Arrow of Gold* as fiction rather than spurious autobiography; they have focused usefully on its subversive treatment of generic conventions, its exploration of gendered identities, and its representations of visuality and the male gaze.[2] The novel has emerged in recent years as a strange hybrid of the romantic adventure tale and the modernist *Künstlerroman*, an aesthetically self-conscious text whose rough-and-ready seafaring hero rubs shoulders with Marseilles bohemia in a landscape crowded with sculptures, painting, curios, and all the paraphernalia of fine art.

Though Conrad's readers have begun to take this novel seriously as a modernist text, relatively little has been said of its linguistic self-consciousness. *The Arrow of Gold* is that rare thing, a Conrad novel that advertises its own status as a piece of writing; it also brings to life speech communities that are strikingly different from those of the eastern fiction or the sea tales. The novel is alive with the chatter of cafés and salons, the polished conversation of artists and connoisseurs, journalists and politicians, but shot through with a certain distrust of the voice. In this novel writing, rather than speech, is privileged as the most authentic resource of self-expression.

The source of this novel, we are told, is a 'pile of manuscript' (p. 3), a book-length reminiscence that began its life as a response to a letter from an unnamed woman, a childhood friend of the hero, M. George. The editor, who frames the text with two Notes, explains that he has suppressed 'all asides, disquisitions, and explanations addressed directly to the friend of his childhood' (p. 4). Although this editor is not explicitly gendered, Robert Hampson argues that the remarks in the Second Note about 'those who know women' (p. 338) invite us to assume that the editor is male.[3] One might also point to the way in which the editor dislodges M. George's female correspondent from her position as the text's 'official' reader and plays up the *Boy's Own* qualities of the narrative. Danger, military struggle, and political intrigue are all emphasized in the First Note as key qualities of this 'great adventure' (p. 4). Given that the editor has 'intercepted' this text, rewritten epistolary as novelistic narrative, and dispatched it to a new, implicitly male audience, one might ask whether M. George's manuscript, in any form, ever reaches its female addressee. '"No woman will read it"' (p. 301), says M. George, of his unwritten valedictory letter to Rita; but he might equally be speaking of the novel's framing narrative, which seems to discourage the participation of the female reader. However, the editor's enthusiasm for narratives of male adventure is itself resisted by the text: Don Carlos's armed struggle, and M. George's role in it as a gun-runner, function as an almost vestigial subplot, entirely subordinated to the social intrigues surrounding Doña Rita.

The First Note of *The Arrow of Gold* sets up a triangular relationship (male writer–female reader–male editor) that prepares us for a series of three-way struggles over language, truth, and interpretation. Groups of three, like the storytelling trio of M. George, Blunt, and Mills, or the 'mounted trio' (p. 32) of Rita, Allègre, and Don Carlos, figure as prominent symbolic structures in this novel, embodying shifting and unstable power-relations. For example, one might say that in the First Note an intimate epistolary relationship between M. George and his correspondent has been disrupted by the narrator, or, on the other hand, that a male writer and male editor have joined forces against a female reader – both readings are possible, though they cannot easily be reconciled. This novel centres on the construction and disruption of idealized binarisms in language, art, and romantic love: letter-writer and addressee, speaker and interlocutor, artist and muse, the pair of isolated lovers – each pairing is challenged by a powerful external force. In particular, the relationship between M. George and Rita is one over which a range of characters –

Captain Blunt, Mrs Blunt, Therese, Ortega, and others – try to exercise linguistic control.

Initially a source of fascination for M. George, storytelling is soon unmasked as an eminently manipulative activity. If the voice is invasive or coercive in this novel, writing appears by comparison to be a more hospitable medium. It is significant that M. George's narrative draws at least in part on extracts from 'notes I made at the time in little black books' that he has salvaged from 'the litter of the past' (p. 87). These 'common little note-books', he says, 'by the lapse of years have acquired a touching dimness of aspect, the frayed, worn-out dignity of documents' (p. 87). The first two excerpts (pp. 88–90, 91–4) cover the recruitment of Dominic, their plans to purchase a balancelle, and M. George's conference with Rita; the third begins with a visit to Rita's villa, where with Mills he learns of her altercation with the financier Azzolati. Conrad does not develop this pretence of diary-as-source as carefully as he might; no clear indication is given of where the final diary excerpt ends and reconstruction through memory resumes, though the end of Part II (p. 105) would seem the most likely point.

M. George begins his diary soon after he commits himself to smuggling arms for the Carlists; this is not simply a new phase in his life but also a shift in his relationship to the linguistic communities of the novel. 'My life had been a thing of outward manifestations', he writes; but he leaves Doña Rita's villa 'committed to an enterprise that could not be talked about' (p. 87). These missions 'close my lips', he confides, and cut him off 'from my usual haunts and from the society of my friends; especially of the light-hearted, young, harum-scarum kind' (p. 87). He begins to keep this 'irregular, fragmentary record' because he is 'thrown back upon my own thoughts and forbidden to seek relief amongst other lives' (pp. 87–8). Exiled from his primary speech community, and unable to converse openly with his new comrades – Mills is 'too old for me to talk to him freely' (p. 88) – M. George takes up writing to 'keep a better hold of the actuality' (p. 88). The necessity of secretive inwardness is forced upon M. George for the first time; he has exchanged a dialogic for a textual model of subjectivity. The moment when a Conrad hero picks up a pen and begins to write is usually one of personal and textual crisis: Martin Decoud's journal letter in *Nostromo*, Razumov's secret diary in *Under Western Eyes*, even Cosmo Latham's anxiously meditated letter to his sister in *Suspense*, each of these texts reproduces the 'fall' from orality into textuality that pitches the Conrad subject from an open speech community into the prison-house of *écriture*. The diary in Conrad is a crisis-text, begun in moments of exceptional pressure or danger, yet in *The Arrow of Gold* the private textual self of the diarist has the virtue of being free from dialogic interference.

It would be no exaggeration to dub *The Arrow of Gold* a dialogic novel – with the proviso that its many conversations tend to be egregiously one-sided. Indeed, the entire novel might be said to turn on the imbalance between a near-voiceless hero and his talkative social world. Early on M. George is set apart from the 'bedlamite yells of carnival' (p. 13), and lost for words when a costumed reveller pokes her tongue out at him – as though to emphasize the particular significance of his subsequent en-counters with *female* language. With the striking exception of M. George, everyone in this novel has a story to tell. 'In no Conrad novel', Daniel R. Schwarz remarks, 'do we learn so little about the characters' pasts.'[4] Its hero has no official identity ('M. George' is a *nom de guerre*), no family, no nationality, no professional career – 'he pretended rather absurdly to be a seaman' (p. 5) – no political allegiances; he has acquaintances but no real friends. Apart from voyages to the West Indies that have left no trace on his sensibilities – they were 'other men's adventures' (p. 8) – his past is a blank page. This hero with no story and no voice becomes passion-ately involved with a woman about whom no end of stories are voiced. Their shared adventure might be seen as a concerted bid to escape the narratological positions in which they seem trapped – M. George as the eternal narratee, bombarded with dialogue from all quarters, Rita as the degraded object of false idealizations and prurient gossip-narratives.

Scarcely the 'hyperactive adolescent'[5] Schwarz makes him out to be, M. George does almost nothing but listen in the first hundred pages of the novel. The act of listening defines George's position in the text, his relationships with others, and his relationship with language. His adventure as a listener begins in a 'legitimist drawing-room' in Marseilles crowded with 'women eating fine pastry and talking passionately' (p. 10). Ill at ease in this community of female speakers, M. George's interest is stirred by the mention of male adventure: a female party-goer describes Mr Mills, who is also present, as '"*un naufragé*"' (p. 10). Mills confirms that '"this is hardly the place to enter on a story of that kind"' (p. 11); the prospect of hearing this tale of shipwreck at a different venue seems to promise M. George an escape from drawing-room chatter into a more expansive and exciting world of male nautical storytelling.

The protagonist is drawn by Mills into a typically Conradian scene of male storytelling, begun in a Marseilles café, and continued late into the night over a '*bivouac* feast' in Blunt's rooms on the street of Consuls. Except that the storytelling double act of Blunt and Mills is more elaborately stage-managed than anything we might find in, say, 'Youth' or 'Falk'. This pair of raconteurs, a shipwreck-survivor and a professional soldier, have M. George on 'tenterhooks of expectation' (p. 11). But the emphasis of their story falls neither on Mills's nautical adventure nor on Blunt's military career but rather on Doña Rita's life-story. The 'discovery' of Rita, her emergence into fashionable Paris circles, and her vulnerability as beautiful heiress – all of this is reported, apparently disinterestedly, by Blunt. The story is designed to provoke M. George's fascination, to stir feelings of gallant protectiveness towards her. Like so many Conrad characters, Rita is a 'floating outline' (p. 31) conjured up by the evocative words of a storyteller, a source of narrative fascination, like Kurtz or Jim, commanding the interest of an audience eager to know more. 'For these two men had *seen* her', M. George recalls, 'while to me she was only being "presented", elusively, in vanishing words, in the shifting tones of an unfamiliar voice' (p. 31; italics in original). At this stage in the novel M. George does not attempt to dissociate the intrinsic elusiveness of Rita from the shifting indeterminacy of Blunt's words: he is content to listen naïvely, 'open-mouthed' (p. 30), 'staring and listening like a yokel at a play' (p. 58), his head swimming with new names and stories.

M. George's development as a character might be measured in terms of his gradual shift from eager, naïve listening into a more sceptical relationship with words. He describes his younger self as 'infinitely receptive' (p. 8), with a limitless appetite not only for adventure, but also for narrative. When he visits Doña Rita's villa in the company of Blunt and Mills the occasion is dominated by the talk of a Paris journalist to whom George listens intently, even though the others are studiously unattentive, like 'a very superior lot of waxworks' (p. 69). But M. George's openness to language and narrative narrows as he learns to distrust the stories he is told and to be wary of the storytellers who produce them.

The text positions M. George at the heart of a repellent polyphony of social and political gossip. Whenever Therese is in his presence, she turns on the 'tap of her volubility' (p. 246). When Mrs Blunt, who speaks with the same 'drawing-room tone' (p. 176) as her son, spouts 'the most appalling inanities of the religious-royalist-legitimist order' (p. 173), M. George listens 'deferentially... yet with every nerve in my body tingling in hostile response to the Blunt vibration' (p. 175). He recalls her 'holding me with an awful, tortured interest' (p. 189), an image of captivity and bodily discomfort that sums up the plight of the involuntary narratee:

[F]or a long time I heard Mme. Blunt *mère* talking with extreme fluency and I even caught the individual words, but I could not in the revulsion of my feelings get hold of the sense. She talked apparently of life in general, of its difficulties, moral and physical, of its surprising turns, of its unexpected contacts, of the choice and rare personalities that drift on it as if on the sea; of the distinction that letters and art gave to it, the nobility and consolations there are in aesthetics, of the privileges they confer on individuals and (this was the first connected statement I caught) that Mills agreed with her in the general point of view as to the inner worth of individualities and in the particular instance of it on which she had opened to him her innermost heart. (p. 179)

M. George feels 'bitterness of contemptuous attention' (p. 182) – a phrase worthy of Razumov – as he 'listens' to Blunt's mother; his written narrative might even be seen as an act of belated vengeance on her overbearing voice. M. George won't quote a single word of Mrs Blunt's extended monologue, though every indication of its platitudinous qualities is given in his catalogue of half-remembered truisms from her 'innermost heart'. When he does quote from her dialogue, he does so in a satirically selective fashion, breaking up her speech into a garbled stream of consciousness:

Educated in the most aristocratic college in Paris . . . at eighteen . . . call of duty . . . with General Lee to the very last cruel minute . . . after that catastrophe – end of the world – return to France – to old friendships, infinite kindness – but a life hollow, without occupation . . . (p. 182)

Mrs Blunt's version of her son's life-story comes across as dialogue overheard rather than heard, reduced – once it has passed through the filter of M. George's scepticism – to a few choice examples of snobbery and sentimentality.

Female voices seem to antagonize M. George with peculiar intensity. The wife of a distinguished financier associated with the legitimist movement is another gossiping voice that plagues him. The financier has briefed his wife on M. George – '*Il m'a causé beaucoup de vous*' (p. 244) – and she regards Conrad's hero as nothing more than a source of priceless drawing-room gossip:

I confess that I was so indifferent to everything, so profoundly demoralized, that having once got into that drawing-room I hadn't the strength to get away; though I could see perfectly well my volatile hostess going from one to another of her acquaintances in order to tell them with a little gesture, 'Look! Over there – in that corner. That's the notorious Monsieur George.'

At last she herself drove me out by coming to sit by me vivaciously and going into ecstasies over '*ce cher* Monsieur Mills' and that magnificent Lord X; and ultimately, with a perfectly odious snap in the eyes and drop in the voice, dragging in the name of Madame de Lastaola and asking me whether I was really so much in the confidence of that astonishing person. '*Vous devez bien regretter son départ pour Paris,*' she cooed, looking with affected bashfulness at her fan ... (pp. 244–5)

An excitable name-dropper, this flirtatious society hostess is obviously insincere in her expressions of familiarity as she angles tactlessly for personal revelations from the hero. As is often the case in this novel, the narrative shifts from English to French when particularly hollow or pretentious dialogue is reported. M. George's disgust at the sound of Rita's name on other people's lips brings to mind the words of Barthes: 'I do not want the Other to speak of you.'

The Arrow of Gold begins with M. George eagerly seeking out voices, and staying up all night to listen to them; but those voices soon begin to seek him out, interrupting his sleep and forcing themselves on his attention. Part IV opens with him waking to the sound of Therese's voice, listening to which is likened by George to 'the prolongation of a nightmare: a man in bonds having to listen to weird and unaccountable speeches against which, he doesn't know why, his very soul revolts' (p. 155). M. George feels trapped by the language of his housekeeper, as though domestic space and domestic language are acting in concert to immobilize him.

The Arrow of Gold displays a singular fascination with houses, rooms, and their contents, especially the sumptuously appointed chambers of Rita's property on the street of the Consuls – the studio, the fencing-room, and the converted drawing-room. Entry into this building marks the beginning of M. George's initiation into adult life, though he will ultimately acquire a 'horrid mistrust of the whole house' (p. 312). Houses in this novel impose suffocating limits on language and action; even the 'rose-embowered hut of stones' (p. 339), where M. George enjoys a brief period of secluded happiness with Rita, is only a temporary refuge from gossip. The intimate association between physical enclosure and subjection to language is most tellingly revealed in the following heated exchange between Blunt and Rita:

'More space. More air. Give me air, air.' ... 'I envy you, Monsieur George. If I am to go under I should prefer to be drowned in the sea with the wind on my face.' ...

A short silence ensued before Mr Blunt's drawing-room voice was heard with playful familiarity.

'I have often asked myself whether you weren't really a very ambitious person, Doña Rita.'

'And I ask myself whether you have any heart.' She was looking straight at him and he gratified her with the usual cold white flash of his even teeth before he answered.

'Asking yourself? That means you are really asking me. But why do it so publicly? I mean it. One single, detached presence is enough to make a public. One alone. Why not wait till he returns to those regions of space and air – from which he came.' (p. 148)

Blunt and Rita's references to 'regions of space and air' gesture towards the sea as a space of openness and unlimited freedom, a world away from the enforced intimacies of drawing-room culture, the fixed social rituals, private salons, and locked doors of this novel's confining architecture. Blunt, a 'drawing-room person' (p. 33) with a 'drawing-room tone' (p. 47), is so much a creature of this elegantly airless environment that it seems to define his very voice. Rita says of Blunt's talk that '"the words of tradition and morality as understood by the members of that exclusive club to which he belongs"' are '"parrot language"' (p. 208). The superficial elegance and finesse of Blunt's conversation is undermined by his parrot-like repetition of self-admiring mottos: '"*Je suis Américain, catholique et gentilhomme*"', '"I live by my sword."'

Whereas the 'regions of space and air' constantly beckon M. George as a means of escape from the suffocating banalities of 'parrot language', no such route is available to Rita. The quarry of journalists, gossips, and fortune-hunters, Rita moves constantly between Tolosa, Paris, and Marseilles, driven by a fear of capture and closure. The first thing we learn of her is that she has '"fled here [Marseilles] for a rest"' (p. 17). '"[Y]our life"', says George to Rita, '"seems to be a continuous running away"' (p. 293). Like many Conrad heroes, Rita is acutely conscious of her own vulnerability to language. '"I stand here with nothing to protect me from evil fame"', she says, '"a naked temperament for any wind to blow upon"' (p. 84). The voice of 'evil fame' fastens particularly on her relationships with men, such as her 'Venetian episode' (pp. 57–8) with Don Carlos, written up as fiction by the poet Versoy and repeated as 'fact' in the newspapers. Another twice-told tale is the story of her 'capture' in the garden of Allègre's pavilion. According to Blunt, Allègre happened upon Rita as she sat reading in the garden: 'She raised her eyes and saw him looking down at her thoughtfully over that ambrosian beard of his, like Jove at a mortal. They exchanged a good long stare, for at first she was too startled to move; and then he murmured,

"*Restez donc*'' (p. 34). This version of the story presents Rita as the startled captive of the male artist's Olympian gaze. Rita emphatically contradicts this: '"I could have run away. I was perfectly capable of it. But I stayed looking up at him and – in the end it was HE who went away and it was I who stayed"' (p. 216). Rita's task resembles that assigned to women critics and artists by Sandra M. Gilbert and Susan Gubar: 'women must kill the aesthetic ideal through which they themselves have been "killed" into art'.[6] Even the idealistic representations of Rita in painting and sculpture reduce her to the status of an exquisite *objet trouvé*; whilst the versions of her identity current in gossip transform her into a human equivalent of the headless dummy in Blunt's apartment.[7]

Perhaps the most vehemently contested Rita-narrative is that of her pursuit through the rocky countryside of Lastaola by the young Ortega. Therese's version of this story paints Ortega as the victim of Rita's shameless flirtations: '"the poor dear child drove her off because she outraged his modesty"' (p. 158). For Rita herself, this story is one of trauma: when chased by Ortega she would take refuge in a shelter and he would sit outside with a heap of stones, and '"rave and abuse me"' (p. 112). The final confrontation with Ortega is a recapitulation of that trauma. Ortega plays the role of storyteller-as-nemesis: he comes to Marseilles threatening to spark off an 'explosive scandal' (p. 275) with vicious gossip about Rita's many lovers and her infidelities. The climax of the novel is not the unseen duel between George and Blunt, but the altogether more fraught three-way confrontation between Ortega, George, and Rita. The confrontation unfolds as a 'ferocious farce' (p. 322), a deadly game of hide-and-seek in a suite of adjacent rooms with communicating doors. The two lovers are ultimately brought together as the captive audience of Ortega's savage threats and abject pleas for recognition. Dominating the novel's climax is the shrill and manic voice of this insane storyteller on whose lips language is devalued and profaned. Just as the 'Blunt' vibration generated nerve-tingling hostility in George, so too does Ortega's voice provoke a physical ordeal: '[Ortega] positively bellowed: "Speak, perjured beast!" which I felt pass in a thrill right through Doña Rita like an electric shock' (p. 313). This image of listening as the bodily experience of traumatizing noise – the thrill is empathetically registered by George – establishes the voice as a weapon far more deadly than the barbaric armoury of spears, choppers, swords, and knives in the fencing room.

Though Ortega ultimately succeeds only in wounding himself, his violent incursion from Rita's past into her present is powerful evidence of the irrepressibility of gossip; not even her flight to the Alps with M. George has any effect on the stories that continue to circulate about them. When Rita complains that '"I can't run away unless I got out of my skin and left that behind"' (p. 107), she reaches the same conclusion as many of Conrad's fugitives from language – that any attempt physically to outdistance gossip is futile. Except that she *does* finally evade narrative closure in a way that confirms the truth of Madame Léonore's verdict: '"She is for no man! She would be vanishing out of their hands like water that cannot be held"' (p. 135). If Rita vanishes mysteriously into an unknown future, M. George escapes into a nautical world that has always been dimly visible on the margins of the text. On leaving one particularly tedious legitimist soirée, he visits the balancelle and, with silent approval and admiration, watches the shipwrights at work: 'From the way they went about their business those men must have been perfectly sane' (p. 245). M. George's implied contrast between the talkative female socialites of the legitimist salon and the hard-working male artisans couldn't be more pointed; a similar juxtaposition is made in 'Heart of Darkness', between the back-biting 'pilgrims' and the engineers in the Central Station.

Although the sea is the location of positive value in *The Arrow of Gold*, the text itself can find very little representational room for this 'region of space and air'. 'But how and why did he get so far from the scene of his sea adventures', as M. George asks himself when listening to Mills, 'was an interesting question' (p. 16). This question might usefully be redirected to Conrad, who has pushed maritime adventure to the very margins of narrative vision. George's sea-expeditions are described in a remarkably perfunctory way: one of them is 'carried out without a hitch' (p. 125); another is 'an extremely successful trip' (p. 229). Each trip is made to seem a formality; even the final three months, which are full of hair's-breadth escapes from danger and culminate in a dramatic shipwreck, are condensed into just three pages (pp. 254–6). The condensed style of M. George's diary jottings – 'Parted with Mills on the quay' (p. 88), 'Hearty handshake. Looked affectionately after his broad back' (p. 89) – reduces the 'adventure' side of the narrative to an absolute minimum. Maritime space is squeezed out, limited to perhaps a dozen pages, as though the novel itself is hemmed in by its claustrophobic social world, and obliged to 'parrot' the 'drawing-room tones' of Mrs and Captain

Blunt speak. Unseen, and as it were unrepresentable, the sea in *The Arrow of Gold*, is, to borrow Frederic Jameson's words, a 'non-place'.[8] The hero escapes from the novel's drawing-room people and drawing-room voices into this utopian, gossip-free non-place – 'The faithful austerity of the sea protected him from the rumours that fly on the tongues of men' (p. 351) – but the text remains problematically house-bound to the end.

PART II

Marlow

CHAPTER FOUR

Modernist storytelling: 'Youth' and 'Heart of Darkness'

'Of all the many narrators within novels', writes Barbara Hardy, 'perhaps none combines caring with impartiality more zealously than Conrad's Marlow.'[1] I suspect that for many readers Charlie Marlow does indeed linger in the memory as an eminently scrupulous and sympathetic narrator whose genius for friendship and exemplary open-mindedness illuminate 'Youth', 'Heart of Darkness', *Lord Jim*, and *Chance*. The very antithesis of Schomberg, for whom storytelling is always and only an outlet for vindictive mendacity, Marlow is presented by his creator as an impeccably scrupulous narrator. But not everyone would agree with Conrad's estimate of Marlow as a 'most discreet, understanding man'.[2] Indeed, in the light of recent criticism it would not be too difficult to paint an altogether less flattering picture of Conrad's nautical raconteur: Marlow as arch-misogynist, monologic imperial speaker, casual racist. In fact, literary theory has only sharpened the long-standing suspicion over Marlow's credentials as a plausible and trustworthy narrator. Ever since word got out that Henry James (whose good opinion Conrad would have cherished) was in the habit of referring to Marlow as 'that preposterous master mariner',[3] many critics have sought to rescue him from the incredulous disdain of his detractors. Conrad called 'Heart of Darkness' his 'Apologia pro Vita Kurtzii';[4] and much that has been written on Marlow belongs to the same genre. William York Tindall's 'Apology for Marlow' typifies the perception that the function of Marlow, far from being self-evident, requires strenuous justification. Most critics who write on Marlow find themselves defending his outrageous long-windedness, portentous obscurity of diction (the notorious 'adjectival insistence' diagnosed by Leavis), or other evidence of artistic perversity.[5]

The sheer quantity of words spoken by Marlow (close to a thousand pages of narration) exceeds many times over the amount of dialogue spoken by any other Conrad character – indeed, few individuals in any literature can have been quite so prodigiously talkative – yet Marlow's biographical details remain curiously thin on the ground. Fully fledged characters tend to be fleshed out with personal history, family background, home address; apart from a solitary aunt in Brussels, Marlow has none of these. He is something of a ghost compared to such robust figures as the Captains MacWhirr and Allistoun – neither of whom, moreover, speaks the same language as Marlow. Like some characters in Dickens, Marlow seems to have developed his own eccentric personal dialect, an idiosyncratic blend of bluff sailor's talk and amateur metaphysics that James, Leavis, and others have found hard to swallow.

Conrad's own reflections on Marlow are as politely unhelpful as we might expect from his Author's Notes, where he affects a certain reluctance to concede that there is anything strange, radical or difficult in his fiction. His tantalizingly brief description of the genesis and function of his nautical raconteur is no exception. Marlow is 'a most discreet, understanding man', a tactful confidant who has Conrad's ear in the lonely hours of literary composition. Various descriptions of his role ('a clever screen, a mere device, a "personator", a familiar spirit, a whispering "daemon"'[6]) are casually dismissed; his presence in these texts is not the effect of premeditated formal artistry – instead, Conrad would have us believe that he merely stumbled across Marlow, and that their acquaintance 'ripen[ed] into friendship' in much the same way that, in the tales themselves, Marlow's chance acquaintances become intimate comrades. Responding to the charge of long-windedness, Conrad claims in the Note to *Lord Jim* that far from exhibiting superhuman narratorial stamina, his nautical raconteur could quite plausibly have narrated his share of the novel during an evening's yarn-swapping. Before we dismiss these remarks as mere anecdotal whimsy, it is worth reflecting on Conrad's strategy – conscious or otherwise – of encouraging us to regard Marlow as a real person. Like any fictional character, Marlow is a construct, a linguistic entity rather than a flesh-and-blood human being; but Conrad's Notes encourage us to respond to him as a sympathetic personal presence. By speaking of Marlow as if he were real, Conrad exhibits a fidelity to the integrity of his fictional world that most readers share to some extent when they are immersed in that world. Given the extraordinary strains placed on the artifice in *Lord Jim* and *Chance*, however, it seems likely that for most readers the sense of Marlow as a human presence is frequently qualified by a more sceptical perception of Marlow as a 'mere device', a textual construct, a set of words on the page.

Because Marlow is a 'transtextual' character, there is a question mark over the continuity (or otherwise) of his personality between four discrete texts. Robert Hampson wonders if we are right 'to talk of "Marlow" as if there were a single, consistent character, or should we rather think of four separate Marlows?' Is the maudlin raconteur of 'Youth' the same person as the flippant sexist of *Chance*? There is no consensus on this question: Jakob Lothe insists that the relationship between the four Marlows is purely nominal, whereas Cedric Watts, ingeniously if unconvincingly, reads the Marlovian quartet as a 'vast biographical narrative'.[7] Marlow is a discontinuous character – hardly a 'character' at all, in the conventional sense – made and unmade in the reader's imagination; and our readerly efforts to 'recuperate' Marlow, to salvage a coherent personality from a mass of conflicting textual evidence, reproduces his own efforts as a 'rescuer' of the lost souls he encounters.

Probably the most tempting means of stabilizing Marlow's flickering mirage of personality is to anchor him in Conrad's own identity. Some critics have spoken of 'Conrad–Marlow' or 'Conrad/Marlow' as though the two are interchangeable. This is, of course, a serious misrepresentation of Conrad's art. Marlow is not Conrad, and although Conrad may at times appear to endorse Marlow's opinions, Marlow is contradicted by his listeners (and by himself) frequently enough for the gap between creator and persona to be obvious to any moderately attentive reader. It would be wrong, of course, to suppose that Marlow is a mere pseudonym for Conrad. The Marlovian narratives are dramatic monologues in prose, and it would be as facile to ascribe Marlow's opinions to Conrad as it would to identify Robert Browning too closely with any of his beguiling monologuists. More persuasive is Vincent Pecora's suggestion that Marlow is Conrad *sous rature*: Marlow is Conrad's fictive proxy, who permits the author to absent himself from the texts. In a letter written during his time in Africa, Conrad suggests to Marguerite Poradowska that '"L'absent" sera mon appelation officielle à l'avenir"'[8] (an epithet, incidentally, that would be a more than adequate replacement for the desperately overworked 'homo duplex'). Given that Marlow permits Conrad to relinquish the vantage-point of supervisory authorial presence, one might even suggest that the invention of Marlow anticipates the deconstruction of the Author performed in different ways by Roland Barthes and Michel Foucault.[9]

Conrad is the very type of the modern writer as exile: displaced from his Polish homeland, a country that officially didn't exist in 1857, he was destined never to feel at home, never to belong exclusively to one national culture or tradition. Not unlike that other great modernist, James Joyce, Conrad is also 'exiled' from his own fictive world; but the contrast between these two instances of modernist self-fashioning is instructive. Whereas Joyce's alter ego is embroiled in a cultural and religious heritage that his creator wants to abandon, Conrad's Marlow represents a culture to which his creator wants to belong. Stephen is, in all important respects (language, religion, nationality), Joyce's former self; Marlow is Conrad's future self. As John Batchelor suggests, Marlow is '*the kind of Englishman whom Conrad would have liked to have been*'.[10] In psychological terms, Conrad seems to have been selling himself to the British public in a form they would recognize; by masquerading as a native English speaker he bids to assuage any lingering doubts about his own fluency. However, rather than viewing Marlow as a symptom of Conrad's faltering self-confidence, I prefer to see him as a *transitional* persona: he functions as Conrad's passport to the mainstream of British literary culture, but also as a 'Trojan Horse' figure, smuggling an outlandish literary voice into the conservative pages of *Blackwood's Magazine*.

Popularly known as 'Maga', *Blackwood's* was pitched to an audience of naval officers, colonial administrators, and British expatriates. (It has often been noted that Marlow's audience in 'Youth' and 'Heart of Darkness' represents a cross-section of likely *Blackwood's* readers.) 'One was in decent company there', Conrad later wrote to J. B. Pinker, 'and had a good sort of public. There isn't a single club and messroom and man-of-war in the British Seas and Dominions which hasn't its copy of Maga.'[11] Having found this snug middlebrow niche, however, Conrad does not simply pay his obeisances to British literary culture and maritime tradition; indeed, surely nothing could be less ingratiating in this context than the tales he went on to produce. It now seems remarkable that *Blackwood's*, the colonial gentleman's favourite light reading, should have been so accommodating to a writer who subjects imperial dreams of heroism to withering irony and takes such hair-raising liberties with narrative technique.

In what is probably the most influential modern discussion of the origin and functions of Marlow, Ian Watt discerns behind Conrad's nautical raconteur not the captains courageous of Victorian romance, but the supersubtle heroes of Henry James's novels of the 1890s – novels which Conrad devoured with supreme admiration. One of James's most significant legacies to modern theories of fiction lies in his evident preference for 'showing' over 'telling'. James suspected that a seamless aesthetic illusion will be irreparably damaged if punctuated by the *ex cathedra* moral judgements of a disembodied, omniscient narrator. Accordingly, in *The Spoils of Poynton* (1897) and *What Maisie Knew* (1897), he pioneered the use of the 'registering consciousness', whereby the novel's dramatic substance is filtered through the fugitive, fragmentary impressions of a subjective witness. This method, which enabled James to navigate a middle-way between the extremes of cold Flaubertian detachment and intrusive authorial omniscience, is emulated by Conrad in the Marlow narratives.[12] Marlow permits his creator to enjoy the best of both worlds: he functions as a Jamesian 'registering consciousness'; but he also lavishes on recorded experience the kind of expansive moral commentary and analysis that had seemed banished from modern fiction with all the other discredited tropes of high Victorian realism. It is not difficult to appreciate the thinking behind James's suavely flabbergasted reaction to Conrad. After all, what possible kinship could there be between the refined creatures of the Jamesian drawing-room and the washed-up derelicts of Conrad's God-forsaken colonial outposts? Conrad saw nothing incongruous in describing James's rarefied fiction in robustly masculine terms: likening artistic creativity to 'rescue work carried out in darkness against cross gusts of wind',[13] he succeeds in making James's fiction sound like an episode from 'Typhoon' or *The Nigger of the 'Narcissus'*.

Conrad's audacious assertions of aesthetic kinship rest on his perception that he shares with James a concern to salvage enduring impressions from the bewildering flux of experience. The hallmark of the Marlow narratives is a complex interplay between breakdown and rescue, deconstruction and restoration, that finds its most literal expression in the narratives of nautical breakdown and heroic rescue, but also extends powerfully into questions of moral, psychological, and linguistic deconstruction. Marlow's vocation is rescue work: the objects of his compassionate curiosity are, invariably, *in extremis*: Mr Kurtz, hell-bent on gratifying his base appetites, is too far gone in his self-destructive orgy for Marlow's intervention to save his life, although he does his best to salvage Kurtz's reputation; 'Lord' Jim is contemplating suicide when Marlow intervenes on his behalf; Flora de Barral, the troubled heroine of *Chance*, is also on the brink of disaster (quite literally, for she is perched on the edge of a hundred-foot quarry) when she first encounters Marlow. Conrad's fictive proxy is the custodian of damaged reputations and fractured narratives: Marlow's self-appointed task is to rescue the objects of his narratorial curiosity from the kind of ravenous textuality that swallows up Axel Heyst. Indeed, one might say that 'Marlow' is the name given by Conrad to a privileged editorial discourse that gathers to itself countless subsidiary narratives (island gossip, sailors' yarns, deathbed confessions), delivering them up, suitably embellished with moral commentary, for his audience. But Marlow does not only enjoy editorial control over a wide range of speech genres, he also cites and translates a variety of different languages. His tale in 'Heart of Darkness', although reported in English, records his encounter with French, Latin, Russian, German, and a number of unidentified African languages. As Robert Hampson has noted, 'Heart of Darkness' is 'heteroglot experience ... rendered into a largely monoglot text'.[14] Not that this process of translation is free from linguistic or cultural problems. Marlow's storytelling discourse operates as a privileged 'metalanguage' that is never entirely free from contamination by other languages or speech genres; his tales are themselves prone to structural 'breakdowns' that involve the audience – or the reader – in challenging acts of interpretative recuperation.

Rescue work of a more literal kind is the theme of Marlow's debut, 'Youth', a tale which confirms that Conrad was no mean exponent of magazine fiction, especially the genre of male nautical reminiscence. As Jacques Berthoud reminds us, the sea was in the 1890s nothing less than a national obsession, and, on the face of it, 'Youth' might seem a fairly innocent product of the late-Victorian appetite for rousing maritime fiction.[15] It is Conrad's most light-hearted, buoyant tale, in which a middle-aged Marlow celebrates the boundless optimism and reckless courage with which Youth goes forth to encounter experience. Although Marlow's nostalgia is tempered with affectionate irony, there is a degree of sentimental desperation in his rekindling of the spontaneous exuberance of youth, a desperation manifest in the tale's fatiguingly irrepressible style – a side-effect, no doubt, of the fact that our storyteller is generously lubricated with claret.

Even if it now seems a surprisingly innocuous overture to his full-dress narrations, 'Youth' anticipates some of the key traits of the bleaker Marlow tales. For all its buoyancy of tone, 'Youth' is a tale of delay, frustration, and shipwreck. Transporting a cargo of coal from Tyneside to Bangkok, the *Judea* runs aground once, is held up for a month waiting for its cargo on the Tyne, returns to Falmouth three times after springing leaks, and ultimately sinks in the Indian Ocean. Hardly the stuff of epic adventure, this stop–start voyage provokes Marlow to an ecstasy of retrospective affirmation: '"O youth! The strength of it, the faith of it, the imagination of it! To me she was not an old rattle-trap carting about the world a lot of coal for a freight – to me she was the endeavour, the test, the trial of life"' (p. 12). This comically ramshackle vessel acquires for Marlow, in his youthful naïveté, a freight of symbolic significance under which it ultimately founders. The famous description of the 'death' of the *Judea* (pp. 34–5) is, crucially, witnessed only by Marlow, as the men 'dozed, waked, sighed, groaned' around him. The image of a ship abandoned to an opulently picturesque death by fire, a consciously elaborate set-piece description, raises the intriguing problem of the aestheticization of work in Conrad. Marlow's private epiphany – the picturesque conflagration of the *Judea*'s final moments represents the burning fire of youth – is obtained only at the expense of the failure of the *Judea*'s mission. Its cargo of coals does not reach its appointed destination but is appropriated rather to fuel the tale's symbolism.

Conrad's work ethic, the ideology of selfless commitment to physical labour as an end-in-itself, seems incompatible with his tendency to privilege those moments where prosaic routine is transcended.[16] Frequently in his fiction and prose writings, Conrad praises the iron discipline and clockwork routines of maritime culture. But in 'Typhoon', *The Nigger of the 'Narcissus'*, and *The Shadow-Line* Conrad is obliged to stage-manage storms, shipwrecks, disease, and mutiny, because without dramatic conflict there can be no story. Routine is, in itself, the antithesis of narrative, or, to borrow D. A. Miller's useful term, the 'nonnarratable equilibrium' against which 'narratable' aberrations become visible.[17] For Conrad, the breakdown of order and the disruption of routinized perceptions are the preconditions of the redemptive possibilities of art. Behind the idealized artist-as-rescuer lurks the shadowy figure of the artist-as-saboteur whose secret affinities are with the dissidents and *agents provocateurs* of the political fiction, and whose task is, to borrow a phrase from 'An Outpost of Progress', the 'negation of the habitual'. The restoration of routine, the strategies whereby breakdowns in language, sanity, ideology are patched up, is a task that devolves to Marlow: it is no coincidence that his 'first command' is the job of piloting a lifeboat to shore as the *Judea* founders.

The fragile nostalgia of 'Youth' is formal as well as thematic. Hankering after a lost era when genial raconteurs enjoyed an easy rapport with like-minded good fellows, Conrad's written text masquerades as human speech. Marlow enjoys the kind of direct, face-to-face relationship with his audience of which the modern novelist can only dream. When Marlow concludes by asking whether youth was not the best time of his listeners' lives, his sentiments are confirmed in a moment of wordless communion:

we all nodded at him: the man of finance, the man of accounts, the man of law,
we all nodded at him over the polished table that like a still sheet of brown water
reflected our faces, lined, wrinkled; our faces marked by toil, by deceptions, by
success, by love; our weary eyes looking still, looking always, looking anxiously
for something out of life, that while it is expected is already gone – has passed
unseen, in a sigh, in a flash – together with the youth, with the strength, with
the romance of illusions. (p. 42)

Just as the table reflects back their faces, so the narrator's incanta-
tory repetitions echo the very cadences and phraseology of Marlow's
yarn, as though Marlow's personal lexicon has spilled over into the language of the frame narrator. Not that this corroborative recapitulation
of Marlow's sentiments should come as any surprise; after all, this is no
scratch audience, but a group of ex-sailors whose civilian careers have
brought them lucrative, if not exactly glamorous, postings in the city of
London, the commercial and administrative heart of empire. In 'Youth',
as in 'Heart of Darkness', Marlow's audience comprises the anonymous frame narrator, an accountant, a company director, and a lawyer.
Edward Said describes the group as 'Conrad's way of emphasizing the
fact that during the 1890s the business of empire . . . had become the empire of business.'[18] With its proud tributes to English pluck and resilience,
and its shamelessly nostalgic evocation of youthful high spirits, Marlow's
tale is sure to find an appreciative audience in this group of middle-aged
veterans of the seafaring life, even if a mischievous reader might suspect
that Marlow's audience is nodding in bemused tolerance of his maudlin
sentimentality, or even, like the suspiciously torpid audience of 'Heart of
Darkness', nodding off.

As I have already suggested, there is no better introduction to the
textual nostalgia which Marlow incarnates than Walter Benjamin's elegy
for traditional storytelling. Benjamin's comments on the subtle interplay
between the storyteller's illusory presence and imminent absence are
particularly redolent of Marlow. It would be misleading, however, to
read Benjamin's storyteller as a kind of belated blueprint for Conrad's
Marlow, since Marlow's tales contravene the 'norms' of storytelling as
laid down by Benjamin: Marlow has no homespun wisdom or practical
counsel to impart to his listeners, though his tales do abound in the kind
of psychological speculation that Benjamin praised traditional stories for
lacking. Advance notice of such oddities is given by the frame narrator
in 'Heart of Darkness':

The yarns of seamen have a direct simplicity, the whole meaning of which
lies within the shell of a cracked nut. But Marlow was not typical (if his

propensity to spin yarns be excepted), and to him the meaning of an episode was not inside like a kernel but outside, enveloping the tale which brought it out only as a glow brings out a haze, in the likeness of one of these misty halos that sometimes are made visible by the spectral illumination of moonshine. (p. 48)

This slippery double simile, worthy of Marlow himself in its resistance to simple paraphrase, carries a sting in the tail. Marlow is credited by the frame narrator with a rare observational subtlety, but his reference to 'moonshine' could well be a coded warning to the effect that our storyteller's words may not always be as pregnantly meaningful as they appear. Marlow's friends seem to tolerate, rather than relish, his eccentric storytelling habits. '[W]e were fated', remarks the frame narrator, incapable of mustering even the most perfunctory enthusiasm for his friend's impending anecdote, '– we were fated, before the ebb began to run, to hear about one of Marlow's inconclusive experiences' (p. 51). Marlow seems less a western sailor than an eastern mystic – 'a Buddha preaching in European clothes' (p. 50) – whose ascetic demeanour is compounded by his reluctance to talk about himself. The Marlow of 'Heart of Darkness' is a haggard convalescent whose narrative conspicuously lacks the life-affirming *bonhomie* of 'Youth' or the timeless wisdom of Benjamin's storyteller: his yarns announce not the resurrection of the storyteller, but his death throes.

Ian Watt claims that 'Marlow's story can be considered as an abortive quest to escape from the breakdown in society's modes of reciprocity.'[19] 'Heart of Darkness' is a compendium of breakdowns: from the ignominious collapse of Enlightenment values in the Dark Continent and the wreckage of imperial dreams of progress in the luxuriant Congolese wilderness, to the mental breakdowns of Fresleven and Kurtz and the scuttling of Marlow's steamer by his own colleagues in a shabby plot to destroy Kurtz. Marlow, our first-hand witness on the scene of this devastation, is professionally committed to the colonial system even as he sees only too clearly the horrors perpetrated in its name. Ultimately, this contradiction causes Marlow's own storytelling procedures to break down. Writing cedes authority to speech – Marlow is postulated as an originating voice of which the texts are mere transcripts – yet that very speech exhibits many of the flaws and imperfections commonly imputed to writing. Marlow's presence is no guarantee of determinate meaning; he proves to be, as it were, an obscure, ambiguous, illegible speaker whose narrative 'seemed to shape itself without human lips in the heavy night-air of the river' (p. 83).

Because my emphasis will be on linguistic breakdowns in the text, it is as well to take note of objections to such readings of 'Heart of Darkness'. The poststructuralist tendency to ignore the tale's historical context has led an exasperated Owen Knowles to declare:

For some exponents of Yale-speak it matters little whether *Heart of Darkness* is set in Africa, Chipping Ongar, Saratoga or Baden Baden: its moral, political and geographical *données* – indeed its whole complex of 'surface' features – are simply irrelevant accidentals or immaterial figments in a general atemporal 'drama of narratability' or 'web of linguistic self-begettings'.[20]

One might object that Conrad himself seemed fairly unconcerned as to the geography of his tale. Africa and the Congo are never named in 'Heart of Darkness': Marlow himself calls the place 'some ghastly Nowhere' (p. 148). Not, of course, that Marlow's topographical ignorance licenses historical amnesia on the part of his readers. Indeed, Knowles's allegations are all the more serious if one reflects that formalist criticism, or the neo-formalism of deconstruction, colludes in the racist and imperialist attitudes that some readers impute to the story itself. Marlow's 'ghastly Nowhere' can be transformed at a stroke into the Unconscious, the maternal body, or a vast unreadable text; but, in stripping the tale of its historical context, the formalist critic emulates Marlow's own culpable ignorance of African history.

Whilst I share Knowles's misgivings about the critical imperialism of deconstruction, I do not believe that formalism is automatically ahistorical. To focus on the acute linguistic self-consciousness of Conrad's novella is not automatically to exclude its 'moral, political and geographical *données*'.[21] There is no question that 'Heart of Darkness' is obligingly susceptible to deconstruction; but the gentle pleasures of textual indeterminacy are, in this tale, treacherously intertwined with the violent falsehoods of colonial discourse. As Marlow very soon discovers, language is as much a weapon of colonial exploitation as the French man-of-war firing blindly into the continent or the Winchester rifles of the trigger-happy pilgrims on his steam-boat. His narrative puns grimly on the many forms of 'report' he encounters: the fusillades of the pilgrims firing at the natives, the salvos of the French warship, the 'objectless blasting' of the cliff at the Company station. This last puts Marlow in mind of a different form of report:

'Another report from the cliff made me think suddenly of that ship of war I had seen firing into a continent. It was the same kind of ominous voice; but these men could by no stretch of imagination be called enemies. They were called criminals, and the outraged law, like the bursting shells, had come to them, an insoluble mystery from the sea.' (p. 64)

Marlow fully appreciates that of all the weapons at the colonists' disposal, language is the most insidiously powerful. The 'ominous voice' of the law is every bit as brutal and dehumanizing as the arsenal of conventional weapons used to subjugate the colonized African people. Implicit in Marlow's storytelling is a struggle to free his own discourse from the over-arching authority of the 'ominous voice' of colonialism. Whether Marlow successfully articulates his own humanitarian opposition to empire, or whether his protests are ultimately recuperated to the impotent liberal conscience of imperialism, is a moot point; but any reading of 'Heart of Darkness' that makes it out to be straightforwardly pro- or anti-colonialist must inevitably turn a blind eye to its textual *dynamic* – the deepening obscurity and equivocality of Marlow's discourse as it is painfully compromised by the appalling revelation that the man on whom he pins his hopes is the very personification of empire's 'ominous voice'.

Anxious as he is to maintain the role of neutral observer, Marlow is caught up in a power-struggle between two factions: the 'sordid buccaneers' whose motives are unapologetically mercenary, and the 'gang of virtue', for whom the imperial project ought to be guided by some higher philanthropic purpose. Marlow is suitably dismayed when he finds that his aunt has been taken in by the sentimental effusions of their cheerleaders in the European press:

'There had been a lot of such rot let loose in print and talk just about that time, and the excellent woman, living right in the rush of all that humbug, got carried off her feet. She talked about "weaning those ignorant millions from their horrid ways", till, upon my word, she made me quite uncomfortable.' (p. 59)

To his consternation, Marlow finds himself conscripted to the 'gang of virtue', a gang whose hypocrisy he denounces even as he feels an involuntary and inexplicable affinity with their figurehead: Mr Kurtz. At the Central Station, Marlow lets the company brickmaker believe that he is affiliated to the gang of virtue; and, more significantly, that he is in league with Kurtz. Much as he deplores the atmosphere of poisonous mendacity in the company stations – '"I hate, detest, and can't bear a lie"' (p. 82) – Marlow's own truth-telling enterprise is compromised by his willingness to perjure himself for the man who might represent an enlightened alternative to the cynical profiteering of the other Company agents.

As he journeys up the Congo, Marlow encounters talk of Kurtz from every quarter: news of his success as an agent, hints about his political destiny, and misinformation about his predicament at the Inner Station. '*Vox et praeterea nihil*' (as First Secretary Vladimir nearly describes the lazy *agent provocateur* Verloc[22]) aptly describes many critics' view of Marlow: the idea that Marlow is only a voice, a mouthpiece for Conrad, a spokesman for imperialism, a traditional storyteller, is one of the half-truths deplored by Owen Knowles in his attack on deconstructive Conradians. Certainly Conrad's readers have largely ignored the fact that Marlow is also an exemplary *listener*. As I have already suggested, Conrad's characters can be roughly divided into two opposing camps: the garrulous verbal narcissists and the reticent, vulnerable 'overhearers', traumatized by other people's aggressive loquacity; but Marlow is unique in that he belongs to both categories. He can be an aggressive speaker, making no secret of his low opinion of the interpretative competence of his listeners. If his Congolese nightmare is too outlandish to swallow, the blame is firmly ascribed to their own anaesthetized urban sensibilities:

'You can't understand. How could you? – with solid pavement under your feet, surrounded by kind neighbours ready to cheer you or to fall on you, stepping delicately between the butcher and the policeman, in the holy terror of scandal and gallows and lunatic asylums – how can you imagine what particular region of the first ages a man's untrammelled feet may take him into by the way of solitude – utter solitude without a policeman – by the way of silence – utter silence, where no warning voice of a kind neighbour can be heard whispering of public opinion?' (p. 116)

Marlow's polemical statement of the unbridgeable differences between London and Africa transforms itself into a revelation of their uncanny resemblance. The huge leap of imagination that his audience can't make (from London to Africa) becomes the repression they can't lift (the 'holy terror' lurking beneath the surface of metropolitan life). Bette London's claim that Marlow's 'act of narration constitutes the audience as a collective yes-man'[23] is quite misleading. The more alert members of Marlow's audience on the *Nellie* will recognize that there is, of course, no 'solid pavement' under their feet; nor will the Accountant or the Director of Companies be reassured by Marlow's treatment of bureaucrats in his tale. The imagery he uses to berate his audience – butchers, policemen, public opinion, and terror of the gallows – will reappear in a later Conrad text, *The Secret Agent*, which might almost be read as a book-length expansion of Marlow's glimpses of gothic London.

Marlow will not be satisfied, it seems, until he can make his metropolitan listeners share the same aural trauma that defined his Congolese experience. He is, as it were, the hypersensitive eavesdropper at large in the text, the uninvited guest lurking on the fringes of other people's conversations. John Vernon, in an essay on overhearing and eavesdropping in fiction, remarks that for the narrator to be positioned as eavesdropper enhances the illusion that the world of a novel exists not by authorial fiat, but externally and objectively.[24] However, the conversation Marlow overhears between the General Manager and his uncle offers no such reassurance. The 'revelation' of this scene – the plot to abandon the fever-racked Kurtz to the jungle by sabotaging Marlow's relief mission – emerges so obliquely and elliptically as to have passed unnoticed until Cedric Watts picked up on it.[25] This conspiracy is all but suppressed by Marlow's own narrative: in narratological terms, Marlow's *sjuzhet* strenuously resists the emergence of its *fabula*. This scene emphasizes the sense of distance and belatedness that plagues our understanding of Kurtz, not least because Marlow supplies no gloss for these garbled snatches of overheard dialogue. 'I heard: "Military post – doctor – two hundred miles – quite alone now – unavoidable delays – nine months – no news – strange rumours"' (pp. 90–1). If there is a scarcity of hard information, there is no shortage of 'strange rumours', unconfirmed hints and coded messages about Kurtz's fate. The nephew actually quotes Kurtz: '"Each station should be like a beacon on the road towards better things, a centre for trade of course, but also for humanizing, improving, instructing." Conceive you – that ass!' (p. 91). Intriguingly, Kurtz's rhetoric reverses the governing image of the entire tale: his vision of imperialism as a highway to illumination precisely reverses Marlow's journey into thickening obscurity. But, paradoxically enough, Kurtz's luminously charismatic rhetoric intensifies the obscurity of Marlow's experience. Because Kurtz's words (which comprise the longest verbatim sentence we have from him) are filtered through the aggressive cynicism of the general manager and the milder scepticism of Marlow, it is impossible to gauge whether they were originally uttered in a spirit of naive idealism, flagrant hypocrisy or nascent megalomania. This scene of overhearing, with its structure of embedded quotations, shows the Chinese-box structure of 'Heart of Darkness' (concentric tales nestling snugly within one another) transformed into an echo chamber of decentred voices in search of an origin.

Even the humble British nautical manual that Marlow stumbles upon some fifty miles below the Inner Station will not yield up its secrets.

Marlow initially greets Tower's (or Towson's, or Towser's – Marlow is curiously forgetful and indecisive on this point) *Inquiry into some Points of Seamanship* as a comforting fragment of a world of cast-iron certitudes he has left behind. With its illustrative diagrams, tables of technical data, and unambiguous language, the book is hailed by Marlow as something '"umistakably real"' (p. 99), a text securely anchored in the practical realities of physical labour and professional technique. Inexplicably, however, it is defaced by what looks like cipher but is presently identified as Cyrillic script in the hand of the 'Harlequin', the rogue Russian trader who has affiliated himself to Kurtz. As we learn more about the book's owner, Marlow's enthusiastic reception for the *Inquiry* comes to seem a little premature. An English sailors' manual is unlikely bedside reading for the Russian devotee of Kurtz, himself a gratuitously incongruous presence in Conrad's wilderness. A set of wildly disparate Conradian motifs coalesce bizarrely in the figure of the bepatched youth. Decked out in vivid primary colours against the tenebrous shades of the wilderness, the Harlequin feels like the tale's mockery of its own mournful sobriety. He is an interloper in the narrative with the temerity to hog our attention when Kurtz should by rights be occupying centre-stage.

Perhaps there is a perverse logic to the fact that Kurtz's hagiographer should resemble a fugitive from the enclave of revolutionary mystics in the Geneva of *Under Western Eyes*, because in Conrad's imagination Russia is a by-word for mystic verbiage. Doubtless the Harlequin would be as intoxicated by the revolutionary mysticism that flourishes in the salon of Madame de S– as he is by the 'splendid monologues' of Kurtz. The Harlequin's dual obsessions, with the practical wisdom of the *Inquiry* and the idolatrous cult of Kurtz, precisely replicate Marlow's curious indecision over whether imperialism's saving grace is 'efficiency' or 'the idea'. These divergent principles are yoked together in the person of the Harlequin, who cherishes the manual (a veritable Bible of efficiency) but also adulates the Kurtzian 'idea'.

Marlow fondly imagines work to be an end in itself, an ideal that Towser appears to confirm; but no text, it seems, is innocent of the interpretative designs of its owners and readers. This innocent sailor's handbook partakes of the cryptic illegibility of Africa, but also supplies the technical expertise for the whole business of colonial exploitation. Indeed, the Harlequin's marginal scribbles resemble nothing so much as the '"valuable postscriptum"' appended to Kurtz's report to the International Society for the Suppression of Savage Customs: 'Exterminate all the brutes!' (p. 118). The Harlequin's cryptic marginalia and Kurtz's deranged postscriptum are dangerous supplements which undermine the self-sufficiency of their primary texts.[26] Walter Benjamin's famous observation that 'There is no document of civilization which is not at the same time a document of barbarism'[27] might almost have been coined to describe Kurtz's pamphlet – a hymn to progress that doubles as a prospectus for genocide.

Benjamin's dictum might equally serve as unofficial epigraph for the novella as a whole, especially if one agrees with Chinua Achebe's denunciation of the 'racism' of 'Heart of Darkness'.[28] Achebe alleges that 'Heart of Darkness' participates in the imperial 'dehumanization' of Africa: the continent is reduced to a 'metaphysical battlefield', where white Europeans play out their existential dramas of psychic disintegration, whilst African people are reduced to a supporting cast of mute 'savages' (given intelligible speech only on two occasions in the tale). Achebe has no time for what he calls Marlow's 'bleeding-heart sentiments': such insipid humanitarian decency is no substitute for articulate political opposition to empire and the racism that nourishes it. Yet Achebe does appear to curb the ferocity of his polemic in his closing paragraph: 'Conrad saw and condemned the evil of imperial exploitation but was strangely unaware of the racism on which it sharpened its iron tooth' (p. 13). The view that Conrad criticizes imperialism without wholly transcending its xenophobic ideology is reiterated in dozens of books and articles on the theme.[29]

There is much to take issue with in Achebe's essay. In one of the most judicious discussions of Conrad and empire, Edward Said notes that even if Conrad's fiction is informed by a Eurocentric world-view, its formal and linguistic self-consciousness pre-empt the complacent assumption that such a world-view is natural or inevitable.[30] For example, the allegation that African people appear in 'Heart of Darkness' only as voiceless 'extras' in a Eurocentric drama requires careful scrutiny. Certainly Marlow's reports of howling, shrieking, jabbering Africans tend to reduce non-European languages to the status of non-language. But as Robert Hampson has pointed out, this act of reduction is Marlow's, not Conrad's; the Harlequin, who confesses that he doesn't '"understand the dialect of this tribe"' (p. 137), displays an awareness of real language differences that is at odds with Marlow's tendency to relegate non-European languages to the status of 'pre-verbal, pre-syntactic sound'.[31] In short, there is an awareness in 'Heart of Darkness' of cultural and linguistic differences that is wider and more subtle than Marlow's.

Also contentious and problematic is Achebe's reading of the significance of Kurtz: 'Can nobody see the preposterous and perverse arrogance in thus reducing Africa to the role of props for the break-up of one petty European mind?' Mistakenly, I think, Achebe takes 'Heart of Darkness' to be a novel about the psychological disintegration of Kurtz (the 'petty European mind'); but Conrad's interest is focused on the *myth* of Kurtz rather than his psychological condition. Kurtz is the vanishing-point of 'Heart of Darkness', at which the trajectories of readerly expectation and Marlovian travelogue converge with the gossip and conjecture voiced by nearly everyone Marlow meets; yet when Kurtz does finally appear *in propria persona* he is a shadow of his own reputation. Marlow intuitively associates Kurtz's voice with 'real presence'; but it is the ghostly non-presence of Kurtz that permeates the atmosphere of the tale. '"He was just a word for me"', Marlow attests. '"I did not see the man in the name any more than you do"' (p. 82). The 'original Kurtz' is dissolved into the myth of Kurtz; his Intended symbolizes his unfulfilled intentions, unrealized potential, ruined ambitions – all the enormous promise in politics, commerce, and art that Kurtz so extravagantly squandered. The Kurtz who crawls on all fours through the jungle, whose deathbed ramblings haunt Marlow's downstream voyage, seems incommensurate with the Kurtz who commanded the veneration of an entire Congolese community, and who posthumously dominates Marlow's imagination.

The stature of Kurtz is radically unstable. His name (*kurz* is German for 'short', according to Marlow's translation) belies his true size: he looked '"seven feet long"' (p. 134); conversely, however, his giant reputation – particularly his reputation for charismatic oratory – is scarcely borne out by his meagre, disconnected whispers to Marlow. We have only the Harlequin's word for it that Kurtz's words were exceptionally powerful; and it is especially curious moreover that Marlow should credit Kurtz with supreme vocal prowess long before he has heard either Kurtz or the Harlequin speak: '"The man presented himself as a voice"', Marlow remembers. '"[O]f all his gifts the one that stood out preeminently, that carried with it a sense of real presence, was his ability to talk, his words"' (p. 113). That Kurtz is only a voice is an intuitive hypothesis which Marlow never gets to test against reality – since Kurtz is a profoundly diminished figure when the steamer arrives. Anthony Fothergill has suggested that the shift from an early emphasis on Kurtz's professional achievements to a 'new and emphatic centring on Kurtz's voice', suggests that 'Marlow, confronting the "meaningless" wilderness, seeks an audible and comprehensible voice to explain it. He is ready to endow Kurtz's voice ... with that power and authority.'[32] In other words, Kurtz becomes an incarnation of the wilderness and, quite literally, its spokesman. This transmutation of silent African wilderness into eloquent European individual is short-circuited by the baffling presence of the Harlequin, whose devotion to Kurtz is matched only by his admiration for British seamanship. As spokesman for Kurtz – and hence the spokesman for a spokesman – he permits Kurtz to remain in the background, his 'splendid monologues' unheard.

Marlow hesitates between pursuing a detective-like interrogation of the enigma of Kurtz and a circumspect acquiescence in indeterminacy. Nowhere is this tension between revelation and repression felt more powerfully than in Marlow's halting account of the extent of Kurtz's depravity:

'his – let us say – nerves, went wrong, and caused him to preside at certain midnight dances ending with unspeakable rites, which – as far as I reluctantly gathered from what I heard at various times – were offered up to him – do you understand? – to Mr Kurtz himself.' (pp. 117–18)

'Unspeakable' in this context may be taken to indicate both 'disgusting' and 'inexpressible', though precisely why language has faltered at this moment is a moot point. Is it because Marlow wants to spare his audience the appalling details of Kurtz's plunge into turpitude, or that his experience in the Congo belongs to an order of experience that is genuinely ineffable? Perhaps Marlow realizes that some things are best left to the imagination, that his listeners, noticing those tell-tale gaps and consciously lame euphemisms, are free to interpolate whatever imaginary abominations gratify their own prurience. The reader, too, is at liberty to step in where Marlow fears to tread. '[T]he reader collaborates with the author',[33] as Conrad once wrote of his fiction; but friendly co-operation may entail political collusion, especially if one is too busy juggling with different interpretative options to grasp the historical reality – the horror of genocide and torture in King Leopold's Congo – behind Marlow's narrative.

'"All Europe"', Marlow remarks, '"contributed to the making of Kurtz"' (p. 117) – which of course implies that all Europe must bear some of the blame for his downfall; moreover, just as the entire cast of 'Heart of Darkness' contributes to the making of the myth of Kurtz, so its readership continues that process of mythologization. The reader of 'Heart of Darkness' is invited to participate in the making of Kurtz, to join Marlow, the Harlequin, and all the rest of them in the construction of his myth. Serious questions about the pleasures derived from reading 'Heart of Darkness' – so forcefully articulated in Nina Pelikan Straus's feminist critique of the novella[34] – hinge decisively, I think, on the interpretative possibilities generated by Marlow's sketchy and evasive portrait of Kurtz. Conrad implicates his readers in the elevation of Kurtz to the dubious position of all-purpose anti-hero. Those gaps in his narrative ensure Kurtz a built-in longevity inasmuch as generations of readers will reinvent him in the image of their own interpretative strategies, as a Faustian 'hero of the spirit', as 'the protean mnemonic of an arbitrary quality about the relationship of morality to experience',[35] or as the lost primary voice behind the infinite play of *différance*.

Rather than attempting to recuperate an 'original' Kurtz, or deploring Marlow for the absence of documentary factuality in his own version, it is better, I think, to ponder the uses of the myth of Kurtz – and, in particular, Marlow's own strategic use of Kurtz to underwrite the failures of his own narrative. Marlow is accorded the terrible privilege of hearing Kurtz's last words, as well as the unenviable task of transmitting an expurgated version of his career to the bereaved family and colleagues who hover like vultures in the novella's closing pages. Marlow's decision not to shatter the illusions of the Intended is, of course, notorious; but an equally grave transgression of his truth-telling ethos is his decision to excise the postscriptum from Kurtz's report before he delivers it up to a Company official. Marlow's loyalty to Kurtz means that, by the end, he deals not in the truth, but in half-truths, misinformation, and censorship.

In a lengthy meditation on the meanings of 'The horror! The horror!', Marlow contrasts his own blurred, ambivalent, half-hearted recollections of his upriver crisis with the terrible deathbed epiphany that he imagines was granted to Kurtz:

'I was within a hair's-breadth of the last opportunity for pronouncement, and I found with humiliation that probably I would have nothing to say. This is the reason why I affirm that Kurtz was a remarkable man. He had something to say. He said it . . . He had summed up – he had judged. "The horror!" He was a remarkable man. After all, this was the expression of some sort of belief; it had candour, it had conviction, it had a vibrating note of revolt in its whisper, it had the appalling face of a glimpsed truth – the strange commingling of desire and hate . . . he had made that last stride, he had stepped over the edge, while I had been permitted to draw back my hesitating foot. And perhaps in this is the whole difference; perhaps all the wisdom, and all truth, and all sincerity, are just compressed into that inappreciable moment of time in which we step over the threshold of the invisible. Perhaps! I like to think my summing-up would not have been a word of careless contempt. Better his cry – much better. It was an affirmation, a moral victory paid for by innumerable defeats, by abominable terrors, by abominable satisfactions. But it was a victory!' (p. 151)

Previously, Marlow has equated lying with dying, but in this passage he makes a much more traditional claim: a dying man's last words are the most absolutely truthful of his life. 'Last words', famous or otherwise, have long captured the imagination since they offer tantalizing glimpses of a finality that is not available in the midst of life. In 'The Storyteller', Walter Benjamin lays very striking emphasis on the link between storytelling and death, likening the storyteller's audience to listeners who cluster attentively around the bed of a dying man to hear his last words. It is traditionally thought that a definitive verdict on one's life only becomes possible at the moment of one's death: everything that has gone before has been tentative, premature, provisional. Benjamin suggests that the storyteller 'has borrowed his authority from death'[36] inasmuch he speaks of life with an authority comparable to that of the dying. For Benjamin, it would appear that the full significance of the storyteller has become visible only now that he is on the threshold of extinction: the death of the storyteller is the precondition of the counsel offered in Benjamin's essay.

Kurtz's dying cry resonates with the finality of a definitive verdict on an entire lifetime. 'The horror! The horror!' is a definitively monologic utterance inasmuch as it admits of no rejoinder. Marlow imputes to Kurtz's words an unanswerable finality he would rather do without. Kurtz has summed up, Kurtz has judged; but Marlow would prefer to do neither. No words of his can rival the resounding authority of 'The horror!'

Marlow's discovery that he has 'nothing to say' belies that fact that, on the face of it, he has plenty to say. '"[M]ine is the speech that cannot be silenced"' (p. 97), he declares; his long-suffering listeners could indeed be forgiven for thinking that Marlow is excessively fond of his own voice. To extend this comparison, Marlow is like an (apparently) terminally ill patient who, stubbornly refusing to give up the ghost, outlives his doctor's most sanguine prognostications. Conrad's ancient mariner continues to speak under a kind of compulsion whereby the burden of authoritative finality is palmed off on Kurtz; the authority of death that underwrites his last words is abdicated by Marlow. If death is equated with truth then lying is equated with *living*: Kurtz is the alibi for the lies Marlow has told, and must continue to tell.

Given its obsession with speech and writing, presence and absence, 'Heart of Darkness' might well be seen as a text that plays all too easily into the hands of deconstruction, a text only too happy to lead the reader into an epistemological cul-de-sac. What I have attempted to show here – and the generalization holds good for *Lord Jim* and *Chance* – is that the failures of language and vision in 'Heart of Darkness' are as it were forced on Marlow's narrative by a wider ideological crisis. Any interpretation of 'Heart of Darkness' that reads it purely as an endlessly self-referring textual artefact succeeds merely in adding a further layer of obfuscation to the narrative. Admittedly, the tale is awash with linguistic and narratological failure, but the tales Marlow cannot tell, the truths he cannot utter – in short, the 'unspeakable' life-story of Kurtz – are not fully ousted from the narrative; rather, they lurk in its interstices, ensuring that Marlow's colonialist apologetics can be read at one and the same time as *post*colonial critique.

CHAPTER FIVE

The scandals of Lord Jim

Conrad's novel of maritime scandal has left no end of scandalized readers in its wake, from the early reviewers who scoffed at the implausible length and wilful obscurity of Marlow's tale, to the more sophisticated readers who complain that the second half of Conrad's broken-backed narrative capitulates to the very romantic errors that the first half clinically diagnoses. In the primary scandal of *Lord Jim*, the Mecca-bound pilgrim ship *Patna*, dilapidated and on the point – or so it seems – of sinking, is abandoned by its white officers. Miraculously for its human cargo of 800 pilgrims (and mortifyingly for its officers), the vessel's rusty bulkhead holds out, and the ship is towed to harbour with no lives lost other than that of the engineer who suffers a heart attack in the initial panic. With two officers hospitalized, and the captain fled to America, only the chief mate Jim stays to face the official inquiry, enduring the full glare of professional disgrace, as well as the gleeful curiosity of the novel's very considerable cast of gossiping sailors. Far more than is commonly recognized, *Lord Jim* is a drama – and, in a particularly cruel sense, a comedy – of *embarrassment*. Overwhelmingly, it is embarrassment rather than guilt that Jim exhibits in the aftermath of the *Patna* affair; as he blushes and stammers his way through his excruciating debriefings with Marlow, it becomes clear that the only victim of Jim's criminal negligence was the narcissistic confidence in his own potential for heroism that he imbibed from popular adventure literature. In his own eyes at least, Jim's jump from the *Patna* thus takes on the character of an horrendous gaffe that he can never live down, rather than a morally reprehensible dereliction of duty.

As Marlow rightly suggests, the *Patna* incident is, in a sense, a diabolical '"practical joke"' (p. 108) that leaves its victim physically intact but his dignity in tatters. In his essay on *Othello*, where he views Iago as 'a practical joker of a peculiarly appalling kind', W. H. Auden discovers surprising affinities between practical-joking and experimental science.[1] Like the scientific investigator, the practical joker constructs an artificial situation in which the object of his curiosity – the folly of human self-deception – is fully knowable and controllable. *Lord Jim* similarly orchestrates a situation in which its hero's delusions are mercilessly laid bare. Indeed, Conrad's adaptation of his source material is indicative of a ruthless sharpening of focus on Jim's culpability. The real-life scandal that inspired Conrad – the notorious *Jeddah* affair of 1880 – is closely followed in *Lord Jim*: a pilgrim ship carrying close to a thousand Muslims from Singapore to Jeddah is abandoned by its white officers who are convinced it is about to sink, and who inform the authorities that the ship went down with all its passengers.[2] However, Conrad is careful to eliminate all the extenuating circumstances that emerged at the official inquiry: the heavy seas and hurricane-force winds, the scuffles between officers and passengers, the presence of the captain's wife on board (enabling him to argue that her personal safety was his first concern), and the fact that Augustine Podmore (the prototype for Jim) was actually *thrown* overboard by some pilgrims. No such shreds of mitigating evidence disguise Jim's naked culpability, which is exposed with all the ruthless clarity of a laboratory experiment.

Marlow's appearance in chapter 4 of *Lord Jim* could scarcely be more timely; as he assumes the position of narrator, he transforms what might have been a painfully systematic study in the psychology of cowardice into something far more subtle, open-minded, and open-ended. Not that his generosity towards Jim is entirely altruistic. Marlow recognizes that embarrassment is contagious, that the story of Jim's failure of nerve makes for desperately uncomfortable listening; accordingly, his version of the story is oblique to the point of evasiveness. One of the favourite stooges of *Lord Jim*'s critics, the *New York Tribune* reviewer who confidently informed his readers that the *Patna* did in fact sink, stands as a salutary reminder of the confusions and misdirections that figure so powerfully in any first-time reader's experience of the novel. Conrad's narrative tactics oblige us to share the sense of bafflement that looms so large in Marlow's response to Jim. Rather persuasively, Mark Conroy has expressed the suspicion that '[Marlow's] bafflement is often strategic: the story may have counsel neither Marlow nor his audience/readership would wish to heed.'[3] For all Marlow's lengthy, searching meditations, Jim's identity remains as '"prodigiously inexplicable"' (p. 98) as the non-shipwreck of the *Patna*. In spite of Marlow's best efforts to grasp the essence of the *Patna* enigma, some *je ne sais quoi* of Jim's identity inevitably slips through his fingers.

The idea that Jim resists narrative explanation is a necessary part of Marlow's own resistance to the epidemic of gossip sparked off by Jim's disgrace:

'[T]his affair . . . had an extraordinary power of defying the shortness of memories and the length of time: it seemed to live, with a sort of uncanny vitality, in the minds of men, on the tips of their tongues. I've had the questionable pleasure of meeting it often, years afterwards, thousands of miles away, emerging from the remotest possible talk, coming to the surface of the most distant allusions.' (pp. 137–8)

Marlow intervenes with a certain reluctance in this ceaseless, ubiquitous conversation: after all, by retelling Jim's story, he is only becoming the most recent of a chain of innumerable gossip-figures whose fascination with the *Patna* affair amounts to a permanent unofficial inquiry in which every loafer and hanger-on qualifies as an expert witness. On the other hand, Marlow is equally convinced that the court of inquiry, with its hard-nosed empiricism, can offer no genuine insights: '"You can't expect the constituted authorities to inquire into the state of a man's soul"' (pp. 56–7). Certainly the court's sentence – the cancelling of Jim's certificate – is an impersonal bureaucratic decision that scarcely throws much psychological light on the affair. There is more than a grain of truth in Chester's blunt opinion that Jim shouldn't torment himself over the loss of '"A bit of ass's skin"' (p. 161).

Having queried the authority of collective speech (gossip) and bureaucratic writing (the law), Marlow launches his own inquiry, which aims to navigate scrupulously between these two extremes. In a marvellously evocative preamble, the narrator locates Marlow's tale on the borderland between speech and writing:

And later on, many times, in distant parts of the world, Marlow showed himself willing to remember Jim, to remember him at length, in detail and audibly.

Perhaps it would be after dinner, on a verandah draped in motionless foliage and crowned with flowers, in the deep dusk speckled by fiery cigar-ends. The elongated bulk of each cane-chair haboured a silent listener. Now and then a small red glow would move abruptly, and expanding light up the fingers of a languid hand, part of a face in profound repose, or flash a crimson gleam into a pair of pensive eyes overshadowed by a fragment of an unruffled forehead; and with the very first word uttered Marlow's body, extended at rest in the seat, would become very still, as though his spirit had winged its way back into the lapse of time and were speaking through his lips from the past. (p. 33)

Neither the verbatim transcript of a one-off oral performance, nor an abridged version of many such tellings, Marlow's yarn hovers indecisively between the two. Whilst conceding that Marlow's yarn has a 'vaguely plural status', Ian Watt emphasizes what most readers probably feel: that this is a 'new and intensely committed venture by Marlow at understanding and conveying the full meaning of Jim's story'.[4] My own view is that whilst the 'plurality' of Marlow's narrative is rapidly forgotten, Conrad does want to keep in view the structural origins of the single written text in the plurality of oral narratives. To this end, Marlow's frequent retelling of the same tale is emphasized, as is the fact that everyone in the Archipelago has his own version of it. One critic terms *Lord Jim* 'an art novel, a novelist's novel, a critic's novel'[5] – which might suggest that the finished article is a polished and finely wrought affair, when in fact *Lord Jim* does its best to flaunt its own generic archaeology. Its roots are in the world of informal conversation and yarn-spinning, and in the ancient genre of the story-collection famously instanced by Chaucer, Boccaccio, and the *Arabian Nights*; and the novel enacts the evolution of collective storytelling, through clique storytelling, into the epistolary narrative sent by Marlow to the 'privileged man' that occupies chapters 36–45. The transition from oral to written narrative signals that the mass oral dialogue has finally been whittled down to a one-to-one exchange. Curiously, however, the shift to writing seems to be implicated in the disappointing moral and narratological simplifications of the novel's second phase.[6]

Alone among those who express an interest in the *Patna* affair, Marlow is able to listen sympathetically to the man at the heart of the scandal. The compassionate attention he extends to Jim is explicitly contrasted with the hearing Jim receives at the court of inquiry. Because of the very inflexible limits on its investigational remit, the court is constitutionally incapable of listening to the particular story that Jim wants to tell: when he strays from unadorned factual recollections into an impressionistic evocation of his state of mind on the *Patna*, he is brutally cut short. Deprived of the opportunity to tell his side of the story, Jim begins to despair of language itself:

For days, for many days, he had spoken to no one, but had held silent, incoherent, and endless converse with himself, like a prisoner alone in his cell or like a wayfarer lost in a wilderness. At present he was answering questions that did not matter though they had a purpose, but he doubted whether he would ever again speak out as long as he lived. The sound of his own truthful statements confirmed his deliberate opinion that speech was of no use to him any longer. (p. 33)

Jim is caught between two forms of futile pseudo-communication: the inquiry, whose rigid question-and-answer procedures preclude the spontaneity of authentic dialogue, and the claustrophobic inwardness of 'dialogue with himself'. It is obviously no coincidence that, just as Jim's dilemma is becoming intolerable, Marlow is glimpsed for the first time in the public gallery, set apart from the crowd by his appearance of intelligent sympathy. The scene is thus set for Marlow's entrance as the patient auditor who will free Jim from moral and linguistic isolation and heal the rift the *Patna* scandal has opened up between Jim and his erstwhile comrades. Marlovian dialogue is thus presented as an ideal norm of dialogue in a text where speech and writing all too frequently fall short of performing the daunting task of explaining Jim's career.

Jim's fate resembles that of the outsider or eccentric in the gossipy neighbourhoods of nineteenth-century realist fiction. D. A. Miller, analysing the function of gossip in *Middlemarch*, discerns a deeper motive behind the prurient *Schadenfreude* on which gossip ostensibly thrives: gossip functions as an informal system of moral surveillance that monitors 'improper' behaviour. As Miller puts it: 'Characters who are felt to threaten the ideology of social routine enter immediately into the network of chatter and gossipy observation that promotes their eccentricities to a state of story-worthiness.'[7] Gossip trades on what 'everybody knows/says', an illusory but powerful consensus that has affinities with Heidegger's description of the 'They-self' (*das Man*) into which authentic Being constantly risks being dissolved.[8] The gossiper borrows the authority of the 'They' in order to reinforce the 'timeless' values of the speech community: '[T]he logic of gossip', writes Miller, 'makes it the inevitable practice of a community that would remain unhistorical.'[9]

Unlike the narrator of *Victory*, who enjoys a lofty vantage-point from which 'chatter and gossipy observation' can be deplored, Marlow is situated in the same discursive world as the sailors for whom Jim has become a laughing-stock. Marlow is both the eloquent conscience of the community and its gossip-in-chief; for all his disapproval of the jeering, gloating voice of quayside gossip, he too is ubiquitously loitering with intent to listen, observe, and talk. To a certain extent Marlow's emphasis on the widespread talk about Jim is another means of enlisting our sympathy for the hero: if Jim has been grossly misrepresented by the promiscuous gossip of the 'deck-chair sailors', then it falls to Marlow's audience, or Conrad's reader, to reach a more sympathetic verdict on his case.

Marlow is quietly adamant that Jim is not a laughing-stock, a pariah, or a source of shame: he is 'one of us'. These words comprise the refrain of Marlow's apology for his protégé: '"I liked his appearance; I knew his appearance; he came from the right place; he was one of us"' (p. 43). 'One of us' is shorthand for a complex sense of professional and national belonging; it signifies approved membership of the elite community of officer-class sailors and expatriates whose moral credentials are visible in their very deportment. 'Us' signifies the non-narratable equilibrium of the novel, the loose aggregation of European sailors and colonial expatriates who gossip about Jim, and for whom he has become public property: '"he did after a time become perfectly known, and even notorious, within the circle of his wanderings (which had a diameter of, say, three thousand miles), in the same way as an eccentric character is known to a whole countryside"' (pp. 197–8). As more and more members of the speech community queue up to pass judgement on Jim, it begins to seem that his case might be nothing more than a flimsy pretext for canvassing as many opinionated, anecdotal voices as the Archipelago has to offer. This ulterior motive is hinted at in a letter Conrad wrote to Hugh Clifford, who had read, and criticized, some of the early serial instalments:

Your criticism is just and wise but the whole story is made up of such side shows just because the main show is not particularly interesting – or engaging I should rather say. I want to put into that sketch a good many people I've met – or at least seen for a moment – and several things overheard about the world. It is going to be a hash of episodes, little thumbnail sketches of fellows one has rubbed shoulders with and so on. I crave your indulgence; and I think that read in the lump it will be less of a patchwork than it seems now.[10]

For all its breezy diffidence, this letter confirms that Jim enables the novel to transform the scattered harbours and trading-posts of the Archipelago into a homogeneous neighbourhood united by the same epic conversation. The speech communities of *Lord Jim* are so densely populated that the novel has earned the dubious compliment of a book-length study of its *minor* characters.[11] Indeed, one might suggest that *Lord Jim* is a portrait not of its eponymous hero but of Brierly, Jones, the French Lieutenant, Bob Stanton, Chester, Old Robinson, and all the other members of the narratorial ensemble – a portrait, in short, of 'us'.

The stubborn longevity of the *Patna* scandal makes it all the more urgent for Marlow to produce a definitive version of Jim, a kind of variorum edition with apocrypha and corruptions properly subordinated. But Marlow's tale hesitates continually on the brink of uttering the 'last word' on Jim. Originally planned as a short story of 20,000 words, *Lord Jim* grew in the telling as it appeared in serial form in *Blackwood's* between October 1899 and November 1900. And, on the evidence of his letters in the intervening months, Conrad was as surprised as his publishers to find the finished article was nearly seven times longer than his original estimate. Naturally, the novel bears traces of this unplanned expansion: '"My last words about Jim shall be few"' (p. 225) is Marlow's confident assertion in chapter 22; notoriously, however, the remainder of his spoken narrative runs to tens of thousands of words – as does its epistolary supplement. The *Sketch* reviewer termed the novel 'a character sketch, written and rewritten to infinity'.[12] Leavis similarly views *Lord Jim* as 'neither a very considerable novel, in spite of its 420 pages, nor one of Conrad's best short stories'.[13] Marlow's unconscionably protracted anecdote seems as resistant to closure as the gossip that inspires it. The impulse to finalize, to frame Jim as definitively as one of Stein's entomological specimens, is sabotaged by Marlow's reluctance to part company with his friend, or to cast anything so crass as a 'verdict' on Jim. These contradictory impulses produce an anecdotal narrative run riot, which despite its unnatural length falls exasperatingly short of telling the whole story.

In his Author's Note, responding to reviewers who described *Lord Jim* as an overgrown short story, and who objected that 'no man could have been expected to talk all that time, and other men to listen so long', Conrad mounts a curiously literalistic defence of his novel:

Men have been known, both in the tropics and in the temperate zone, to sit up half the night 'swapping yarns.' This, however, is but one yarn, yet with interruptions affording some measure of relief; and in regard to the listeners' endurance, the postulate must be accepted that the story *was* interesting . . . As to the mere physical possibility we all know that some speeches in Parliament have taken nearer six than three hours in delivery; whereas all that part of the book which is Marlow's narrative can be read through aloud, I should say, in less than three hours. (p. vii)

Whether or not this is an accurate estimate of the duration of Marlow's marathon tale, the analogy with the inordinate length of some political speeches is revealing, for Marlow's tale, like the parliamentary filibuster, exploits length for its own sake. The filibustering speaker attempts to sabotage the legislative process by using up all available debating time, exhausting subject-matter and listeners alike in a bid to derail new legislation; the process might be seen as the revenge of oral open-endedness on textual closure.[14] Like any storyteller, Marlow is eager to command the rapt attention of his audience; but in *Lord Jim* another part of him wants rid of his audience, wants to exhaust their patience and curiosity and hence lay the gossip about Jim to rest.

Conrad's own compositional procrastination only confirms what we already suspect: that in *Lord Jim* the aesthetic of delay creates a text which is less a novel than a short story that refuses to end, that procrastinates over its own closure and imperfectly conceals its own anecdotal germ, thus retaining structural affinities with the hinterland of gossip and rumour in which it originated. The discrete elements of the narrative are determined to resist being integrated into some over-arching teleological superstructure. The primary anecdote breeds subsidiary anecdotes, subsidiary enigmas – stories that might have been told, that have been excised from some imaginary, comprehensive *ur*-text, leaving only such tantalizing traces as the near-confession of the French Lieutenant:

'"Take me, for instance – I have made my proofs. *Eh bien!* I, who am speaking to you, once . . ."

'He drained his glass and returned to his twirling. "No, no; one does not die of it", he pronounced, finally, and when I found he did not mean to proceed with the personal anecdote, I was extremely disappointed; the more so as it was not the sort of story, you know, one could very well press him for.' (p. 147)

Marlow's tale would have been still longer, it seems, were it not for the reticence of some of his more discreet acquaintances. Marlow himself indicates that he is mining selectively from an inexhaustible seam of dialogue. Having described Jim's stints under Denver and Egström, Marlow remarks that '"There were many others of the sort, more than I could count on the fingers of my two hands"' (p. 197). The effect of this is, as Watt puts it, to make the novel's chronological sequence lapse into an 'undefined iterative limbo'[15] in which Jim drifts from one dead-end job to another in a career that threatens to become listlessly episodic rather than heroically progressive.

Marlow's encounter with the French Lieutenant who helped to tow the abandoned *Patna* to shore (pp. 137–49) is one of the major disruptions of lucid, linear, teleological narrative in the novel. *Lord Jim* at this point becomes a 'bilingual' text, written in English but interspersed with parenthetical French. It is possible that the entire conversation between Marlow and the French officer was originally conducted in French – after all, the Marlow of 'Heart of Darkness' speaks passable French – but the precise balance of languages is not specified. What is remarkable about Marlow's recollection of the conversation is the very strong residue of French it contains. Rarely is the encounter between two languages quite so intensively marked in Conrad's prose. His habit of obscuring foreign tongues by implicitly rendering them into English has been conspicuously abandoned at this point in the novel. Consider, for example, the following passage:

'He clasped his hands on his stomach again. "I remained on board that – that – my memory is going (*s'en va*). *Ah! Patt-nà. C'est bien ça. Patt-nà. Merci.* It is droll how one forgets. I stayed on that ship thirty hours . . . "' (p. 140)

If the Lieutenant's memory is faltering, Marlow's seems positively super-human. Not only does he record precise details about the Lieutenant's body language, but he produces a more-or-less verbatim record of their conversation that juggles confidently between French and English, effortlessly translating (and often parenthetically untranslating) the Lieutenant's words, and all the while displaying a gift for verbal mimicry that captures even the Lieutenant's distinctively 'French' pronunciation of *Patna*. To a certain extent Marlow seems to be according French linguistic parity with English – the kind of parity that is not enjoyed by, for example, the language of Patusan, which is never specified in *Lord Jim*. But, if anything, the Lieutenant's French seems be all too perfectly and transparently translatable; the language barrier is negotiated far more easily in this scene than it will be in Marlow's interview with the German-speaking Stein. It hardly seems necessary, for example, for Marlow to inform his audience that 'is going' is '*s'en va*', any more than it is necessary for 'doubtless' to be glossed as '*sans doute*', 'mind you' as '*notez bien*', or 'to keep an eye open' as '*pour ouvrir l'oeil*' – none of these phrases is complex or ambiguous in a way that might warrant reference to its French original. Marlow seems to be very carefully placing himself in confident editorial control of the French Lieutentant's potentially devastating testimony – because if anyone in the novel is qualified to cast a damning verdict on Jim, it is the sailor who performed the very act of heroism of which Jim was incapable. Face-to-face with the French Lieutenant in a Sydney café, Marlow produces a rather sheepish defence of Jim; but his fluent retrospective command of the French language suggests that the veteran officer's dauntingly inflexible Gallic code of honour can be readily assimilated (and therefore subordinated) to English values and discourse. But there is a price to pay for this illusion of authority. Nowhere else is *Lord Jim* so conspicuously *written* as in the exchanges between Marlow and the Lieutenant: littered with italics, parentheses, aposiopetic breaks, and diacritical marks, these pages unmask Marlow the Anglophone racon-teur as 'Marlow' the effect of writing. It seems to be no coincidence that the monologic English voice that dominates *Lord Jim* yields to a poly-glot *écriture* at the very moment that its highest values are being most profoundly and searchingly reappraised; and this 'breakthrough' from traditional storytelling to modernist textuality can be traced directly to the ideological crisis that Jim's cowardly act has triggered.

No less problematic than the complex relations between speech and writing in this text is Marlow's experience of listening to Jim. Indeed, Marlow more than once maintains that a talent for listening, rather than a flair for words, is the single most important attribute of any would-be storyteller:

'I know I have him – the devil, I mean . . . He is there right enough, and, being malicious, he lets me in for that kind of thing . . . the kind of thing that by devious, unexpected, truly diabolical ways causes me to run up against men with soft spots, with hard spots, with hidden plague spots, by Jove! and loosens their tongues at the sight of me for their infernal confidences; as though, forsooth, I had no confidences to make to myself, as though – God help me! – I didn't have enough confidential information about myself to harrow my own soul till the end of my appointed time. And what I have done to be thus favoured I want to know. I declare I am as full of my own concerns as the next man, and I have as much memory as the average pilgrim in this valley, so you see I am not particularly fit to be a receptacle of confessions. Then why? Can't tell – unless it be to make time pass away after dinner.' (p. 34)

Marlow is the lay confessor, or, in secular terms, the itinerant psycho-analyst on whom the lost souls of the Malay Archipelago offload their harrowing life-stories. Listening to the unbidden confidences of his fellow men is the hard part of Marlow's job; by comparsion, his role as an after-dinner raconteur is represented as nothing more than a hobby.

Of course, Marlow has his reasons for elevating the act of listening above that of speaking. At times, it suits his purposes to present himself in an almost submissive relationship to language, overwhelmed by the power of other people's words:

'He was not speaking to me, he was only speaking before me, in a dispute with an invisible personality, an antagonistic and inseparable partner of his existence – another possessor of his soul. These were issues beyond the competency of a court of inquiry: it was a subtle and momentous quarrel as to the true essence of life, and did not want a judge. He wanted an ally, a helper, an accomplice. I felt the risk I ran of being circumvented, blinded, decoyed, bullied, perhaps, into taking a definite part in a dispute impossible of decision [. . .] It seemed to me I was being made to comprehend the Inconceivable [. . .] I was made to look at the convention that lurks in all truth and on the essential sincerity of falsehood [. . .] He swayed me. I own up to it, I own up.' (p. 93)

Marlow presents himself as a 'weak' listener, so awestruck by the tantalizing undecidability of Jim's case that the distinction between truth and falsehood falls by the wayside. Philosophical hyperbole is never far from the surface of Marlow's narrative in *Lord Jim*, and for all those protestations of intellectual passivity – he is *made* to look, *made* to comprehend, much like the reader of the Preface to *The Nigger of the 'Narcissus'* – his words are more manipulative by far than Jim's. Marlow ascribes to Jim qualities that better describe his *own* words: his audience is decoyed into believing the *Patna* sank, blinded by the dazzling obscurity of his portrait of Jim, and bullied by Marlow's own petulant hints to the effect that he deserves a better audience. ' "I could be eloquent" ', he declares, ' "were I not afraid you fellows had starved your imaginations to feed your bodies" ' (p. 225). Marlow's frustration with the stolid imperviousness of his well-fed audience is a corollary of his own pretence of heightened susceptibility to language.

Marlow's most painful auditory ordeal in *Lord Jim* is brought about by Jewel's account of her mother's death:

'It had the power to drive me out of my conception of existence, out of that shelter each of us makes for himself to creep under in moments of danger, as a tortoise withdraws within its shell. For a moment I had a view of a world that seemed to wear a vast and dismal aspect of disorder, while, in truth, thanks to our unwearied efforts, it is as sunny an arrangement of small conveniences as the mind of man can conceive. But still – it was only a moment: I went back into my shell directly. One *must* – don't you know? – though I seemed to have lost all my words in the chaos of dark thoughts I had contemplated for a second or two beyond the pale. These came back, too, very soon, for words also belong to the sheltering conception of light and order which is our refuge.' (p. 313)

The whole process of Marlovian storytelling is recapitulated in this passage: Marlow hears a disturbing narrative, and copes with his disturbance by telling stories, by translating alien experience into comfortable, familiar words. The contention that listening is more serious and risky than speaking re-emerges here in Marlow's rather self-congratulatory dramatization of himself as someone who has been exposed to narratives of shattering intensity, shaken to the very roots of his being, and lived to tell the tale. His ordeal by language is considerably less taxing than Jim's: words fail Jim constantly, and when they don't fail him, they seem to conspire sadistically against him, whereas Marlow finds words in abundance to construct his shelter.

When Marlow invites Jim to dinner at the Malabar House hotel, the dining room is full of a lively party of tourists whose merriment provides an awkward counterpoint to the strained intensity of Marlow and Jim's tête-à-tête: ' "[N]ow and then a girl's laugh would be heard, as innocent and empty as her mind, or, in a sudden hush of crockery, a few words in an affected drawl from some wit embroidering for the benefit

of a grinning tableful the last funny story of shipboard scandal"' (p. 77).
Marlow's recollections of dinner are interspersed with sidelong glances at
the 'squad of globe-trotters' whose superficial chatter, by a cruel stroke of
dramatic irony, revolves around a 'shipboard scandal'. Jim is constantly
being found out – if not by people, like the *Patna*'s second engineer who is
employed at Denver's rice-mill – then by language itself, which pursues
him with mocking echoes of his disgrace.

For a theoretical perspective on Jim's auditory ordeal, I would like
to borrow some ideas from Frank Kermode's *Genesis of Secrecy*. Writing
on the relationship between interpretation and error, Kermode cites the
case of Henry Green, a novelist who, because he was slightly deaf, frequently misheard or misidentified words. When a *Paris Review* journalist
described his fiction as 'subtle', Green thought she said *suttee* (the suicide
of a Hindu widow on her husband's funeral pyre) and proceeded to re-
assure his interviewer that Mrs Green wasn't likely to commit suicide
when he died.[16] Green has made what is, on the face of it, a random
error; but his mistake is taken by Kermode to be an instance of creative
mishearing, a strong misinterpretation that redeems what would otherwise be a routine, unenlightening interview. Kermode considers this to
be a salutary instance of strong interpretation because it emphasizes the
playful instability of language which soberly schematic models of interpretation are too apt to dismiss as irrelevant to serious usage. Novelty
in interpretation, according to Kermode, often requires that our ordi-
nary criteria of intelligibility – not least the idea that the spoken word
is a transparent expression of preverbal intent – be temporarily waived.
In his discussion of the difference between the general reader and the
professional interpreter, Kermode, borrowing his metaphor from the
apocryphal Epistle to Barnabas, says that specialists have 'circumcised
ears'.

Many of Conrad's more troubled heroes, especially Jim and Razumov,
might be said to listen with circumcised ears, although in Conrad's world
of linguistic violence this is a decidedly mixed blessing. Acutely conscious
of the risks of auditory error in his own life – 'I always mistrust my
ear', he confessed, when asked to comment on the poetry of his friend
E. L. Sanderson[17] – Conrad turned that mistrust to his advantage in the
fiction. Marlow and Jim are first brought together by a slip of the ear.
When a casual acquaintance of Marlow's notices a native dog outside the
courthouse his remark ('Look at that wretched cur') is overheard by Jim,
who assumes that the words were spoken by Marlow in reference to him.
The obvious psychological explanation for his slip of the ear would be

that it is a piece of involuntary self-revelation, an attempt at self-assertion that backfires in the most mortifying fashion possible by revealing that Jim feels *himself* to be a cur. But I prefer to see the wretched cur incident as an instance of creative misinterpretation rather than sheer error. It is as though Jim has overheard the novel itself articulating its suppressed residue of hostility towards its morally wretched hero. The stringent criticism that Jim perhaps deserves is on the whole smothered by the indulgent generosity of Marlow's narrative, but resurfaces in the form of this vein of grim wordplay.

On the courthouse veranda Jim betrays his inability *not* to hear echoes of the *Patna* affair in other people's words. Whenever Jim is within earshot, language seems to acquire new dimensions of cruel irony; even random scraps of overheard dialogue or the banalities of phatic conversation become urgently meaningful in his presence. At Egström and Blake's he overhears some especially wounding remarks about the *Patna* affair in an exchange between Egström and some clients:

'[W]e all struck in. Some said one thing and some another – not much – what you or any other man might say; and there was some laughing. Captain O'Brien of the *Sarah W. Granger*, a large, noisy old man with a stick – he was sitting listening to us in this arm-chair here – he let drive suddenly with his stick at the floor, and roars out, "Skunks!" ... Made us all jump. Vanlo's manager winks at us and asks, "What's the matter, Captain O'Brien?" "Matter! matter!" the old man began to shout; "what are you Injuns laughing at? It's no laughing matter. It's a disgrace to human natur' – that's what it is. I would despise being seen in the same room with one of those men."' (pp. 193–4)

Captain O'Brien, incapable of tolerating even the mention of the *Patna*, departs with the exit-line: ' "It stinks here now." ' The idea of discourse as a form of pollutant is crucial in *Lord Jim*. Tony Tanner describes gossip in *Victory* as a form of linguistic 'mud' that sticks to Axel Heyst. What is intriguing about *Lord Jim*, however, is not so much the adhesive properties of the 'verbal mud' – powerful though they are – as the magnetic qualities of Conrad's hero. Like a lightning-rod, Jim attracts the violent energies of the verbal atmosphere in which he lives and breathes. Egström's outburst is a case in point:

'I turned to him and slanged him till all was blue. "What is it you're running away from?" I asks. "Who has been getting at you? What scared you? You haven't as much sense as a rat; they don't clear out from a good ship. Where do you expect to get a better berth? – you this and you that." I made him look sick, I can tell you. "This business ain't going to sink," says I. He gave a big jump.' (p. 195)

Egström's words are full of unpremeditated innuendo. Reaching for the most venerable of nautical clichés – the idea that rats abandon a sinking ship – he strikes home with devastating precision on the raw nerve of Jim's guilt, causing Jim, once again, to jump. A fugitive from his own reputation, Jim is determined to get out of earshot of the entire Archipelago; but, in the *Patna* section at least, he inhabits a curious limbo, hovering uneasily at the fringes of other people's conversations, ready to jump at the first (imagined) mention of the *Patna*. Jim's jumpiness seems quite understandable when other people's words are riddled with startling *double entendres*. Egström's question – 'What is it you're running away from?' – does not receive a reply from Jim; but the answer is, of course, *language*. Jim will only stop running when he is placed by Stein in an environment that is securely insulated from quayside gossip.

Throughout *Lord Jim* there is a complex trade-off between visions of Jim as immaculate and dazzlingly bright and damning comments to the effect that he is soiled and polluted by his past. Initially, the disjunction between visual and auditory apprehension is ironic: Jim's scrupulously maintained attire belies his inner moral and psychological deficiencies. In Patusan, however, the novel exhibits a renewed faith in surfaces and their ability to signify unambiguously. Now that the would-be imperial hero is relocated in his preferred habitat of exotic jungle, Jim's appearance can once again signify courage and integrity:

'He was white from head to foot, and remained persistently visible with the stronghold of the night at his back . . . For me that white figure in the stillness of coast and sea seemed to stand at the heart of a vast enigma. The twilight was ebbing fast from the sky above his head, the strip of sand had sunk already under his feet, he himself appeared no bigger than a child – then only a speck, a tiny white speck, that seemed to catch all the light left in a darkened world . . . And, suddenly, I lost him . . . ' (p. 336)

Fused in this passage are two hitherto contradictory versions of Jim: he remains 'persistently visible', a beacon of light against the kind of ominous crepuscular backdrop of which Conrad was so fond; but, in his dazzling inscrutability, Jim invites symbolic interpretation to the extent that he defies forensic scrutiny. This moment of transfiguration corroborates the moral redemption that Jim appears to have found in Patusan; but it also hints at the price he pays for that redemption. Shrinking from full adult stature to the size of a child, and then receding into invisibility, Jim is infantilized by Marlow's imagery, just as his adventures in Patusan are not the stuff of adult experience. The reader, too, is obliged to regress from literary 'adulthood' if s/he is to derive any pleasure from the rather straightforward adventure narrative that follows.

As a boy, Jim nourished his fantasies of heroism on a diet of 'light holiday literature' (p. 5); as a trainee sailor, he daydreams of becoming 'as unflinching as a hero in a book' (p. 6); but, as many readers have protested, surely the second half of *Lord Jim* is an instance of the very 'light holiday literature' that the first half exposes as dangerously disengaged from reality. It is possible to see the novel as a miniature version of Conrad's career, or, rather, a version of Thomas C. Moser's 'achievement and decline' model of Conrad's career: a phase of challenging innovative fiction lapses abruptly into a palpably inferior tale of romance and adventure. That Jim's fantasies, subjected to such withering scepticism in the novel's first half, should be so spectacularly vindicated in its second is a matter of serious critical consternation. In a discussion of Paul de Man's reading of Rousseau, Jonathan Culler makes some observations that are extremely suggestive of the 'division' of *Lord Jim*:

One might say ... that works that turn boring and sentimental or moralistic in their second halves, such as *Julie*, *Either/Or*, or *Daniel Deronda*, and seem to regress from the insights they have attained, are allegories of reading which, through ultimately incoherent ethical motives, display the inability of deconstructive narratives to produce settled knowledge ... The problem, it seems, is 'that a totally enlightened language ... is unable to control the recurrence, in its readers as well as in itself, of the errors it exposes'.[18]

Lord Jim undergoes a similar regression from 'deconstructive' to 'sentimental' narrative. In the Patusan section the novel reneges on its own scepticism, betraying the readers whom it has so assiduously schooled in the ways of reflexivity.[19] It is as though, by turning itself into an heroic adventure, the novel is attempting to compensate generically for Jim's ontological failures. Conrad's failure to prosecute his sceptical narrative to a convincing conclusion is a failure of nerve as catastrophic in its own way as Jim's.

Lord Jim is a novel that repeats itself: the first time as farce, the second as tragedy. Jim is given the opportunity to make the same mistake in a more honorable context, and the source of his opportunity, Stein, is the pivotal figure in the novel's problematic transition. The novel's shift to romance is licensed by Stein, whose *deus ex machina* arrival in the narrative, which coincides with echoes from Goethe, *Hamlet*, and Calderón, lends romance some of the intellectual respectability of Romanticism. Stein bears many intriguing resemblances to Kurtz: he is a Germanic polymath, the cryptic resonance of whose words promises some visionary insight into matters that have baffled Marlow. Stein and Kurtz are speakers whose eloquence rivals his own: in the shadow of Kurtz or Stein, he can seem once again to be engagingly down-to-earth and honestly confused. Stein reaches a surprisingly swift and unequivocal diagnosis of Jim: "'I understand very well. He is romantic'" (p. 212). Ian Watt rightly cautions us to be sceptical of this 'miracle of taxonomic clairvoyance',[20] because, if anything, Stein's insights only serve to intensify the unreadability of Jim. Stein's famous parable of the swimmer, for example, combines nebulous existential metaphors in a way that defies literal paraphrase:

"'A man that is born falls into a dream like a man who falls into the sea. If he tries to climb out into the air as inexperienced people endeavour to do, he drowns – *nicht wahr?* . . . No! I tell you! The way is to the destructive element submit yourself, and with the exertions of your hands and feet in the water make the deep, deep sea keep you up.'" (p. 214)

The irreducible metaphoricity of Stein's parable forestalls any clear-cut message we might hope to extract from it.[21] In another mood, Conrad might deplore such wanton indeterminacy, but in *Lord Jim* it fortifies the philosophical 'shell' into which Marlow retreats on being exposed to the historical crisis of the *Patna*. The parable's metaphorical incoherence enacts the impossibility of reconciling its conflicting frames of reference. Guerard suspects that Conrad 'produced without much effort a logically imperfect multiple metaphor, liked the sound of it, and let matters go at that'.[22] Guerard wasn't the first to call Conrad's bluff. Some thirty years earlier, E. M. Forster complained that Conrad's prose gestures grandly to some revelation that never happens.[23] My own view is that the 'destructive element' is language itself, which destroys the settled meanings we assign to experience. As Marlow remarks, '"a word carries far – very far – deals destruction through time as the bullets go flying through space"'(p. 174).

Stein advocates an indulgent view of Jim that implicitly challenges the severity of the verdict cast by the French Lieutenant. Stein is more generous, tolerant, and forgiving than the French officer – but also far more cryptic. He shares with the French Lieutenant the privilege of having his native tongue accorded a degree of parity with English in Marlow's narrative; but, unlike the Lieutenant's French, many of Stein's German words and phrases are left untranslated by Marlow. Whereas much of the Lieutenant's discourse is informational, Stein's interventions take the form of metaphysical conjecture – they are scarcely designed to be transparently intelligible. Because it is not fully rendered into English, Stein's discourse is insulated from the promiscuous gossip that thrives elsewhere in the novel. Stein's wisdom is constituted *as* wisdom through the density and complexity of its linguistic texture. Elsewhere in the novel 'Jim' has become effortlessly narratable in a way that devalues the language applied to him; his identity has become nothing more than an ice-breaking conversational gambit, sure to provoke lively but superficial banter in any social context throughout the Archipelago. Stein restores sophistication, complexity, and opacity to the Jim-discourses of the novel, not least through the polyglot nature of his advice: '"That was the way: To follow the dream, and again to follow the dream – and so – *ewig* – *usque ad finem* ..."' (pp. 214–15). The shifts in language here seem to correspond to progressive refinements in Stein's formulation of a general truth from a specific case-study: he moves from English (workaday reality), through German (the language of metaphysics), and Latin (timeless, 'classical' wisdom), to a silence marked only by aposiopeses that hint at an order of truth beyond words. Declining to gloss non-English words, and evidently reluctant to complete the gaps in his friend's pronouncements, Marlow obviously respects the integrity and otherness of Stein's discourse; we have never been further from the world of 'quayside gossip'. Ironically, however, Marlow's audience with Stein does not lift the novel to a new level of philosophical sophistication, but prepares rather for a glamorous simplification of Jim's fate in Stein's 'empire': Patusan.

After Stein's mesmeric intervention, the novel itself 'falls' into the dream of Patusan (note, too, how Stein 'rewrites' a voluntary jump as involuntary fall just as Jim has already done: '"I had jumped ... it seems"' (p. 111). In Patusan an amazing but highly deceptive reversal takes place in the relationship between Jim and language. Whereas gossip once preyed on his weaknesses, fantastic legends now flourish about his heroic military endeavours. The fisher-folk claim that the tide turned early to speed Jim's boat to Patusan (pp. 242–3); the 'simple folk' claim that the guns used for the onslaught on Sherif Ali were carried up the hill '"on his back two at a time"', although one old sorcerer claims that Jim raised them up there with '"powerful charms and incantations"' (p. 266). A reputation of '"invincible, supernatural power"' (p. 361) speeds his political ascendancy. Whereas in the world of the *Patna* textual constructs are cruelly mocked by experience, in Patusan imagination magically coincides with reality. In the *Patna* section a community ponders the obscure implications of an undisputed fact; in Patusan we are shown a community quite happily modifying facts to square with a preconceived hypothesis about Jim's supernatural powers. For Marlow, the whole process is a pleasing alternative to the unimaginative world of 'civilization':

'[D]o you notice how, three hundred miles beyond the end of telegraph cables and mail-boat lines, the haggard utilitarian lies of our civilization wither and die, to be replaced by pure exercises of imagination, that have the futility, often the charm, and sometimes the deep hidden truthfulness, of works of art?' (p. 282)

There is an extremely potent irony in this contrast between 'utilitarian lies' and 'pure exercises of the imagination'. The technological paraphernalia of imperialism is dedicated to the dissemination of scientific empiricism; but, beyond the visible perimeters of imperialist expansion there remain enclaves of rich, charming, and profound oral culture where the language of fact is properly subordinated to the freedom of imagination. Ironically, however, the 'deeply truthful' rumours that emanate from this unsullied region of forest are in profound complicity with the entire colonial project. The 'simple folk' of Patusan do Jim the profound service of providing an extremely picturesque rationale of his own position, which is dedicated to securing the region as a profitable trading zone. Thus Jim is the herald of the very 'utilitarian lies' by which Patusan seems untainted. This complicity with colonialism is part of the elementary credulity posited by Marlow among the Patusan natives. Inexplicable phenomena are attributed to occult causes and simple facts are distorted to accommodate a view of Jim as superhuman. The Jim whom Marlow encounters on his visit to Patusan is a reluctant Prospero, mildly exasperated by the adulation he receives but conscious that he can wield the resulting power in the best interests of Doramin's people. The honeymoon period enjoyed by Jim in Patusan, where the speech community collaborates with his own dreams, is only a temporary reprieve. As Martin Ray notes, the world of Patusan 'is both the playground and the graveyard for Jim's heroic imaginings'.[24]

In the Patusan section of *Lord Jim*, Marlow's generalizations are more sweeping, his eye for detail less keen, and his ear for dialogue less sharp. The problem of linguistic difference – which looms so large in his interviews with Stein and the French Lieutenant – is largely ignored. Marlow converses freely with the headman of a local fishing village (p. 242), Sura the sorcerer (p. 266), Doramin (pp. 273–5), the Rajah's scribe in a village south of Patusan river (p. 280). The first phase of *Lord Jim* brings to life a remarkable range of idiosyncratic voices; but Marlow lets us hear very little of the actual dialogue of Patusan. To a certain extent the wheedling voice of Cornelius is made audible, as well as the asthmatic invective of Gentleman Brown; but in general the speakers in this second phase of the novel speak with the same stagey and stilted formality that characterizes most Malay noblemen in Conrad's fiction. Patusan is clearly a different kind of speech community: a place to glean information rather than a place to contemplate linguistic and idiomatic differences; it is a place where the voice of fame has displaced the voice of gossip in a way that leaves Jim elevated, ennobled, but radically simplified.

Patusan never loses its aura of make-believe and childish wish-fulfilment: the villagers' collective suspension of disbelief is shared by the novel itself. There is one 'astonishing rumour' which Marlow encounters from several sources hundreds of miles from Patusan, about '"a mysterious white man in Patusan who had got hold of an extraordinary gem – namely, an emerald of an enormous size, and altogether priceless"' (p. 280):

> 'Most of my informants were of the opinion that the stone was probably unlucky, – like the famous stone of the Sultan of Succadana, which in the old times had brought wars and untold calamities upon that country. Perhaps it was the same stone – one couldn't say. Indeed the story of a fabulously large emerald is as old as the arrival of the first white men in the Archipelago.' (p. 280)

This legend bears intriguing similarities to the tales of the ill-fated gringos of Azuera in *Nostromo*, which also concerns the advent of European traders intent on acquiring precious local commodities. Just as Charles Gould and Nostromo seemed destined to re-enact the fate of the gringos, so Jim's acquisition of the jewel – presently identified as his lover Jewel – seems to portend 'wars and untold calamities'. Current events are accommodated to the folkloric model offered by the venerable legends of the Sultan's stone, a curse-narrative that balefully 'accommodates' Jim's heroic biography to its own predetermined pattern of crisis and failure.

In the *Patna* world the normative version of reality was established by bureaucratic authority; in Patusan it is created by collective oral narratives. Hard information is a precious commodity, all too vulnerable to malicious distortion, especially during Jim's absence in the interior, which creates a vacuum in power promptly filled by fatalistic rumours of blood-soaked violence. Energetically fanned by the Rajah's wily spokesman, Kassim, these rumours spread like wildfire: '"Wild and exaggerated rumours were flying . . . They were coming with many more boats to exterminate every living thing"' (p. 363). This linguistic utopia, which has reflected back on Jim a supremely flattering image of his own achievement, is left in Jim's absence to reflect on its own fragility. The spell is broken, the magical coincidence between language and reality is shattered. '"The social fabric of orderly, peaceful life, when every man was sure of tomorrow, the edifice raised by Jim's hands, seemed on that evening ready to collapse into a ruin reeking with blood"' (p. 373). I have argued that Conrad is curious about the 'gossiping crowd' for its own sake; no such curiosity is extended to Patusan, which is conjured up purely as a backdrop for Jim. After Jim's death it fades into irrelevance. The helplessness felt in Jim's absence is the necessary obverse of the villagers' colourful exaggerations of his benevolent power. Jim is held hostage to the collective fantasies of Patusan, and held responsible when those fantasies fail.

Brown's incursion into Patusan resembles nothing so much as the blackmail narratives of nineteenth-century fiction, where the repressed past of a pillar of the community returns in the person of a familiar scoundrel intent on procuring money in exchange for silence.[25] The novel flirts with, but ultimately rejects, the pattern of informational blackmail, displacing attention from language's informational content onto its rhetorical forms as the agent of Jim's downfall. Brown brings no compromising information to Patusan; he has nothing that could possibly undermine Jim's standing in the settlement – apart from a diabolically serendipitous way with words that discomposes Jim just as surely as if Brown had been there with him on the *Patna*. In Conrad's modernist revision of the blackmail narrative, the first half of the novel avenges itself on the second, as though Brown brings to Patusan the attitudes of a more cynical reader of the *Patna* section of *Lord Jim*.

Gentleman Brown, who, like Egström, has no precise knowledge of Jim's past, hits upon just the right expressions to disarm him. His phraseology during their parley exhibits the same kind of linguistic serendipity as Egström's: '"This is as good a jumping-off place for me as another. I am sick of my infernal luck. But it would be too easy. There are my men in the same boat – and, by God, I am not the sort to jump out of trouble and leave them in a d – d lurch"' (pp. 382–3). Dead metaphors have an alarming habit of springing back to life in Jim's presence. The experience of mishearing in Conrad is an act of pre-emptive counter-interpretation that ascribes a startlingly precise meaning to an otherwise vague or banal expression. John Batchelor notes that 'metaphors or similes in the *Patna* half become concrete reality in the Patusan half'.[26] In Brown's language this process is secretly reversed: the metaphors Conrad puts in his mouth are literal representations of Jim's past career. The process that seemed like a redemptive transformation of Jim's ignominious lapse on the *Patna* is turned on its head, as Brown's stale metaphors yield up all too literal realities. Jim's tragedy originates in his naively literalistic relationship to fiction: his belief that the stuff of adventure fiction could be translated into real life ruins his maritime career. In the aftermath of the scandal, his tendency to literalize and personalize every utterance he (over)hears ensures that his torment continues. Jim has nothing at his disposal equivalent to the linguistic resources of Marlow or Stein. Compare, for example, Marlow's prodigious bout of letter-writing in chapter 15 to Jim's abortive valedictory epistle – '"An awful thing has happened . . . I must now at once"' (p. 340) – in which language splutters out into a poignant silence that foreshadows the permanent silence of his impending death.

Jim begins the novel as a bad reader, naively literalistic in his response to popular romance fiction; he ends the novel as a failed author with a case of terminal writer's block. Marlow's own narrative might also be described in terms of failure: his words frequently fall short of conveying his full meaning; his rhetoric never quite delivers the momentous revelations that it seems to promise; his stories fail to offer the customary satisfactions of moral certainty and formal closure. *Lord Jim*, too, might be said to 'fail' in its bid to deconstruct the myths of imperial adventure. Except that categorical judgements of this sort, couched in a binary language of success and failure, provide only a radically simplified understanding of the startling narrative innovations of *Lord Jim*; instead we ought to read this novel as a brilliant *transvaluation* of ideas of moral and narrative failure, in which 'embarrassing' jumps, breaks, silences, gaps, and inconsistencies are transformed into the very language of modernist fiction.

CHAPTER SIX

The gender of Chance

Chance is Conrad's problem novel. Published in 1914, it occupies an ambiguous position between his most celebrated creative phase, which culminated with *Under Western Eyes* (1911), and the comparatively neglected work of his 'decline'. It is the most 'feminine', or female-oriented, of Conrad's novels, but its engagement with issues of gender is tainted by the arch misogyny of Marlow, whose clumsy and unsympathetic line in anti-feminist repartee is never convincingly challenged or dialogized in the text. Also problematic is the novel's unwieldy narrative structure, which, with its convoluted time-scheme and strange ensemble of variously limited or unreliable narrating voices, presses the techniques of 'Heart of Darkness' and *Lord Jim* dangerously close to self-parody. Any serious reading of *Chance* must begin by confronting these problems, not in a bid to explain them away, but in order to move to a fuller understanding of the vexing *relationship* between the novel's curious structure and provocative substance.

The notion of Conrad as an irredeemably homocentric, even '*macho*'[1] writer has been challenged so forcibly in recent years that it is worth reminding ourselves of the kind of material that gave rise to it in the first place.[2] The following remarks, by the narrator of 'Because of the Dollars', suggest that the view of Conrad's world as an exclusively masculine environment is not without foundation in the texts themselves: 'Ours, as you remember, was a bachelor crowd; in spirit anyhow, if not absolutely in fact. There might have been a few wives in existence, but if so they were invisible, distant, never alluded to.'[3] These words might equally apply to a number of Conrad's stories where the central characters are a 'bachelor crowd', and women are 'invisible, distant, never alluded to'. The shipboard communities of men in 'Youth', 'Typhoon', 'The End of the Tether', *The Nigger of the 'Narcissus'*, or *The Shadow-Line* tend to marginalize female experience; the emphasis on male friendship in 'The Secret Sharer', 'Heart of Darkness', and *Lord Jim* leaves precious little room for male–female or women-only relationships; and the generic conventions of espionage novels like *The Secret Agent* and adventure stories like *The Rover* and *The Rescue* assign male characters to the prominent active roles. Conrad's women, meanwhile, are often marginal or passive, voiceless or nameless, with no subjectivity outside that granted to them by male narrators.

Of course, we can recognize that Conradian narrative deals in a generic language of masculine adventure without denying that Conrad finds ways to disrupt the authority of that language. *Chance* is his most systematic attempt to engage with female experience; it does so by addressing the feminist controversies of its time, and by courting the attention of women readers. Conrad appears deliberately to have played up the romantic content of his 'girl-novel'[4] in order to appeal to a female readership; prior to serial publication in the *New York Herald*, *Chance* was trailed as 'A sea story that appeals to women'. The *Herald* also ran an 'interview' with Conrad under the heading: 'World's Most Famous Author of Sea Stories Has Written "Chance", a Deliciously Characteristic Tale in Which, He Says, He Aimed to Interest Women Particularly.'[5] This change of emphasis and address has led Susan Jones to read *Chance* as a novel that moves towards what might be called a 'feminine' modernism.[6]

Jones's generous treatment of *Chance* is surprising, given that Marlow's narrative tone in this novel is so often marked by hostility towards women and feminism. The 'ingratiatingly humane'[7] storyteller of 'Youth', 'Heart of Darkness', and *Lord Jim* has been replaced by a devil's advocate who likes to scandalize his earnest interlocutor with flights of provocatively opinionated conversation. 'In my estimation', writes one impatient critic, 'the Marlow of previous narratives is a person with whom I would gladly participate in a convivial dinner-party. In contrast, if the Marlow of *Chance* offered me his company, I would seek an excuse for a quick exit.'[8] It is a measure of Marlow's capacity to exasperate his readers that C. B. Cox should dispense with analytical detachment to vent his frustration with Marlow in this very personal way. One suspects, moreover, that the Marlow of *Chance* would take a certain pleasure in being struck off Cox's imaginary guest-list: controversy, not clubbability, is his goal.

Particularly controversial and unsympathetic are the outrageous generalizations about women that Marlow drops into his narrative. '"[T]here is enough of the woman in my nature"', he claims, '"to free my judgement of women from glamorous reticency."'[9] But few readers will be grateful to learn that 'compunction' is '"rare in women"' (p. 158); that women have '"never got hold of"' honour (p. 63); that they crave '"Sensation at any cost"' (p. 63); they '"always get what they want"' (p. 63); they are not 'rational' but 'acute' (p. 145); they '"often resemble intelligent children"' (p. 171); that a woman is '"seldom an expert in matters of sentiment"' (p. 330). Marlow's 'anthology of misogynic clichés'[10] is so transparently spurious that it scarcely requires detailed refutation. The best that can be said of these remarks is that they are opportunistic rather than systematic, outrageous squibs rather than deeply held beliefs, and that Marlow is being quite deliberately 'placed' as an unreliable narrator whose opinions are too manifestly objectionable to be ascribed to his creator. Perhaps for this reason *Chance* has received surprisingly lenient treatment from women readers.[11]

Beyond the unsympathetic tone of Marlow's narrative, there is a wider problem with the structure of his story, which reads at times like the product of a sensibility that has acquired a curious allergy to first-hand experience. A chapter-heading in Jakob Lothe's *Conrad's Narrative Method* presents a stark assessment of Conrad's technical achievement in this novel: '"Heart of Darkness" Contrasted with *Chance*: Narrative Success and Narrative Failure'.[12] Some might demur from the brutality of this comparative valuation, but many readers have found themselves singularly unconvinced by the narrative experiments of *Chance*. Thomas C. Moser argues pointedly that this novel is a work of factitious virtuosity, intrinsically *less* complex than *Lord Jim* and *Nostromo*: 'Its apparatus of several narrators and seeming time shifts makes it superficially complex, but in fact, the machinery does little more than irritate the reader.'[13] Arguing along similar lines, Daniel R. Schwarz describes the novel's structure as a 'sophisticated scaffolding'.[14] Whether we prefer to describe the structure of *Chance* as 'scaffolding' or as 'machinery', the purport of such images is clear: that there is nothing in the dramatic substance of this text to warrant the obtrusive visibility of its structure – the novel is, to borrow the language of 'Heart of Darkness', all shell and no kernel.

'Postmodern' readers of *Chance*, such as Robert Siegle and Daphna Erdinast-Vulcan, have been quick to point out that the novel's privileging of 'textuality' might well be its saving grace.[15] Erdinast-Vulcan finds in the novel a radical challenge to naïve conceptions of referentiality: 'the distinction between the word and the world is no longer upheld. Reality is viewed as a construct of language.'[16] The visibility of Marlow and his crew of subordinate raconteurs and informants, and the interference of the text's linguistic structure in its dramatic substance, should therefore only trouble readers who are nostalgic for the false transparency of Victorian realist fiction. This postmodern interpretation of *Chance* provides a useful corrective to the somewhat naïve model of form/content relations underpinning the strictures of Moser and Schwarz, though it sheds little light on the curiously rebarbative *tone* of Marlow's convoluted narrative.

Perhaps the best way to approach the strange narrative structure of *Chance* is through a reconsideration of Henry James's influential response to the novel. In his essay 'The New Novel', James makes his discussion of Conrad's work the centrepiece of a sceptical survey of a group whom he dubs, with suave condescension, 'the younger generation'.[17] The nub of his argument is that the fiction of the younger generation has been damaged by its 'disconnection of method from matter',[18] the most visible symptom of which is the formless accumulation of realistic detail in the novels of H. G. Wells and Arnold Bennett. The other extreme, according to James, is represented by *Chance*, a work whose formal experiments are so ambitious and conspicuous as to place their creator 'absolutely alone as a votary of the way to do a thing that shall make it undergo the most doing'.[19] Whether this remark is to be taken as a sincere tribute to the technical inventiveness of Conrad's novel is not immediately obvious; if James is dissatisfied by the vulgar realism of Wells and Bennett, he can summon up only the faintest praise for the thoroughgoing formalism of *Chance*, as though he regards it as nothing more than a delightfully idiosyncratic curiosity. Still, James writes on Conrad's 'eccentricities of recital' and 'circumferential tones' with a felicity that few others have matched; it would be difficult, moreover, to improve upon his description of Marlow's involvement as reflective narrator as a 'prolonged hovering flight of the subjective over the outstretched ground of the case exposed'.[20]

It seems reasonable to assume that the rather condescending treatment of Conrad in 'The New Novel' owes something to the very obvious affinities between *Chance* and James's own fiction, which have been explored by many readers, including E. E. Duncan-Jones, Susan Jones, and Ian Watt.[21] I have already touched in an earlier chapter on the 'Jamesian' qualities of the Marlow narratives; but in *Chance* the influence of James is a matter of dramatic substance as well as technique. Leaving aside 'The Return', which is very much a failed experiment, *Chance* is Conrad's only substantial venture into the territory of 'society' fiction that James had made his own. Its story of the matrimonial prospects of a vulnerable young woman, and its vision of the placid rituals of middle-class life being disturbed by tremors of financial scandal and sexual impropriety, are unmistakeably Jamesian; indeed, the echoes of James are so clearly audible that Conrad's novel has been dismissed by Frederic Jameson as a 'mediocre imitation'[22] of the Master. But Conrad's relationship to James is far more complex than one of mere servile imitation. James himself no doubt recognized that he had in Conrad an enormously gifted disciple, and that *Chance* represented an audacious attempt to annex his jealously guarded fictional territory. *Chance* might well be seen as a novel in which the adventures of a 'Jamesian' heroine are framed by and subordinated to those of a typical Conrad hero in a way that subjects the sumptuous world of Jamesian melodrama to rigorous scrutiny from the vantage-point of austere Conradian values. If we were looking for a visual aid to describe the James–Conrad relationship in *Chance*, we could do worse than consider the renovations to the *Ferndale*'s living quarters where, after Captain Anthony's unexpected marriage, a plush Jamesian drawing room is constructed within a Conradian sailing vessel, incorporating the world of *What Maisie Knew* into the world of 'The Secret Sharer' or *The Shadow-Line*. In the light of these intertextual relationships, we ought to read 'The New Novel' as James's attempt to distance himself from Conrad.[23] On a personal level, he succeeded in wounding Conrad, who later confessed to John Quinn that James's review was 'the *only time* a criticism affected me painfully'[24] – not least, one imagines, because James patronizingly classed him with the 'younger generation', which was a chronological as well as artistic demotion for the fifty-six-year-old author of *Chance*. James also succeeded in asserting his cultural authority on Conrad: the irresistible quotability of 'The New Novel' has ensured that it is far more widely cited than Conrad's own Author's Note, which it has effectively displaced as indispensable ancillary material for *Chance*.

By imposing his critical and cultural seniority on 'the younger generation', James reproduces a pattern of intergenerational conflict that is visible in the text of *Chance* – the forceful reassertion of patriarchal authority on the lives of wayward children. Much more than has been commonly recognized, *Chance* is a novel of family life, or, to be more specific, a novel of intergenerational conflict and genealogical crisis, haunted by those tyrannically possessive patriarchs, Carleon Anthony and the 'Great' de Barral. A celebrated poet, but a cold-blooded husband and father, Carleon Anthony casts a long shadow over the lives of his children Zoe and Roderick, both of whom bid to escape his influence, the former by eloping with Fyne, the latter by going to sea. De Barral, the disgraced tycoon, is an even more sinister patriarch; insanely possessive, he wields a powerfully negative influence over his daughter Flora. But de Barral and Carleon Anthony have something more in common: their success, power, and status is obtained through the abuse of language:

Carleon Anthony is heartless in his dealings with real women but produces poetry that is idealistically devoted to them; de Barral is a reckless investor who preaches a gospel of thrift. Given that *Chance* problematizes paternity and patriarchal language, we might usefully read Marlow's quasi-paternal role in the novel, and his engagement with feminism and gender, as extensions of that complex 'dialogue' between masculine language and female experience.

Before we examine the domestic relations of *Chance*, I would like to cite some suggestive comments on the novel of family life from Mikhail Bakhtin's essay, 'Forms of Time and of the Chronotope in the Novel'. In the first schema, of which *Tom Jones* is Bakhtin's primary example, the family provides an environment of support and affection for the hero who has successfully negotiated the vicissitudes of the wider world and is ready to settle down to a life of stable domesticity. In the second, exemplified by the fiction of Samuel Richardson, the family is a domestic sanctuary under threat from alien forces that intrude into the 'cozy little world' of domestic life. Bakhtin crystallizes this argument in terms that are richly suggestive of *Chance*:

What is important here is precisely the stable family and material goods belonging to the heroes, how they overcome the element of chance (random meetings with random people, random situations and occurrences) in which they had initially found themselves, how they create fundamental, that is, *family* connections with people, how they limit their world to a well-defined place and a well-defined narrow circle of relatives, that is, to the family circle. It often happens that in the beginning the hero is homeless, without relatives, without means of support; he wanders through an alien world among alien people; random misfortunes and successes happen to him; he encounters random people who turn out to be . . . his enemies or his benefactors (all this is later decoded along family or kinship lines). The novel's movement takes the main hero (or heroes) out of the great but alien world of random occurrence into the small but secure and stable little world of the family, where nothing is foreign, or accidental or incomprehensible, where authentically human relationships are re-established, where the ancient matrices are re-established on a family base: love, marriage, childbearing, a peaceful old age for the in-laws, shared meals around the family table.[25]

In both models, the 'family circle' is a form of institutional and narratological closure, a self-contained community that offers permanent shelter from the dangerous unpredictability of the wider world. The discrepancy between this tradition and Conrad's versions of family life could scarcely be more conspicuous. The absence of an affectionate and supportive family may be a significant loss for such characters as Jim and Razumov,

but Conrad's vision of family life is never idyllic. Anyone familiar with
the Bacadous in 'The Idiots' or the Verlocs in *The Secret Agent* will know
that Conrad had a flair for creating unhappy families and disastrously
mismatched couples; but *Chance* takes apart myths of domesticity even
more systematically than those texts – it is a black comedy of family life
gone awry. Full of disintegrating or dysfunctional families, it formally enacts the disintegration of the classic novel of family life. The idea that the
family subsumes randomness into genealogical continuity is forcefully resisted by *Chance*. Randomness, as Marlow observes, seems to be the very
condition of family life. The 'runaway' marriages of the Fynes ('"there
was no design at all in it"', remarks Marlow (p. 37)) and of Flora and Anthony owe as much to chance as to careful forethought. Whatever control
one exercises over one's choice of spouse does not extend to one's choice
of in-laws: marriage brings with it a raft of in-laws, to whom one is legally
if not emotionally tied. Marlow, whose acquaintance with Anthony's
brother-in-law John Fyne draws him into the whole affair, remarks that
'"a brother-in-law"' happens into a man's life '"without intelligent design"' (p. 36). At best, the family is a random cluster of individuals
brought together by spur-of-the-moment alliances or the arbitrary con-
junctions of social life; at worst, it is predatory and parasitic on its weaker
members. On the evidence of this novel, it would be no exaggeration to
say that for Conrad 'the alien world of random occurrence' *is* the family.

Nothing could be less 'cozy' than the claustrophobic domestic regimes
of *Chance*: Carleon Anthony's two wives were '"chivied and worried into
their graves"' (p. 51); de Barral's wife also dies prematurely – '"absolutely
from neglect"' (p. 72); whilst the Fynes, themselves an oddly mismatched
couple, co-habit with a sisterhood of 'girlfriends', which is not a set-up
that meets with Marlow's approval. His sardonic description of mealtimes
at the Fynes' provides a useful counterpoint to Bakhtinian idealization
of the family circle:

'I played chess with Fyne in the late afternoon, and sometimes came over to the
cottage early enough to have tea with the whole family at a big round table . . .
Mrs Fyne smiled mechanically (she had splendid teeth) while distributing tea and
bread and butter. A something which was not coldness, nor yet indifference, but
a sort of peculiar self-possession gave her the appearance of a very trustworthy,
very capable and excellent governess; as if Fyne were a widower and the children
not her own, but only entrusted to her calm, efficient, unemotional care. One
expected her to address Fyne as Mr.' (pp. 41–2)

Here we have a strange parody of an authentic family, with the wife
as governess, the husband as widower, and their offspring as foster

children – unrelated individuals engaged in a mechanical performance of traditional domestic roles, as though the Fyne family has become its own surrogate.

A family tree of *Chance* would reveal that those of its thirty or so named characters who are not connected by family relationships of blood or marriage are often drawn into a larger, unofficial family tree through some form of surrogacy or pseudo-kinship. Surrogacy, the substitution of conventional relationships for natural ones, is a powerful source of crisis in *Chance*.[26] Having been displaced from her natural family by the death of her mother and the imprisonment of her father, Flora is shunted between a series of surrogate families where she undergoes a long apprenticeship in unhappiness, suffering indignity and abuse at the hands of every guardian with whom she is placed, from the Brighton governess and de Barral's '"atrocious East-End cousins"' to the '"respectable"' German couple by whom she is dismissed after the husband fails to seduce her. The Brighton household offers a notably disorientating instance of family roles in baffling permutation, with Eliza '"playing . . . the part of mother"' (p. 96), and Charley (posing as Eliza's cousin) playing Flora's beau. Eliza has designs on Charley – for whom she nurses 'maternal' (p. 105) as well as sexual sentiments – and is using Flora as bait. De Barral's daughter is forced to inhabit domestic structures in which a perverse interchangeability of roles, a confusion of familial with sexual relations, and a distortion of generational gaps have become the 'norms'.

Flora is barely sixteen when her father is imprisoned and her innocence shattered by the savage verbal mauling she receives from Eliza. Although in some ways she has to grow up quickly, she is nevertheless infantilized both by Roderick's refusal to consummate their marriage and by the suffocating possessiveness of her ex-convict father. She is obliged to play a double role in which untimely adulthood is telescoped with child-like helplessness: as a teenage girl she is prematurely impelled into adulthood, whilst seven years later, as a grown woman, she is treated as a helpless waif. It is as though the world can't forgive Flora for being her father's daughter, but neither will it allow her to become anything else. The superimposition of the sixteen-year-old girl upon the twenty-three-year-old woman is also conveyed by the prison-imagery that overshadows her relationship with de Barral. With its central picture of the innocent young girl in the shadow of the prison, *Chance* reads at times like a modernist revision of *Little Dorrit* in which incarceration functions as a *temporal* metaphor. De Barral's seven-year sentence is 'frozen' time for him, a period of '"dead stillness"' (p. 355): on his release he expects

Flora to be the same teenage girl whom he left in the custody of the malevolent governess. De Barral is not the only father-figure who experiences strangely mixed reactions to Flora. In a curious reversal of roles, Flora's husband comes to adopt a paternalistic attitude to her, renouncing his 'conjugal rights' and acting merely as guardian and source of economic and social support; whilst her German employer and would-be seducer '"set about his sinister enterprise in a sentimental, cautious, almost paternal manner"' (p. 181). Marlow himself experiences a similar confusion of sexual and paternal impulses towards Flora ('"she was an appealing and – yes – she was a desirable little figure"' (p. 201)), whilst the novel's anachronic structure – its oscillation between past and present, between Flora's childhood and maturity – seems to confirm Flora's status as a child-woman, ambiguously suspended between innocence and experience.

If the lives of young Powell – who is an orphan – and Flora de Barral – who is an orphan '"to a certain extent"' (p. 61) – are in any way exemplary, then we might say that family members in *Chance* are subjected to unpredictable hostility and uncontrollable misfortune, whereas those without families are free to experience life's adventures on their own terms. Early in his quest for employment, Powell becomes so disheartened that he 'didn't think himself good enough for anybody's kinship' (p. 8), but on the whole this lack of family links – aside from a solitary aunt – seems positively advantageous. Powell's sense of 'profound abasement' (p. 8) at his failure to obtain a berth quickly leads, in a heavy-handed but instructive pun, to the 'basement of St Katherine's Dock House' (p. 9). Through a mixture of pluck and good fortune, and with a helping hand from his avuncular namesake, Powell finds his way out of this subterranean labyrinth and into the adult world of the sea. He seems to thrive on other people's bad luck – like that of the *Ferndale*'s second mate, hospitalized with broken limbs after a traffic accident, or Captain Anthony, whose death leaves the way open for Flora to remarry. Powell's search for a berth functions as a rehearsal of Flora's own labyrinthine journey through abasement into adult identity, though female adventure – caught up as it is in perverse family structures – proves to be more much more fraught with difficulty and misfortune than its male equivalent.

Marlow's account of Flora's adventures is a typically self-conscious act of modernist storytelling, in which the challenge of understanding Flora is compounded by the problem of finding an authentic language for her story. In his bid to make Flora narratable, Marlow has to pick his way carefully through disreputable and discredited languages: the sentimental poetry of Carleon Anthony; de Barral's advertising slogans ('"Thrift, Thrift, Thrift"' (p. 78)) and the '"business verbiage"' and '"financial jargon"' (p. 80) of venture capitalism; the newspaper headlines and juridical pronouncements that accompany the de Barral crash; and the ceaseless gossip that surrounds Flora on the *Ferndale*. The image of Marlow caught up in the scrum outside the court where de Barral is tried (pp. 85–6) – so reminiscent of his encounter outside the courthouse in *Lord Jim* – sums up the challenge of reaching a sensitive personal verdict on a case that has become public property. Like Jim and Kurtz, Flora both stimulates and baffles narrative; family secrets – her notorious convict father, her mysterious elopement with the brother of her guardian, the non-consummation of her marriage – are the 'gaps' in her life-story that provoke the gossiping curiosity of others, nowhere more intensely than on her husband's ship.

The *Ferndale* festers with the resentment and suspicion of old hands who can't reconcile themselves to the presence of Flora on the ship – the chief mate Franklin, the shipkeeper, the steward, the cook, the cook's wife, and the carpenter form a little speech community whose petulant obsession with their Captain's marriage intrudes constantly on Powell's attention. As Powell remarks, the *Ferndale* crew were '"always talking of the man [Captain Anthony], making free with him to that extent that really he seemed to have become our property"' (p. 412). When he isn't being plagued by the grievances of the vessel's old hands, Powell has to listen to the malevolent whispers of de Barral himself. 'Young Powell Sees and Hears', the title of chapter 2 of Part II, captures the young sailor's position and predicament: trapped in the delicate position of '"unwilling eavesdropper"' (p. 280), he sees and hears intensely private matters that he is in no position to understand. Faced with Franklin's mutterings about the '"devil-work"' (p. 305) of Flora and her father, and de Barral's dark allusions to Captain Anthony as '"the jailer"' (p. 307), he differentiates only by lucky chance between the relatively innocuous whingeing of the crew members and the murderous intent that lies behind de Barral's words. Structurally, then, Powell's role in this novel is to function as Marlow's eyes and ears in a world that he understands only imperfectly. As Marlow observes: '"The inwardness of what was passing before his eyes was hidden from him, who had looked on, more impenetrably than from me who at a distance of years was listening to his words"' (p. 426). Because Marlow can place Powell's *Ferndale* experience in a wider frame of reference than was available to his informant at the time, he is further from the reality but closer to the truth.

One of the lessons of Powell's ordeal on the *Ferndale* is the difficulty of recognizing genuinely malicious gossip. When Marlow is himself challenged to differentiate between gossip and authentic storytelling, he does so with emphatic confidence:

'But we, my dear Marlow, have the inestimable advantage of understanding what is happening to others,' I struck in. 'Or at least some of us seem to. Is that too a provision of nature? And what is it for? Is it that we may amuse ourselves gossiping about each other's affairs? You, for instance, seem – '

'I don't know what I seem,' Marlow silenced me, 'and surely life must be amused somehow. It would be still a very respectable provision if it were only for that end. But from that same provision of understanding, there springs in us compassion, charity, indignation, the sense of solidarity; and in minds of any largeness an inclination to that indulgence which is next to affection.' (pp. 117–18)

Marlow is unusually impassioned, at this moment, in his defence of storytelling as a unifying expression of moral sympathy. To understand 'what is happening to others' is an honourable purpose for a speech genre that some might lightly dismiss as mere tittle-tattle. However, by interrupting and silencing his interlocutor in this emphatic way, Marlow sharpens the adversarial edge of his narrative. Despite his avowed commitment to solidarity, Marlow is obviously eager not to let his voice be lost in any bland consensus.

Marlow's defence of storytelling implies that there is good gossip and bad gossip, a distinction he reinforces elsewhere in the novel by assigning disreputable gossip a female gender. The pejorative assumption that 'bad' gossip is an exclusively female speech genre has, as George Steiner observes, a long and dishonourable history: 'In every known culture, men have accused women of being garrulous, of wasting words with lunatic prodigality. The chattering, ranting, gossiping female, the tattler, the scold . . . is older than fairytales.'[27] In a survey of male denunciations of 'women's talk', Patricia Meyer Spacks observes that men have traditionally based their low estimation of female discourse on either moral or economic grounds. Women are given to indiscreet chatter, it is traditionally thought, either because of 'mental weakness' – by which logic the Biblical Eve becomes the mother of all gossips – or because, lacking any real occupation, they have nothing better to do.[28] Marlow's idea of gossip as a women-only discourse is rooted in his sense of the shallow partiality of female language and thought: '"The secret scorn of women for the capacity to consider judiciously and to express profoundly a meditated conclusion is unbounded"' (p. 145). Dismissive remarks of this sort are obviously designed to consolidate Marlow's credentials as a judicious and profound storyteller with none of the '"malevolent curiosity"' (p. 281) of women. Take, for example, his remarks about '"a woman's quick power of observation and inference (the putting of two and two together)"' (p. 390). Marlow's apparent tribute to female intelligence is immediately retracted; female reasoning is reduced to the status of elementary arithmetic. He also withdraws an apparent compliment to the late wife of de Barral: '"Mrs de Barral was no foolish gossiping woman. But she made some confidences to Miss Anthony..."' (p. 72). Women's language is an indispensable resource for Marlow – '"putting two and two together"' is an '"old-maiden-lady-like"' (p. 326) activity that he cannot resist – and it is perhaps for this reason that he can't seem to decide whether female storytellers are acute or simplistic, tactful or indiscreet.

The notion that gossip is the preserve of the *unmarried* woman, one of the more curious myths associated with this speech genre, has been strikingly glossed by Jan B. Gordon in his discussion of the gossiping spinsters of Jane Austen. Gordon argues that the Austen heroine who seeks a husband is obliged to become 'a kind of literary critic' who must accurately read every gesture from every would-be suitor. If she fails to read these social signs correctly, she is excluded from 'the final, ultimate text – the marriage contract' and becomes instead 'the impecunious old maid charged with the community's verbal re-presentations rather than its genealogical reproduction'.[29] It seems possible that Marlow's caustic remarks about 'old maiden ladies' might owe something to an uncomfortable sense of his own situation as a sort of 'male spinster' figure, an ageing onlooker, match-maker and recycler of social information who lives vicariously through the pairings-off of the younger generation.

The sheer distance between the storyteller and his subject-matter is the major narrative problem negotiated by *Chance*. Marlow has precious little first-hand contact with any of the leading players and none at all with Roderick. One of Marlow's tasks is to persuade his audience – and himself – that this distance is an advantage rather than a handicap. The early exchanges in the riverside inn establish a creative interaction between the first-hand experience of Powell and Marlow's detached reflections. As a storyteller, Powell brings to mind the Marlow of 'Youth': his narrative is rooted in concrete personal experience, and displays a certain 'contempt of general ideas' (p. 23). Marlow weaves around

Powell's words a moralizing commentary that is often quirkily at odds
with the apparent lessons of the narrative: for example, he claims that it is
'"unwise to admit any sort of responsibility for our actions"' (p. 23), and
also that '"the incapacity to achieve anything distinctly good or evil is
inherent in our earthly condition"' (p. 23). Ironic generalizations of this
sort are part of Marlow's bid to establish the superiority of the armchair
raconteur over the involved storyteller. Powell's job is to unfold a naïvely
autobiographical narrative of events whose deeper significance we can
grasp only if we turn to Marlow. Powell, the Fynes, and his other informants are like so many spies, eavesdroppers, and private investigators
reporting back to Marlow, who inhabits a sort of self-imposed narrative
quarantine where 'information' reaches him only once it has been refined
in multiple retellings. He is openly scornful of those storytellers, like Fleet
Street reporters or gossiping spinsters, who combine a naïve attachment
to 'information', or to superficial visual impressions, with a vulgar habit
of actively seeking out such material. '"Information"', he asserts, '"is
something one goes out to seek and puts away when found as you might
do a piece of lead: ponderous, useful, unvibrating, dull. Whereas knowledge comes to one, this sort of knowledge, *a chance acquisition* preserving
in its repose a fine resonant quality"' (p. 88; my italics). The principle
of chance is a significant part of the metanarrative of legitimation that
accompanies his primary story; he maintains that truth will always seek
out the storyteller, if he has the necessary patience. For him, the best storyteller is an accidental storyteller, a '"chance confidant"' (p. 238) with a
lucky knack of bumping into useful sources of information, or stumbling
across people in desperate need of a sympathetic listener. At the heart
of *Chance* there seems to be a curious intuition that the wretched luck
experienced by women represents a golden opportunity for the male
storyteller.

Marlow's stance as the accidental storyteller will be familiar to readers
of *Lord Jim*; what is new in *Chance* is the air of absolute certainty that is
often present in his narrative. When Mrs Fyne professes herself baffled at
the foul treatment of Flora by her East-End cousins, Marlow experiences
no such interpretative difficulty: '"I, on the contrary, thought it very possible. I could imagine easily how the poor girl must have been bewildered
and hurt at her reception in that household"' (p. 163). This air of effort-
less infallibility is entirely characteristic of the Marlow of *Chance*, perhaps
most strikingly in his extremely detailed description of the psychological
impact of Flora on Roderick: '"This is no supposition"', he concludes.
'"It is a fact"' (p. 159).

A corollary of this new-found certainty is Marlow's contempt for other storytellers; he extols the virtues of his own narration by continually adverting to the failures and limitations of other people's. For example, his interpretation of de Barral's gestures of defiance in court is counterpointed to that of a 'pressman':

'His business was to write a readable account. But I, who had nothing to write, permitted myself to use my mind . . . And the disclosure which so often rewards a moment of detachment from mere visual impressions gave me a thrill very much approaching a shudder. I seemed to understand that, with the shock of the agonies and perplexities of his trial, the imagination of that man, whose moods, notions, and motives wore frequently an air of grotesque mystery – that his imagination had been at last roused into activity. And this was awful. Just try to enter into the feelings of a man whose imagination wakes up at the very moment he is about to enter the tomb . . .' (p. 87)

Typical of the Marlow of *Chance* is the sense of one-upmanship that underpins his opposition between the meditated speech of the raconteur and the thoughtless journalistic writings of a pressman who can see no further or deeper than the '"actualities"' (p. 87) craved by his readers. The journalist deals in mere information, the storyteller in shared experience – the awakening of de Barral's imagination stirs Marlow into imaginative activity and he appeals for his listener to enter into the same process. His insights are articulated in a language of paradox beyond anything the pressman can attempt: this epiphanic moment of 'disclosure', the thrilling shudder of sympathy between Marlow and de Barral, paradoxically depends on the imminent closure of de Barral's life. No 'external' evidence is brought forward to confirm these insights; but any doubts over the accuracy of these suppositions are dispelled when Marlow's interlocutor gasps at their '"absolute verisimilitude"' (p. 102). This vision of de Barral is one of the points where, despite his reliance upon second-, third- or even fourth-hand testimony, Marlow becomes as it were temporarily clairvoyant, vividly reconstructing scenes or states of mind to which he has not even had vicarious access. These moments – de Barral's frame of mind prior to committal (p. 87), the impact of the de Barral crash on Eliza and Charley (pp. 101–7), the initial impact of Flora on Roderick (p. 159), the effects of Carleon Anthony's poetry on his gallant son (p. 328–9) – are associated with moments of crisis, trauma or revelation. Such insights owe less to our storyteller's deductive virtuosity than to the text's willingness to grant Marlow the insight he desires, the rare gift of producing commentary emancipated from fact, knowledge divorced from information.

Insufferable knowingness is probably the keynote of Marlow's story-telling in *Chance*. As in 'Heart of Darkness' and *Lord Jim*, narrative in this text takes the form of an incremental breakdown in confidentiality that the storyteller bids to recuperate or contain, though the process is now gendered in more obvious ways. The actions of a displaced – even unplaceable – woman give rise to gossip, a 'female' speech genre that threatens to infect the male storyteller's own discourse. The waspish ec-centricity of Marlow's narrative tone must be seen as a determined effort to resist the kind of facile consensus on which gossip thrives. But what truly differentiates the Marlow of *Chance* from his previous incarnations is his conjectural omniscience, a gift that transforms the scrupulous, ten-tative raconteur of 'Heart of Darkness' and *Lord Jim* back into one of the all-knowing patriarchs of realist fiction.

PART III

Political communities

CHAPTER SEVEN

Nostromo *and anecdotal history*

'Conrad must have asked himself again and again: Is this novel to be a spoken or a written narrative, a story or a history?'[1] These, according to Albert J. Guerard, are the disarmingly simple either/or questions that vexed Conrad as he worked on his most ambitious novel, *Nostromo* (1904). Not that you would have suspected any such authorial indecision from the novel's magisterial opening pages, where academic history appears to have displaced oral story as the model of Conrad's fictional narrative. The narrator who introduces us to the volatile Latin American republic of Costaguana is well-versed in the region's colonial and commercial history, knows all there is to know about its remarkable landscape and peculiar weather-systems, and doesn't need to borrow the eyes and ears of his characters to witness its tempestuous political affairs. Nor does he choose to draft in a specialist raconteur, a Marlow-figure, to bring those events to life as 'spoken' narrative. Folklore and popular legends of the region are occasionally sampled, but the narrator's interest in oral culture seems broadly 'anthropological' rather than structural, and the novel's marginal storytellers never seem likely to challenge his control of the novel's language.

Conrad's decision to pension off Marlow at this stage of his literary career doubtless has a great deal to do with his growing mastery of the language and fiction of his adopted homeland – with 'Heart of Darkness' and *Lord Jim* to his name, he no longer needed to shelter behind an 'English' *alter ego*. But the particular significance of the absence of Marlovian storytelling from *Nostromo* can only be discovered in the text itself. Frederic Jameson, in a challenging Marxist interpretation of Conrad's 'great historical novel', argues that *Nostromo* systematically undermines 'the individual categories of storytelling in order to project, beyond the stories it must continue to tell, the concept of a process beyond storytelling'.[2] That unnarratable 'process', the impact of capitalism in its imperialist phase on an economically 'backward' province of South

America, is too complex to be entrusted to a single storyteller, not least because oral culture seems to be one of the main casualties of this massive programme of socio-economic modernization. The transformation of Sulaco into an independent republic is accompanied by a remarkable outpouring of writing – letters, front-line reportage, newspaper propaganda, historical memoirs, constitutional documents – as the written word imposes its authority on a raucous oral culture. The telegraph also comes of age in the course of the novel, playing a decisive role in the unfolding military and political drama. The circulation of printed material and the flow of encoded information now seem to matter far more to the modern state, and the modern novel, than the quaint wisdom of traditional speech communities; and this transition from oral to print culture is re-enacted, and as it were confirmed, by Conrad's own switch from oral story to written historical narrative.

Mark Conroy, who writes perceptively on the transition from oral to print culture in *Nostromo*, observes that 'The one epic legend in *Nostromo* has wisdom but no audience prepared to receive it, while the one story-teller figure in the book [Captain Mitchell] has plenty of audiences but no wisdom to dispense.'[3] This is attractively clear-cut, but not quite true to the complexity of the text. Mitchell is indeed Sulaco's most prominent raconteur; but he is not alone. Don José Avellanos, during his tea-time visits to the Casa Gould, 'talk[s] on and on with a sort of complacent virtuosity wonderful in a man of his age' (p. 51). General Barrios regales 'unceremonious gatherings of men' with 'jaguar-hunt stories' and 'tales of extraordinary night rides' (p. 161). Giorgio Viola declaims 'tales of war' (p. 32) to the patrons of the Casa Viola. Military reminiscences are also the subject of Don Pépé's orations to fellow members of the Aristocratic Club of Sulaco (p. 97). Admittedly, these elderly raconteurs make a fairly negligible contribution to the novel's overall narrative; their epic tales of heroism and adventure belong to a precapitalist era whose demise leaves the storyteller as a figure of tragicomic pathos, an antiquated side-show rather than a figure of authority and wisdom. In 'Gaspar Ruiz', written in October 1905, General Santierra, a 'venerable relic of revolutionary times',[4] captivates an audience of English naval officers with his vivid recollections of the South American wars of independence. But the 'venerable relics' of *Nostromo* – Don José, Barrios, Don Pépé, Viola – never enjoy the undivided attention of an entire speech community.

Captain Joseph Mitchell, the Oceanic Steam Navigation Company's superintendent at the harbour, is the only one of Sulaco's garrulous senior citizens to be given a generous hearing in the text. Mitchell seems to have inherited Charlie Marlow's role as the English seaman whose over-seas adventures become the stuff of compelling yarns: he even performs Marlovian 'rescue work', helping to bundle the ladies and gentlemen of Sulaco to safety during an outbreak of mob violence, and lending a hand as Decoud and Nostromo spirit away the consignment of sil-ver from the clutches of the renegade Colonel Sotillo. The resemblance between Marlow and Mitchell is, however, entirely superficial. Through-out *Nostromo*, Mitchell displays irrepressible enthusiasm for storytelling – '"Begad, sir! I could spin you a yarn for hours"' (p. 484) – but abso-lutely none of Marlow's subtlety, irony or self-consciousness. He displays a singular lack of penetration in his commentary on the foundation of the Occidental Republic, which he sees as a straightforward triumph of civilized European values over mob rule. It never occurs to Mitchell that the visitors whom he conducts on gruelling tours of the regenerated town might find his anecdotes baffling rather than vivid or astounding. He manages the unlikely feat of presenting a grossly simplified account of Sulaco's recent past in a form almost incomprehensible to anyone who isn't already acquainted with the region. As Sulaco's oral historian, or one-man 'heritage industry',[5] Mitchell is plainly and comically inept, the novelist's stooge rather than his trusted proxy; but, while it is easy enough to laugh at him, one wonders whether even a more gifted racon-teur could improve much on the efforts of Sulaco's 'merciless cicerone' (p. 486). The problem is not that Sulaco deserves a better storyteller, but that 'the storyteller' simply isn't a viable mouthpiece for historical narratives of such formidable complexity. The task of reshaping the jum-bled chapters of Costaguanan history into a coherent story of economic development or political reform is probably beyond the competence of any individual speaker, however eloquent or incisive.

But we should, nevertheless, be wary of overstating the marginality of voice, storytelling, and oral culture in *Nostromo*. The transparent absur-dities of *Nostromo*'s primary storyteller should not lead us to discount the potential value of the speech genre to which he is addicted, the historical anecdote. As Pedro Montero's fascination with the 'historical anecdotes' (p. 402) found in 'gossipy' historical works (p. 403) might suggest, *Nostromo* doesn't always encourage us to regard anecdotes as serious forms of his-torical narrative. The idea of 'anecdotal history' is suggestive of trivial-ization, of the substitution of colourful apocrypha for hard evidence, or the reduction of serious scholarly enquiry to the level of gossip about well-known personalities. But in his Author's Note of 1917, Conrad re-veals that a 'vagrant anecdote', the story of an American sailor 'who was supposed to have stolen single-handed a whole lighter-full of silver, some-where on the Tierra Firme seaboard' (pp. vii–i), was the germ of the entire novel. This tale was subsequently augmented in his imagination by a curi-ous range of secondary sources: a volume of nautical memoirs purchased in a second-hand bookshop, 'gossip half-forgotten' (p. ix), and a historical work (Don José Avellanos's *History of Fifty Years of Misrule*) that exists only in the world of the novel. He stretches our credulity still further by claim-ing first-hand experience of the Occidental Republic, where, he assures us, he became personally acquainted with old Giorgio, Don José, and Antonia Avellanos. Conrad obviously derives a degree of mischievous pleasure from mocking our solemn curiosity about the historical 'ori-gins' of his novel. Teasingly playful in its intermingling of anecdote and history, fact and fiction, speech and writing, the Note is a metafictional *jeu d'esprit* in which a slender anecdote of dubious provenance is given more authority than a weighty historical text. But, for all its mischievous humour, the Note is a salutary warning against the easy assumption that *Nostromo* subordinates anecdotal narrative to written history.

In the light of Conrad's Note, the presence in *Nostromo* of subhistorical, 'anecdotal' material – local folkore, proverbs, gossip, rumours, sayings – might represent something larger than a passing 'anthropological' in-terest in Costaguana's dying oral culture. The narrator's habit of citing hearsay evidence – 'the story goes that', 'as the sailors say', 'it was said that', 'as the saying is', 'it was related that' – seems to acknowledge the presence of a living speech community on the margins of the text. His 'soundings' from oral culture may have no official place in the annals of Costaguana, but, as the narrator of 'The Warrior's Soul' remarks, 'See how people's mere gossip and idle talk pass into history.'[6] The signs of this contamination of history by hearsay are visible in the first chapter of the novel, where the narrator reaches for the proverbial language of the country's seamen:

[T]hese cloudy nights are proverbial with seamen along the whole west coast of a great continent. Sky, land, and sea disappear together out of the world when the Placido – as the saying is – goes to sleep under its black poncho. The few stars left below the seaward frown of the vault shine feebly as into the mouth of a black cavern. In its vastness your ship floats unseen under your feet, her sails flutter invisible above your head. The eye of God Himself – they add with grim profanity – could not find out what work a man's hand is doing in there. (pp. 6–7)

The vivid panorama of the novel's opening paragraphs becomes in this passage a region of impenetrable darkness, a blindspot in the 'eye of

God'. But, as so often in Conrad, there are voices in the darkness; in this case, the voices belong to sailors who comment grimly that even omniscience has its limits. It is as though the seamen are dimly aware of the limitations of the author's all-seeing gaze: even a narrator perched, as it were, on the summit of Higuerota cannot see everything and must let the voices of his characters conjure up what the eye can't make out. These snatches of sailors' talk, which might strike us as nothing more than the vestigial traces of obsolete oral culture amidst the modernist *écriture* of *Nostromo*, prove to be an indispensable supplement to the impersonality of the written, a vital means of closing the ontological distance between disembodied narrator and created world.

Nostromo modulates constantly between the vivid speech of those involved in the Costaguanan revolution and the authoritative discourse of the detached narrator. The narrative is never entrusted to a single raconteur (aside from Mitchell) for any length of time, but dozens of minor storytellers chip in with their small contributions to the overall storyline. Consider, for example, this exchange between anonymous travellers on the Camino Real:

[S]purring on in the dusk they would discuss the great news of the province, the news of the San Tomé mine. A rich Englishman was going to work it – and perhaps not an Englishman, *Quien sabe!* A foreigner with much money. Oh, yes, it had begun. A party of men who had been to Sulaco with a herd of black bulls for the next corrida had reported that from the porch of the posada in Rincon, only a short league from the town, the lights on the mountain were visible, twinkling above the trees. And there was a woman seen riding a horse sideways, not in the chair seat, but upon a sort of saddle, and a man's hat on her head. She walked about, too, on foot up the mountain paths. A woman engineer, it seemed she was.

'What an absurdity! Impossible, señor!'

'*Si! Si! Una Americana del Norte.*'

'Ah, well! if your worship is informed. *Una Americana*; it need be something of that sort.' (pp. 101–2)

This horseman's-eye view of the San Tomé revolution allows us to inhabit, briefly, the mindset of a traditional community coming to terms with radical but imperfectly understood change. Excitement mingles with apprehension as new landmarks appear on the horizon of a familiar shared world – the twinkling lights of the mine, and the powerful strangers who have overseen its development. The passage is a masterly piece of defamiliarization, both in terms of perspective – Charles becomes 'A foreigner with much money' and Emily 'a woman seen riding a horse sideways' – and in terms of language. The snatches of dialogue in

Spanish compel us to read the Goulds through an unfamiliar language
as well as see them through an unfamiliar pair of eyes, before we are re-
stored to the 'transparent' intelligibility and authority of the Anglophone
narrator's discourse.

Spanish is the first language of Costaguana but the second language
of *Nostromo*: it is rarely quoted at any length, beyond isolated words and
phrases whose presence in the text seems largely decorative. Loan-words
from the region's vernacular – *caballeros, casa, leperos, mozo, posada, salteador,
vaqueros*, and many others – give the novel a broadly 'Hispanic' flavour
without disturbing the authority of English as its primary language. Most
of its dialogue has been 'translated', as it were, from Spanish or from
one of the other non-English languages spoken in the novel – Italian,
German, French, and 'Indian dialect of the country-people' (p. 48). John
Crompton has remarked that the entire novel reads like a 'translation'
in which 'English is a convenient medium for unifying three or four
languages which are being spoken or written.'[7] But the English language is far more than a mere convenience for the narrator. His casual
plundering of the Spanish lexicon to supply 'exotic' local colour for an
English master-narrative reproduces at the level of language the very
Anglo-American political ascendancy that the novel charts.

The linguistic communities of *Nostromo* are more various and the transactions between them more complex than those of any other Conrad
text. The intersections between these communities are often most visible
in the titles and nicknames acquired by Sulaco's prominent citizens. Most
of the novel's major characters have at least two names or nicknames,
current in different speech communities, and reflecting variations in role,
responsibilities, and reputation in different quarters of the province. The
novel's very title is an English mispronunciation of two Italian words:
in the mouths of Captain Mitchell and others, *nostro uomo*, or 'our man',
becomes 'Nostromo'. This act of renaming erases the baptismal name
(Gian' Battista Fidanza) of Sulaco's exemplary citizen and makes him, at
least nominally, the property of the British-owned O.S.N. Charles Gould
is also the object of an ambiguous process of renaming: 'in the talk of
common people he was just the Inglez – the Englishman of Sulaco'
(p. 47); but in Sta. Marta circles he has been christened 'El Rey de
Sulaco', a title with all the ambiguous prestige of 'Rajah Laut' or 'Tuan
Jim'. These linguistic negotiations between different speech communities
now seem to interest Conrad much more than the discursive practices
within a given circle of speakers. Indeed, the very idea of a homogeneous
linguistic community seems to have no place in the world of *Nostromo*.

Even the intimate Casa Viola is a carefully stratified and subdivided discursive space:

[T]he aristocracy of the railway works listened to him [Giorgio Viola], turning away from their cards or dominoes. Here and there a fair-haired Basque studied his hand meantime, waiting without protest. No native of Costaguana intruded there. This was the Italian stronghold. Even the Sulaco policemen on a night patrol let their horses pace softly by, bending low in the saddle to glance through the window at the heads in a fog of smoke; and the drone of old Giorgio's declamatory narrative seemed to sink behind them into the plain. (pp. 32–3)

This little speech community has its own professional, linguistic, and ethnic hierarchies. Non-Europeans are excluded from the Casa Viola; non-Italian Europeans are admitted and tolerated; but only Giorgio's fellow countrymen can become full members of this community of speakers. If different languages are a factor in determining the shape of this discursive space, then so too are different kinds of silence – and the polite silence with which the Italian workers greet the Garibaldino's 'declamatory narrative' suggests that his need of an audience is much greater than their need of a storyteller. One could scarcely ask for a better visual summary of Conrad's idea of modernization than this image of silent technocrats patiently waiting for the old soldier to talk himself into submission.

Although *Nostromo* is haunted by the figure of the redundant storyteller, the narrator often becomes infected by the enthusiasm of his talkative characters; even when there is more urgent business at hand he is only too pleased to turn from official history to intriguing apocrypha. For example, as Barrios and his troops prepare to embark for Cayta, the narrator can't resist an anecdotal digression on the general's colourful reputation:

All his life he had been an inveterate gambler. He alluded himself quite openly to the current story how once, during some campaign (when in command of a brigade), he had gambled away his horses, pistols, and accoutrements, to the very epaulettes, playing *monte* with his colonels the night before the battle. Finally, he had sent under escort his sword (a presentation sword, with a gold hilt) to the town in the rear of his position to be immediately pledged for five hundred pesetas with a sleepy and frightened shop-keeper. By daybreak he had lost the last of that money, too, when his only remark, as he rose calmly, was, 'Now let us go and fight to the death.' From that time he had become aware that a general could lead his troops into battle very well with a simple stick in his hand. 'It has been my custom ever since,' he would say. (p. 162)

Here the narrator relaxes from the rigours of scholarly history into the more expansive gestures of anecdote. Historical specificity is set aside ('once, during some campaign . . .') for the sake of sheer delight in storytelling. But Barrios's night of gambling, which can only be described as a kind of military striptease – horses, pistols, epaulettes, sword all recklessly surrendered – is anything but irrelevant. The General displays an edifyingly nonchalant attitude to material possessions in a world where others are enslaved to precious metal. His compulsive gambling, a habit shared by many characters in the novel, is a minor version of the desperate risk-taking that dominates the political scene in Sulaco – the resurrection of the San Tomé mine, Decoud and Nostromo's mission with the silver, Monygham's 'game of betrayal' with Sotillo (p. 410). And 'gambling' might even serve as a covert metaphor for the speculation and guess-work indulged in by the narrator when the attractive uncertainties of anecdotal narrative tempt him to venture beyond the limits of official history. Recklessly gambling away his possessions, and coming away with only a simple stick and a priceless anecdote, Barrios allows us to reflect on the pleasures and politics of risk-taking as they bear both on Costaguanan history and on Conradian narrative.

Nostromo exhibits the kind of fascination with anecdotal narrative that is sometimes seen as the defining characteristic of the so-called New Historicist movement in literary studies. Stephen Greenblatt, the doyen of the New Historicists, likes to read canonical Renaissance texts in complex juxtaposition with autobiographical reflections and suggestive anecdotes culled from non-literary sources. Inspired in part by the 'postmodern' disenchantment with grand narratives, Greenblatt's idiosyncratic and somewhat controversial method lays special emphasis on those fugitive fragments of the past that can't be neatly subordinated to established narratives of historical change. It would be fairly meaningless to designate *Nostromo* a work of New Historicism *avant la lettre*, but recent debates about the value of Greenblatt's work have generated terms that are surprisingly suggestive of Conrad's work of imaginative historiography. Joel Fineman has nicely described New Historicism's 'characteristic air of reporting, haplessly, the discoveries it happened serendipitously to stumble upon in the course of undirected, idle rambles through the historical archives' (p. 52), and contends that this privileging of the anecdotal enables the literary historian to free the past from the grip of narratives that accommodate every contingent detail to a predetermined teleology. John Lee is much more sceptical of the scholarly credentials of New Historicism: he alleges that the New Historicists play fast and loose with historical fact, and claims that errors in Stephen Greenblatt's scholarship can be attributed to his casual manipulation of anecdotes by master-narratives.[8]

I do not propose to adjudicate between Fineman and Lee, but rather simply to note that the tensions between master-narratives and anecdotes are visible everywhere in *Nostromo*, and that the lessons of New Historicism might sharpen our appreciation of Conrad's own suspicion of grand narratives like 'industrialization' or 'secularization', those big words that say everything and nothing about the changes being wrought in the world of the novel.

Of course, the tensions between master-narratives and anecdotes in *Nostromo* do more than simply illustrate academic debates over historical methodology. Consider, for example, the afterlife of Guzman Bento, a dictator of legendary cruelty, in the collective memory of Costaguana:

> [Bento] reached his apotheosis in the popular legend of a sanguinary land-haunting spectre whose body had been carried off by the devil in person from the brick mausoleum in the nave of the Church of Assumption in Sta. Marta. Thus, at least, the priests explained its disappearance to the barefooted multitude that streamed in, awestruck, to gaze at the hole in the side of the ugly box of bricks before the great altar. (p. 47)

Stealing a corpse is one rather gruesome way of laying claim to the past; however, if the grave-robbers have made off with Bento's remains, the priests retain control of his memory. Their supernatural explanation of Bento's posthumous vanishing-act, which transforms the dictator into a bogey-man who strikes the fear of God into the 'barefooted multitude', puts popular legend at the service of religious piety. As Robert Hampson has observed, the legendary in *Nostromo* 'is used as a displacement or mystification of the political'.[9]

But not all of Costaguana's folklore is at the service of the authorities. The legend of gold in the waterless Azuera peninsula, much the most important of the folk-tales in *Nostromo*, is handed down by an impoverished and marginalized speech community:

> The poor, associating by an obscure instinct of consolation the ideas of evil and wealth, will tell you that it is deadly because of its forbidden treasures. The common folk of the neighbourhood, peons of the estancias, vacqueros of the seaboard plains, tame Indians coming to market with a bundle of sugar-cane or a basket of maize worth about threepence, are well aware that heaps of shining gold lie in the gloom of the deep precipices cleaving the stony levels of Azuera. Tradition has it that many adventurers of olden time had perished in the search. The story goes also that within men's memory two wandering sailors – Americanos, perhaps, but gringos of some sort for certain – talked over a gambling, good-for-nothing mozo, and the three stole a donkey to carry for them a bundle of dry sticks, a water-skin, and provisions enough to last a

few days [...] The sailors, the Indian, and the stolen burro were never seen again. As to the mozo, a Sulaco man – his wife paid for some masses, and the poor four-footed beast, being without sin, had been probably permitted to die; but the two gringos, spectral and alive, are believed to be dwelling to this day amongst the rocks, under the fatal spell of their success. (pp. 4–5)

The 'poor', the 'common folk', the 'peons', 'vacqueros', and 'tame Indians' who share and perpetuate the Azuera legend seem to belong to a prehistoric phase of the region's past, an unspecified 'olden time' long before the calendar of colonial and political events was inaugurated. This apparent exclusion of native South American people from Costaguana's political history has been described by Robert Holton as a form of 'temporal apartheid' in the novel.[10] But the partition between 'mythic' and 'historical' pasts is far more permeable than Holton suggests. New versions of the Azuera legend have emerged in response to the events of recent history: within 'living memory' a self-contained story, almost a first draft of *Nostromo*, has crystallized out of these ancient traditions. The accursed gold deposits of Azuera correspond to the equally deadly riches of San Tomé; and the ill-fated 'gringos' of the legend are the ghostly cousins of those whom the silver emasculates, corrupts, and dehumanizes. The interference of the republic's oral traditions in its modern history gives the lie to Holton's allegation that *Nostromo* 'leaves the incomprehensible native other marginalised, discursively disenfranchised and aphasic'.[11] Costaguanan history is not simply reflected in, but, as it were, scripted by the Azuera legend, a curse-narrative that asserts its authority by tempting the novel's would-be history-makers – Gould, Decoud, Nostromo – to defy its finality. I wouldn't want to overstate the novel's credentials as a 'postcolonial' fiction, but Conrad's use of the voices of the dispossessed to utter a dire allegorical warning about San Tomé is an unmistakeably political gesture, one that aligns *Nostromo* with the 'problematic shared by a number of nineteenth-century British novelists . . . of making an oral culture relevant to a state's future rather than some persecuted tribal past'.[12]

Nostromo opens with a story of recuperation, the gold-diggers' quest, enfolded in a counter-story of enslavement and dehumanization. Images of human agency absorbed and negated by language are a familiar part of Conrad's fictional world; but *Nostromo* massively extends this pattern to encompass an entire community of gossip-provoking, story-worthy personages 'meshed in a web of rumour and legend, record and raconteurship'.[13] This 'web' is strikingly visible in Conrad's sketch of Father Corbelàn:

It was known that Father Corbelàn had come out of the wilds to advocate the sacred rights of the Church with the same fanatical fearlessness with which he had gone preaching to bloodthirsty savages, devoid of human compassion or worship of any kind. *Rumours of legendary proportions* told of his successes as a missionary beyond the eye of Christian men. He had baptized whole nations of Indians, living with them like a savage himself. *It was related* that the padre used to ride with his Indians for days, half naked, carrying a bullock-hide shield, and, no doubt, a long lance, too – *who knows?* That he had wandered clothed in skins, seeking for proselytes somewhere near the snow line of the Cordillera. Of these exploits Padre Corbelàn himself was never known to talk. But *he made no secret of his opinion* that the politicians of Sta. Marta had harder hearts and more corrupt minds than the heathen to whom he had carried *the word of God*. His injudicious zeal for the temporal welfare of the Church was damaging the Ribierist cause. *It was common knowledge* that he had refused to be made titular bishop of the Occidental diocese till justice was done to a despoiled church. (194–5; my italics)

It is ironic that Corbelàn should be pictured spreading 'the word of God', given the absence of absolute truth or hard evidence in this sketch of his past. The omniscient narrator seems to disclaim any kind of editorial authority over the conflicting discourses – popular say-so, common knowledge, 'legendary' rumours, the priest's own publicly voiced opinions, and the voices of his Ribierist critics – in which Corbelàn is conjured up. Which is not to say that we must regard the passage as benignly polyphonic, an echo chamber or Speaker's Corner where every voice is equally valid, every narrative freely interchangeable. Acute political tensions are legible beneath the surface of this 'polyphonic' prose: every phrase is strained and inflected with the contradictory prejudices of rival interest groups. The simple uncertainty over the turbulent cleric's title ('Father Corbelàn' or 'Padre Corbelàn'?) breaks him down into a set of conflicting reputational narratives circulated in different speech communities. Far-fetched rumours of Corbelàn's evangelical journeys are balanced against acerbic whispers about his political beliefs: the fantastically successful missionary of popular legend has become, for the Protestant-backed Ribierists, a trouble-making malcontent who won't be palmed off with an episcopal sinecure. These provocative allegations are uttered with suave diplomacy ('injudicious zeal') or disguised in the bland consensual language of public opinion ('It was common knowledge that . . .'). Even the innocuous phrase 'who knows' is a double-voiced expression: '*Quien sabe?*', as Martin Decoud remarks, is what 'the people here are prone to say in answer to every question' (p. 249), the rueful motto of a speech community accustomed to limited knowledge of the present and the future. But 'who knows' is also the narrator's wry observation – who knows how much further the common people might embellish this improbable portrait of Corbelàn? One could scarcely ask for a better illustration than this passage of Bakhtin's assertion that 'The word in language is half someone else's.'[14]

The intense mediation of Corbelàn's subjectivity by public language is exemplary, rather than exceptional, in this novel. To a remarkable extent, *Nostromo*'s quartet of male heroes – the Capataz, Martin Decoud, Charles Gould, and Dr Monygham – are defined, as human subjects and as political agents, by their response to the pressures and demands of the novel's speech communities. Conrad's scrutiny of their relationships with language and with each other rests on a fundamental opposition between the faith placed in words by Nostromo and Decoud, and the linguistic scepticism of Gould and Monygham. This rudimentary contrast is developed, almost systematically, through the pairing and juxtaposition of the novel's male leads – Decoud and Nostromo on the lighter, Gould and Decoud in the Casa Gould, Nostromo and Monygham at the Custom House – in extended scenes of dialogue.

The typical Conrad hero hates the idea of being talked about, but Nostromo goes out of his way to court publicity in the belief that a splendid reputation is more valuable, in the long term, than a modest salary. Nostromo says comparatively little in the first half of the novel, as though he is content for the voice of the world to speak for him, and of him, with a suitable degree of respect and admiration. He collects praise, those precious epithets 'illustrious', 'incorruptible', 'magnificent', 'indispensable', as another man might hoard money; but this naïve conception of public language as a flattering mirror for his picturesque displays of loyalty and resourcefulness blinds Nostromo to the demands that language makes of him. When hyperbolic acclaim for the Capataz becomes commonplace, and perfection becomes the expected norm of his professional conduct, then anything less than faultless heroism in the performance of his duties will ruin his fictionalized public persona.

The bitter recognition that he has made himself answerable to impossible expectations dawns on Nostromo when he joins forces with Decoud in their perilous night-journey with the silver. This partnership of Sulaco's popular hero with its leading journalist emphasizes just how closely Nostromo's fate is tied to public language. We might note, however, that the linguistic behaviour of Nostromo and Decoud on the lighter runs counter to our expectations. Floating in the darkness and silence of the Golfo Placido, the taciturn man of action becomes restlessly talkative, while the professional wordsmith is uncharacteris-tically reticent. Nostromo talks at length, with grim and embittered bravado, about the 'deadly' trust (p. 263) that has been placed in him, and feels that the presence of Decoud has compromised the mission:

'I told Captain Mitchell three times that I preferred to go alone. I told Don Carlos Gould, too. It was in the Casa Gould. They had sent for me. The ladies were there; and when I tried to explain why I did not wish to have you with me, they promised me, both of them, great rewards for your safety. A strange way to talk to a man you are sending out to an almost certain death. Those gentlefolk do not seem to have sense enough to understand what they are giving one to do. I told them I could do nothing for you . . . But it was as if they had been deaf.' (p. 280)

A new self-consciousness emerges in Nostromo when he realizes that Sulaco's 'gentlefolk' will neither grant him full autonomy nor engage him as an equal in the give-and-take of genuine dialogue: his misgivings, his repeated pleas for recognition, fall on deaf ears. In one important sense it is entirely appropriate that Nostromo should be forced to share his adventure with a journalist: Decoud is the very personification of the public language to which the Capataz has surrendered a significant part of himself. Despite his fiercely self-reliant demeanour, Nostromo is al-most childishly dependent on the approving words of others. One might even argue that his 'fall' occurs not when he resolves to steal the silver, but, much earlier in the novel, when he finds his own voice. Prior to the mission with the silver, Nostromo has been a curiously depthless charac-ter: dynamic, resourceful, and possessed of a certain laconic machismo, he is more of a 'type' than a character, and certainly has none of the complex inwardness of, say, Gould or Decoud. Only when he begins to articulate his own fears and desires does he reveal a subjective interiority in powerful tension with public language.

The gap between Nostromo's private self and his public reputation in Part III is probably the most significant of all the 'startling dispari-ties between action and record' probed by Edward Said in the novel.[15] 'Trumpeted by Captain Mitchell, grown in repetition, and fixed in gen-eral assent' (p. 432), Nostromo's reputation as a man '"worth his weight in gold"' (p. 530) is never more illustrious than in the aftermath of the Monterist coup. However, if the Capataz continues to be showered with undeserved praise, he also becomes prey to disreputable – but not baseless – gossip. Rumours have reached old Giorgio and others that Ramirez, Nostromo's nominated successor as Capataz, is besotted with Giselle Viola. Ramirez, as it were in retaliation, has been making public allegations about Nostromo's suspicious late-night returns from the Great Isabel. Whereas in *Lord Jim* the hero begins his career as the butt of gossip and ends as the stuff of legend, in *Nostromo* Conrad exchanges the pattern of apotheosis for one of anti-climax. The legendary Capataz is drawn into an undignified tit-for-tat exchange of gossip, as he dwindles in stature from citizen-hero to minor coastal entrepreneur, to furtive thief and unfaithful lover. That Nostromo should be ultimately unrecognizable – shot by Giorgio, who takes him for Ramirez – is as much a reflection on the essential anonymity of Conrad's strangely named hero as it is on the fading faculties of the Garibaldino.

If Nostromo's 'fall' into villainy is a case-study in the dangers of renown, the emergence of Dr Monygham as an unlikely hero in the later stages of the novel reveals the potential advantages of notoriety. Known for his abrasive way with words, his limping gait and his careless attire, the Doctor is an unprepossessing and unpopular figure in the town. But reliable information about what lies behind this unfavourable public impression is hard to come by, because the narrator seems conspicuously reluctant to divulge the 'facts' about 'the mad English doctor' (p. 311). Whether there is any truth, for example, in the 'strange rumours' linking him to 'a conspiracy which was betrayed and, as people expressed it, drowned in blood' (p. 45) is an open question. Such tantalizing empty spaces are common in his life-story:

It was known that many years before, when quite young, he had been made by Guzman Bento chief medical officer of the army... Afterwards his story was not so clear. It lost itself amongst the innumerable tales of conspiracies and plots against the tyrant as a stream is lost in an arid belt of sandy country before it emerges, diminished and troubled, perhaps, on the other side. The doctor made no secret of it that he had lived for years in the wildest parts of the Republic, wandering with almost unknown Indian tribes in the great forests of the far interior where the great rivers have their sources. But it was mere aimless wandering; he had written nothing, collected nothing, brought nothing for science out of the twilight of the forests, which seemed to cling to his battered personality limping about Sulaco, where it had drifted in casually, only to get stranded on the shores of the sea. (p. 311)

The narrator cannot – or will not – sift out the truth from the 'innumerable tales' of Monygham's past; our glimpse of the doctor's 'lost years' is obscured by the impenetrable thickets of 'great forests of the far interior'. Monygham's aimless inland odyssey, reminiscent of Father Corbelàn's equally obscure missionary journeys through the same region, might offer a revealing insight into what Fogel calls *Nostromo*'s 'problem geography'.[16] The town of Sulaco is the site of official history, its affairs a matter of public record; but the outlying territories of the Republic, such as the peninsula, the Campo and the interior, are known chiefly through long-distance conjecture, the rumours and legends that reach the seaboard. In Bakhtinian terms, the republic's urban centre and its outlying regions are vividly contrasting chronotopes or 'time-spaces'.[17] The harbour town, with its thrice weekly newspaper, its regular calls from the O.S.N. ferries, its telegraph office, and its lighthouse, has a fixed position on the map and a precisely regulated temporal structure. But the peninsula, the Campo and the interior are unmapped, premodern spaces, beyond the totalizing gaze of the novelist-as-historian, but glimpsed occasionally by the novelist-as-storyteller.

Those characters, like Monygham, Corbelàn, and Hernandez, who have spent time in the unmapped corners of Costaguana, have strayed as it were from a chronotope of official history into one dominated by hearsay and supposition: the doctor's past is clouded by unconfirmed stories, the priest's by 'legendary' rumours, and the bandit's by 'the gossip of the inland Campo' (p. 109). Those who emerge from the text's 'pre-historic' backwoods into the daylight of public scrutiny do so under a cloud of suspicion or uncertainty that takes the form of unflattering rumours about their dubious 'origins'. This division in narrative space, between official history and backwoods hearsay, extends into strange discontinuities between the 'official' and 'unofficial' selves of the novel's characters. As the brothers Montero rise to prominence, one as the Blanco party's Minister of War, the other as its Military Commandant, it is whispered that 'their father had been nothing but a charcoal burner in the woods, and their mother a baptised Indian woman from the far interior' (p. 39). Similar rumours are peddled about Señor Gamacho, who, according to Monygham, '"might have been a Cargador on the O.S.N. wharf had he not (the posadero of Rincon is ready to swear it) murdered a pedlar in the woods and stolen his pack to begin life on"' (p. 321).

Monygham scarcely belongs with the Monteros or Gamacho as one of the novel's unambiguous villains, but the taint of suspicion on his character is never fully erased: '[T]he whole story of the Great Conspiracy was hopelessly involved and obscure . . . Don José Avellanos was perhaps the only one living who knew the whole story of these unspeakable cruelties' (p. 312). We have already seen that the narrator seems to make a virtue of not knowing 'the whole story', preferring not to disturb memories that Monygham himself has sought to repress. And in some senses the eccentric physician welcomes his reputation. He certainly displays a more resourceful and thick-skinned attitude to his own notoriety than his counterparts elsewhere in Conrad. Monygham harbours no illusions about the possibility of escaping language – '"I have lived too long amongst them to be anything else but the evil-eyed doctor"' (p. 517) – but neither does he surrender to its coercive force; rather, he chooses to 'enact' his reputation, playing the part of Sulaco's sharp-tongued misanthropist with a certain relish, and letting those around him believe what they want to believe. Having reached this pragmatic accommodation with his 'evil reputation' (p. 410), the Doctor proves himself a shrewder judge of the politics of reputation than those who try to resist the grasp of unkind gossip.

At the root of Monygham's abrasive cynicism and distrust of language is the traumatic memory of his ordeal at the hands of Father Beron, Guzman Bento's torturer-in-chief. If the Doctor's ordeal was to have words violently forced out of him, Charles Gould's is to have spoken and written language forced upon him. His childhood was dominated by the '"plaintive and enraged letters"' (p. 58) of his father, who was driven close to madness by the seemingly hopeless task of resurrecting San Tomé as a profit-making enterprise. The energies of Gould *père* are displaced, as it were, into letter-writing: full of references to 'the Old Man of the sea, vampires and ghouls', and with the 'flavour of a gruesome Arabian Nights tale' (p. 58), his lengthy and numerous letters to Charles – '"Ten, twelve pages every month of my life for ten years"' (p. 73) – are a kind of epistolary version of the Azuera legend. These embittered texts shape Charles in much the same way that the philosophical writings and conversation of Heyst *père* mould the sensibilities of the young Axel Heyst in *Victory*. However, unlike Heyst, who submits to the authority of his father's writings, Gould's mature professional life begins as a wilful and systematic misreading of patriarchal language. He chooses to read his father's letters as symptoms of the cruel and perverse imbalance between language and action that dominates Costaguana, a place where human potential is extravagantly and tragically squandered in futile words – the hundreds of pages of despairing paternal correspondence, the Gould Concession and the 'worthless receipts' (p. 58) associated with it, and the fatuous political speechifying that reverberates throughout the country.

Gould's defiance of his father's words is a central part of his wider attempt to break the grip of empty language on Costaguana. '"The air of the New World seems favourable to the art of declamation"' (p. 83), he says, as though deeply reluctant to breathe an atmosphere polluted by such language. Like the Russian-born but doggedly Anglo-Saxon narrator of *Under Western Eyes*, Gould regards the language of his birthplace as an alien tongue. In a nation dominated by inflammatory public rhetoric, Gould's is a *sotto voce* revolution, asserting itself in 'rumour of work and safety' that 'spread over the pastoral Campo' (p. 101), and 'faint whispers hinting at the immense occult influence of the Gould Concession' (p. 117). Gould himself is a powerfully reticent figure, one whose habitual silence is a matter of deliberately withheld speech. Few characters in Conrad exhibit anything like the formidable resistance to language displayed by the 'almost voiceless' (p. 59) Gould; but the qualities that make him an indomitable administrator seem to leave him incapable of making intelligent discriminations between kinds and levels of public and private language. With inexhaustible disdain for 'clap-trap eloquence' (p. 83), 'balderdash' (p. 92) and 'empty loquacity' (p. 368), Gould brushes aside Señor Hirsch's business propositions, refuses to join a delegation to negotiate with Pedro Montero, and refuses to read Decoud's Separationist proclamation – different forms of language are lumped together by *El Rey de Sulaco* as just so much Costaguana verbiage. But if Gould succeeds in putting himself beyond the grasp of language, he does so at the cost of sacrificing that part of our human subjectivity which is fundamentally verbal. Gould's final linguistic act in the novel, a telephone message informing Emily that he plans to sleep at the mountain (p. 519), is both confirmation of the death of their marriage, and a valediction to the realm of living speech.

Unsurprisingly, perhaps, the most astute critic of Gould's '"dumb reserve"' (239) is Sulaco's man of letters, Martin Decoud. Gould and Decoud are revealingly juxtaposed in chapters 5 and 6 of Part II, a brilliantly orchestrated sequence of dialogic encounters in the great sala of the Casa Gould, dominated by the contrast between Decoud's impassioned talk with two women – his scandalous tête-à-tête with Antonia Avellanos and his conspiratorial rendezvous with Mrs Gould – and the intimidating silence maintained by Gould as he is besieged by European businessmen. If Gould's career might be seen as a progressive retreat from language into silence, then Decoud's is inspired by the land of declamation to produce an extraordinary torrent of words. Decoud brings to Costaguana a love of droll repartee and a set of unrealized poetic ambitions; but he soon develops into a remarkably prolific and versatile political writer, reporting on Costaguanan affairs for *Semenario* and the *Parisian Review*, dashing

off polemical articles for the Ribierist *Porvenir*, drafting the Separationist
proclamation, and composing a dramatic journal-letter to his favourite
sister during the Monterist insurrection. It is as though Decoud is incapable of not writing; his flurry of literary activity seems to be nothing
less than a single-handed attempt to script Costaguana's emergence into
modernity as an independent republic. His writings on, and scriptings
of, Costaguanan history invite comparison with the efforts of Captain
Mitchell, the region's oral historian. Decoud is in many ways flattered
by this comparison. The vivid fragments of eye-witness reportage in his
journal-letter (pp. 223–49) are sharpened by an intelligent scepticism
that Mitchell so obviously lacks. When Decoud recounts the breakdown
of order in the town, Ribiera's narrow escape from the mob, the shifting
political allegiances of former Ribierists, the urgent news from Esmer-
alda and the railhead, and the frantic preparations for the rescue of
the silver, he does so from a position of radical uncertainty rather than
complacent retrospect. Also, whereas Mitchell is happy with a child-like
language of heroism and villainy, Decoud is refreshingly nuanced in his
appraisal of the leading personalities in the revolution.

On the face of it, this comparison between Mitchell and Decoud can
only lend support to the notion that in *Nostromo* the man of letters un-
problematically supersedes the storyteller. Yet Decoud's fate in the novel
is scarcely auspicious, and even less so when we set it alongside that of the
other prominent writer in the novel, Don José Avellanos. Decoud is very
much a creature of language – he lives by words and through words,
and seems to harbour an obscure fear of the silence that lies beyond
them. As a consequence of his curious addiction to speech and writing,
he compromises for, and is compromised by, language in ways that un-
settle his authority over it. For example, Decoud has to set aside both
his poetic ambitions and his ironic scepticism when he becomes chief
Ribierist slogan-maker, a role than requires him to deal in a language
scarcely more sophisticated than that of the Goulds' parrot. Except that
the parrot's squawks of '*Viva Costaguana!*' are entirely innocuous when
set alongside '*gran' bestia*', the offensive epithet coined by Decoud for
Montero and reiterated '"every second day"' (p. 177) in the *Porvenir*.
When the narrator describes Decoud as 'the voice of the party, or, rather,
its mouthpiece' (p. 200), he slides in a casual reformulation between two
radically opposed notions: Decoud as an originating voice is replaced by
Decoud as a medium for other people's words. As the Ribierists' 'mouthpiece', Decoud assumes a certain personal responsibility for the party's
political language; moreover, he incurs the risk that whatever language

he does broadcast on the party's behalf may be taken down and used in potentially lethal evidence against him – indeed, in the later stages of the novel, he lives in the shadow of an unrevoked death sentence issued by Montero.

Even more disconcerting for Decoud than the possibility that he will become a scapegoat for other people's words is the threat of silence that haunts the quieter moments of his career. We tend to remember his journal-letter as motivated by the dangerous, exhilarating spectacle of insurrection; but it is the *aftermath* of the civil disorder, when an eerie silence descends on the town, that prompts Decoud to write. '"The silence around me is ominous"' (p. 231), he confides at the start of this letter, in which he will dwell on soundlessness and wordlessness with an obscure trepidation. Decoud's lonely vigil in the Casa Viola might be seen as a strange premonition of his experience on the Great Isabel; and the narrator's equation of the end of writing with the end of life offers a precise foreshadowing of the journalist's suicide: 'With the writing of the last line then came upon Decoud a moment of sudden and complete oblivion. He swayed over the table as if struck by a bullet' (p. 249). Involvement in writing, in language, for all its risky compromises, would appear to be indispensable for Decoud, whereas the 'absolute silence' of the Great Isabel – 'the first he had known in his life' (p. 496) – is fatal. To say that Decoud is killed by silence would be an exaggeration; but it seems that he cannot survive without the energizing 'noise' of public language.

Like Decoud, Don José Avellanos is a cultivated 'European' man of letters whose fate in the novel calls into question the ascendancy of writing. Don José is putting the finishing touches to a history of Costaguana's recent past, and has plans for a sequel, 'another historical work, wherein all the devotions to the regeneration of the country he loved would be enshrined for the reverent worship of posterity' (p. 142). Magnanimous in its appraisal of the nation's troubled past, and cautiously optimistic in its vision of the future, Don José's historical opus is a victim of the bruising realities of the moment in which it is written. *Fifty Years of Misrule* is subjected to the very political violence that it hoped to consign to history: after the *Porvenir* offices are stormed by a mob, the mangled and scattered manuscript is seen by its author 'littering the Plaza, floating in the gutters, fired out as wads for trabucos loaded with handfuls of type, blown in the wind, trampled in the mud' (p. 235). Martin Decoud rightly senses that the mutilation of Don José's book prefigures the death of its author: '"he looked so frail, so weak, so worn out. Whatever happens, he will not survive"' (p. 235). Don José's physical vulnerability mirrors and confirms the frailty of the text's body, the fragility of fine writing in this uproariously violent political arena.

The deaths of Sulaco's men of letters cast a pall of tragic disenchantment over the life of writing: Decoud takes his own life when he feels he has lost his audience; Avellanos is all but extinguished by the spectacle of a mob tearing up his life's work in a savage act of non-reading. This novel, which one might initially suppose to be Conrad's valediction to storytelling, becomes on closer reading a meditation on the death of the author and the unexpected persistence of raconteurship. *Nostromo* is framed by the language of storytelling: it opens with an indigenous folk-tale that defines Sulaco as a region of hidden and cursed gold, and closes with the words of the foreign correspondent of *The Times*, who dubs Sulaco 'The Treasure House of the World' – an expression taken up by Mitchell as the banal refrain of his anecdotal history of the region (pp. 480, 483, 489). If Mitchell is an exemplary figure, it is not, of course, because of the quality of his narratives; rather, his sheer indefatigable commitment to telling stories points to the uncanny survival of storytelling in this daunting work of modernist textuality. Storytelling and oral culture have been displaced to the margins of the text, but they continue to exert complex pressures on the novel's central cast of would-be history-makers, and outlive those who envision a breakthrough into a fully textualized modernity. We should not read *Nostromo* as a novel that hovers indecisively between story and history, but one that traces an endlessly intricate dialogue between the traditional wisdom of oral culture and the impersonalities of modernist *écriture*.

CHAPTER EIGHT

Linguistic dystopia: The Secret Agent

According to Geoffrey Galt Harpham, *The Secret Agent* is 'the first, and really the only, *written* text in Conrad's entire *oeuvre*'.[1] One might object that *all* Conrad's tales are, willy-nilly, 'written'; but, prior to *The Secret Agent*, Conrad's fiction is dominated by the 'writing of the voice'. Even *Nostromo*, with its string of references to the folk legends of Azuera and its lengthy quotations from Captain Mitchell's anecdotes, betrays a lingering formal affiliation to oral tradition. Uniquely, however, *The Secret Agent* has no recourse to the utopian myths of transparent communal discourse that sustained the earlier fictions. The tone of impersonal irony that prevails in *The Secret Agent* is a far cry from the cosy atmosphere of 'Youth' or *Lord Jim*, where the reader automatically qualifies as an honorary listener, invited to pull up a chair with Marlow's friends and enjoy a good after-dinner yarn. The utopian dimension in Conrad's fiction previously extended into his conception of the relationship between text and reader, a relationship to which Conrad hoped to restore some of the direct intimacy of that between storyteller and listener. As Conrad's fiction became more sophisticated, however, it became less hospitable. Growing in creative power and ambition, he felt less need of the enabling fiction of a storytelling situation; the novels he composed at the height of his powers – *Nostromo*, *The Secret Agent*, *Under Western Eyes* – make the fewest concessions to the general reader. In *The Secret Agent* Conrad marks the occasion of his first major narrative set in his adoptive homeland by effectively tearing up his old contract with his English readership; readers who expected a sympathetic raconteur and exotic locales are confronted by a cold-blooded ironist narrating a low-key 'domestic drama'.

Equally surprising is Conrad's decision to observe unity of place. Elsewhere his fiction tends to shuttle between two locales (the Thames estuary and the Congo, Geneva and St Petersburg, *Patna* and Patusan), but the action in *The Secret Agent* is confined exclusively to London: the novel denies itself the luxury of an external vantage-point from which the city might be contextualized. The result is an atmosphere of claustrophobia that Winnie Verloc's abortive cross-channel excursion only confirms. Land-locked and text-bound, *The Secret Agent* seems to discount in advance the possibility of discursive or geographical alternatives to the city. The novel locates itself in an environment of such abject banality that one suspects Conrad shares the destructive fantasies of its more unbalanced inhabitants. No less abject than the city's polluted streets and repellently obese citizens is the discourse that flourishes, or rather festers, in it: tawdry pornographic fiction, lurid anarchist propaganda, spurious revolutionary pamphlets, and banal mass-circulation newspapers – this city is, for Conrad, a veritable graveyard of authentic language.

It might however be argued that the change of scene is merely superficial, that *The Secret Agent* reproduces the same pattern of exclusive, men-only verbal interaction that we encounter in the sea fiction and Marlovian narratives. Andrew Michael Roberts, in an essay on what he calls the 'gendered epistemology'[2] of Conrad's fiction, certainly sees the novel in these terms. Following the example of Nina Pelikan Straus, who reads 'Heart of Darkness' as an expression of Conrad's 'dream of a homocentric universe',[3] Roberts discerns in Conrad a relatively stable pattern whereby knowledge is circulated between men, including male narrators, listeners and implied male readers, but withheld from women who, like Kurtz's Intended, are idealized for their very ignorance. Frequently in Conrad a chance encounter between a pair of men leads them to strike up an intimate rapport, a delicate mutual understanding that shades into the homoerotic. The *locus classicus* is, of course, 'The Secret Sharer'; but the same goes for the relationships between Marlow and Kurtz, or Jim and Marlow. Profoundly homosocial in its celebration of such relationships, Conrad's fiction seems to corroborate the tendency of its characters to idealize Woman but exclude real women. As Roberts points out, some of the moments of most profound existential crisis in Conrad occur when a woman acquires, or threatens to acquire knowledge, thus breaking the charmed circle of male cognoscenti.

The Secret Agent is clearly vulnerable to the allegation that it presents male dialogue as its linguistic norm. Its *dramatis personae* comprises the familiar Conradian ensemble of male speakers: civil servants, policemen, detectives, politicians, and spies have replaced the sailors, entrepreneurs, and company agents of the exotic fiction, but the pattern remains the same. Like *Lord Jim*, *The Secret Agent* presents conversation after conversation between men about matters from which women are excluded. For John Hagan Jr, the novel is constructed around a series of seventeen 'interviews',[4] a term which aptly suggests that whilst oral culture hasn't disappeared without trace, what remains of it is sorely lacking in spontaneity, warmth, or candour. One such 'interview', an encounter between the Assistant Commissioner and Toodles (Sir Ethelred's unpaid secretary), yields some keen insights into what I shall call the 'erotics of information' in Conrad – the minor thrills and gratifications obtained by men from the possession and manipulation of secrets.

Toodles, who affects an air of laconic *gravitas* but is clearly an incorrigible gossip, refers with bated breath to the difficult passage of the fisheries bill, and its intolerable burden on Sir Ethelred. Delivered with smug condescension, these morsels of humdrum parliamentary gossip are obviously meant to establish Toodles's proximity to the very nerve-centre of government. The Assistant Commissioner cannot resist trumping the 'apprentice statesman' with a few veiled references to his own investigation. Shrewdly gauging that nothing is more intimidating than a display of offhand omniscience, the Assistant Commissioner drops a couple of hints – just enough to convince an awe-struck Toodles that he has plenty more in reserve:

'What I am after is . . . like a dogfish. You don't know perhaps what a dog-fish is like.'

'Yes; I do. We're buried in special books up to our necks – whole shelves full of them – with plates . . . It's a noxious, rascally-looking, altogether detestable beast, with a sort of smooth face and moustaches.'

'Described to a T,' commended the Assistant Commissioner. 'Only mine is clean-shaven altogether. You've seen him. It's a witty fish.'

'I have seen him!' said Toodles, incredulously. 'I can't conceive where I could have seen him.'

'At the Explorers, I should say,' dropped the Assistant Commissioner, calmly. At the name of that extremely exclusive club Toodles looked scared, and stopped short.

'Nonsense,' he protested, but in an awestruck tone. 'What do you mean? A member?'

'Honorary,' muttered the Assistant Commissioner through his teeth.

'Heavens!'

Toodles looked so thunderstruck that the Assistant Commissioner smiled faintly.

'That's between ourselves strictly,' he said. (p. 216)

In this informational stand-off between the civil servant and the senior policeman, espionage culture is depicted, with obvious satiric intent, as a *Boy's Own* world of furtive secret-sharing where information is a supposedly glamorous accessory of male power. There is a crucial parallel in

The Secret Agent between the circulation of secrets – all those furtive whispers and off-the-record hints – and another secretive, men-only economy: namely, the traffic in pornography between Verloc, his suppliers, and his clientele.

Off-the-record confidences figure prominently in the Author's Note to *The Secret Agent*, where the novel is said to germinate from an unnamed friend's tip-off in the course of a discussion about the Greenwich explosion of 1894: '"Oh, that fellow was half an idiot. His sister committed suicide afterwards."' Conrad wonders how his friend came by this information:

> It never occurred to me later to ask how he arrived at his knowledge. I am sure that if he had seen once in his life the back of an anarchist that must have been the whole extent of his connection with the underworld. He was, however, a man who liked to talk with all sorts of people, and he may have gathered those illuminating facts at second or third hand, from a crossing-sweeper, from a retired police officer, from some vague man in his club, or even, perhaps, from a Minister of State met at some public or private reception. (p. x)

Conrad's imagination frequently strays from the sphere of official history and public record into this vague hinterland of rumour, hearsay, and apocrypha, and he is a canny enough storyteller to sense that the credence we extend to such historically dubious narratives owes less to their factual content than to the frisson of obtaining an 'inside story' whose tantalizing content is yet to be devalued by widespread dissemination. It is as though these glimpses of the inside story of Greenwich – the lurid personal details of madness and suicide behind the dry official accounts – serve to implicate the reader in the same process of secret-sharing and prurient curiosity that the novel itself implicitly associates with pornography. This Author's Note, ostensibly the official version of the novel's genesis, is less a responsible preamble than a subversive postscript to *The Secret Agent*; it does little to allay the suspicions of those readers who believe that Conrad's novel belongs with the soiled volumes in Mr Verloc's shop-window. Perhaps the one felicitous observation in *Country Life*'s remarkably obtuse review of *The Secret Agent* is that the novel is 'indecent'.[5] Conrad, like his shady protagonist, is smuggling subversive material into that stronghold of propriety, the decent, moderate sensibilities of his English readership.

Indecency is the stock-in-trade of Verloc, the shady proprietor of a shop whose merchandise, which we are invited to inspect on the novel's opening page, is a cross-section of the least edifying manifestations of modern print culture:

> The window contained photographs of more or less undressed dancing girls; nondescript packages in wrappers like patent medicines; closed yellow paper envelopes, very flimsy, and marked two-and-six in heavy black figures; a few numbers of ancient French comic publications hung across a string as if to dry; a dingy blue china bowl, a casket of black wood, bottles of marking ink, and rubber stamps; a few books, with titles hinting at impropriety; a few apparently old copies of obscure newspapers, badly printed, with titles like *The Torch*, *The Gong* – rousing titles.

Like Verloc's shop-window, Conrad's novel showcases a collection of degraded discourses – newspapers, pornography, propaganda – which is separated from the narrator (and the reader) by a seemingly impregnable *cordon sanitaire* of irony. The genre of spy thriller is also being ironized here. When it was published in America, the novel was marketed as 'A Tale of Diplomatic Intrigue and Anarchist Treachery'[6] – a manifestly inadequate blurb, but a useful one all the same for creating a false horizon of expectation to disorient the unsuspecting reader. In any case the narrator's deadpan irony soon dampens such generic expectations as the reader may harbour about the potentially 'thrilling' content of the text. The novel's first paragraphs are a decidedly inauspicious opening for a thriller with such a promising title. Nothing could be less 'rousing' than these shabby journals, nothing less glamorous or thrilling than the contents of this seedy emporium; and the novel's protagonist, an overweight shop-keeper with a wife and in-laws to support, is scarcely the stuff of which conventional espionage heroes are made.

Implicitly, anarchist literature is presented as a kind of intellectual pornography that permits extremists to indulge their wild fantasies of destroying capitalism and smashing the state. However, as Brian W. Schaffer suggests, *The Secret Agent*'s ultimate satiric target is the moral panic of puritans who would regard pornography and propaganda as twin symptoms of an imminent plunge into moral and political anarchy.[7] True, Conrad obviously does not believe Verloc's den of vice is likely to corrupt the nation's moral fibre, and neither does he harbour any real anxiety over the political stability of his adoptive homeland. After all, with the honourable exception of the Professor, the subversives who convene in the backroom of Verloc's shop are a risibly innocuous bunch: Yundt, Ossipon, Michaelis – if this coterie of workshy parasites is a representative sample of London's political underworld then nothing could be less likely than the prospect of anarchist revolution in Britain.

Conrad is unconcerned with knee-jerk puritanical objections to pornography, and indeed seems positively to relish the notion of becoming a kind of high-brow Verloc; however, he seems genuinely disturbed by the possible *textual* kinship between his novel and the disreputable publications mongered by its hero. Pornography offers vicarious erotic excitement; revolutionary propaganda likewise substitutes incendiary rhetoric for real political action; the problem, however, is that the novel-form is itself a textual construct incapable of transcending its own writtenness. What is a novelist, after all, if not a purveyor of pseudo-realities for the pleasure of a passive readership? And it is that very readership, with its appetite for counterfeit experience, which bears the brunt of the novel's frustration and self-disgust. It seems no coincidence, for example, that the reader is initially positioned as a potential customer, or at the very least a casual window-shopper, guiltily intrigued by a window-display whose combination of salacious texts and innocuous bric-a-brac prefigures the novel's own dramatic juxtaposition of banal domesticity with the lurid excesses of terrorism. It is difficult, moreover, to read of the flustered adolescent who purchases Verloc's overpriced marking-ink when he really wanted pornography without suspecting that this is a sly allegory of the fate of the reader who enters the world of *The Secret Agent* hoping for some cheap thrills.

Two excellent recent essays by Paul Armstrong and Jacques Berthoud have focused on the challenge *The Secret Agent* poses for the reader – though their emphasis is on the liberal intellectual reader; indeed, Berthoud goes so far as to claim that the novel's 'true subject is the mind-set . . . that the *lecteur moyen intellectuel* brings to it'.[8] For me, however, the text is more double-edged than Armstrong or Berthoud allow; certainly it has its pitfalls for the intellectual, but it does not let the general reader off lightly. Indeed, one could be forgiven for thinking that Conrad, especially in his political fiction, has it in for the man in the street. 'I imagine with pain the man in the street trying to read it', Conrad remarked of *The Spoils of Poynton*. 'One could almost see the globular lobes of his brain painfully revolving and crushing mangling [*sic*] the delicate thing.'[9] Unlike Henry James's novel, *The Secret Agent* has prepared itself for the hamfisted advances of the average reader: its chief defensive weapon is its irony – an aggressive irony that has replaced sympathy as the basis of the contract between Conrad and his audience.

Conrad's irony is far more problematic for his readers than is commonly supposed. Such is the virtuosity of Conrad's ironic narrative that *The Secret Agent* is regarded in some quarters as the author's most consummately unproblematic creation; indeed, it is for this very reason that in Daphna Erdinast-Vulcan's study the novel is consigned to a single footnote.[10] A brief reconsideration of Conrad's 'ironic method' will be necessary for a proper appreciation of the novel's complexity. We might usefully distinguish, first of all, between what I will call 'epistemological' and 'textual' irony. Epistemological irony refers to the narrator's discreet omniscience, whereby the world of the novel is knowable in terms of the errors and inconsistencies of its characters. Irony of this sort involves the subtle perception of discrepancies between appearance and reality, or the witty revelation of contradictions between public conduct and private motive. The ironies multiply at every level of the narrative: the police are hand-in-glove with the anarchists, foreign embassies sponsor political violence in the name of legality, and revolutionists are fêted in high society. The narrator is particularly adroit at teasing out the self-interest that motivates his characters: Verloc is a double agent and police informer because it suits his indolent disposition; the Professor's grudge against humanity is traced back to quarrels with the authorities in his days as a laboratory technician; the Assistant Commissioner tries to exonerate Michaelis because the obese Marxist has been adopted by his wife's social circle.

Textual irony, meanwhile, broadly designates the novel's formal and linguistic strategies, the most notable of which is its transformation of popular genres. *The Secret Agent* borrows liberally from detective fiction, spy thrillers and the language of the popular press, subjecting their crass one-dimensionality to sophisticated critique even as it recoils in disgust from such intimate contact with mass culture. Above all, irony guarantees *distance*, be it intellectual or linguistic, from the object of critique; it ensures that the writer will not be compromised by his proximity to London. Conrad's irony is taken by many readers as the hallmark of a writer confidently disengaged from the object of his critique. Erdinast-Vulcan refers to the narrator's 'barrier of acerbic irony'; Daniel R. Schwarz claims that the linguistic virtuosity of Conrad's novel constitutes an 'alternative to the language of London'; Muriel Bradbrook describes the novel's subject-matter as a 'sordid welter' presented for inspection under the 'glass bell' of the narrator's discourse.[11] For these critics, Conrad's irony enables him to keep this morass of degraded language at arm's length in much the same way that, say, Alexander Pope's scintillating verse is offered as

the antidote to the very 'Dulness' against which it rails. But the assumption that *The Secret Agent* has an immaculately disengaged ironic narrator
tells only half the story, because the novel's ironic strategies embroil it
in the very environment it abhors. Ideally, textual and epistemological
irony ought to work in tandem, since the ironic imitation of other discourses serves to challenge the ideologies that they habitually, and uncrit-
ically, reinforce. In practice, however, there are complex entanglements
in Conrad's text between language and epistemology that preclude a simple disengagement from the object of critique and generate frustration
and disgust that are, ultimately, vented on Conrad's English readership.

Ironic discourse presupposes an audience with the intelligence to dis-
cern subtle differences between literal and implied meanings; and the
reader of *The Secret Agent* is clearly credited with such intelligence. But
the ironist must admit at least the theoretical possibility of a reader on
whom such nuances of meaning would be lost, a reader so deficient in
hermeneutic sophistication that he takes every word at its most obvious literal sense. Of course, *The Secret Agent* dramatizes such a reader
in the person of Stevie, Verloc's retarded brother-in-law. The credulity
that Conrad imputes to the reading public is dramatized through Stevie,
himself an avid and credulous consumer of the newspapers in Verloc's
window. Stevie is incensed by the stories of cruelty and exploitation he
reads in the anarchist papers, just as he responds with inarticulate passion to the vicious polemic of Karl Yundt. Feeble-minded, credulous,
and barely literate, Stevie receives language with a visceral force that
those characters inured to Yundt's rhetorical excesses would find hard to
imagine. It seems to me that Stevie is the most obvious manifestation of
the novel's decidedly unflattering estimation of the general reading public: in his gullible excitability and his woeful lack of verbal or political
sophistication, he stands as Conrad's cruel caricature of 'public opinion'.

The mass-circulation newspaper is for Conrad the symptom *par
excellence* of modern linguistic degeneration; and its readership, that ill-
defined entity known as 'the public', is a pale shadow of the vibrant
linguistic communities to be found elsewhere in his fiction. There could
scarcely be a more graphic counterpoint to the powerful longevity of oral
tradition than the newspapers that litter the landscape of *The Secret Agent*.
When Ossipon and the Professor leave the Silenus club, the narrator's
eye is caught by the newspaper vendors:

In front of the great doorway a dismal row of newspaper sellers standing clear
of the pavement dealt out their wares from the gutter. It was a raw, gloomy day
of the early spring; and the grimy sky, the mud of the streets, the rags of the dirty

men harmonized excellently with the eruption of the damp, rubbishy sheets of paper soiled with printers' ink. The posters, maculated with filth, garnished like tapestry the sweep of the curbstone. The trade in afternoon papers was brisk, yet, in comparison with the swift, constant march of foot traffic, the effect was of indifference, of a disregarded distribution. (p. 79)

Journalism is viewed as a form of linguistic effluent welling up from the gutters: depthless, mass-produced ephemera that will not outlive the day of its publication and indeed resembles rubbish even before it has been purchased. It is as though Conrad is offering sardonic confirmation of Walter Bagehot's famous observation in his essay on Dickens that 'London is like a newspaper.'[12] Trashy, grimy, and repellent, the newssheets are of a piece with the abject metropolis whose quotidian affairs they record. One suspects however that the disgust lavished on newsprint by *The Secret Agent* is a form of deflected self-loathing: the novel heaps odium on a narrative mode that it all too clearly resembles.[13] The novel has closer generic affinities with the mass-circulation newspaper than with the kind of oral narrative that Conrad's fiction so frequently masquerades as. Like the newspaper, the novel is implicated in the break-up of traditional speech communities; both newspaper and novel address themselves to that collective anonymity known as the 'public' – an invisible, homogeneous mass of nameless city-dwellers. *The Secret Agent* is haunted by the notion of the public as an anonymous, undifferentiated mass of strangers, figured either as 'public opinion' or the urban crowd. The public is conceived either as capriciously volatile – in thrall to the whims of newspaper editors – or in the grip of a bovine inertia that even the most bloodthirsty outrages will fail to stir. The former view is roughly that of the Assistant Commissioner; the latter, that of the Professor, who nurses a private terror of the faceless multitude who threaten to ignore his megalomaniacal career out of existence. It is possible to see these wildly divergent conceptions of the 'public' as expressions of Conrad's contradictory attitudes to his own readership. On the one hand he wants to please his invisible audience; on the other, he violently resents the constraints placed on his artistic autonomy by the requirements of a mass market. The notion of a 'disregarded distribution' would have been only too familiar to Conrad, whose sales, prior to the success of *Chance*, were a constant disappointment. Exerting a profound influence on politicians, anarchists, and policeman, as well as on the novelist himself, the 'public' may be seen as the text's absent protagonist.

The link between novel and newspaper is reinforced by *The Secret Agent*'s stylistic affinities with journalism. Just as its landscape is littered with newspapers, so its text is laced with mock-journalistic prose and brief citations from press reports. The following description of Ossipon is conspicuously indebted to journalistic phraseology:

Comrade Alexander Ossipon – nicknamed the Doctor, ex-medical student without a degree; afterwards wandering lecturer to working-men's associations upon the socialistic aspects of hygiene; author of a popular quasi-medical study (in the form of a cheap pamphlet seized promptly by the police) entitled 'The Corroding Vices of the Middle Classes'; special delegate of the more or less mysterious Red Committee, together with Karl Yundt and Michaelis for the work of literary propaganda. (p. 46)

There is a certain deadpan exorbitance to Conrad's appropriation of journalistic phraseology; and this parenthetical pen-portrait is certainly quite a mouthful. Comically prolonged beyond anything we might encounter in a real newspaper, Ossipon's curriculum vitae deliberately clogs the narrative flow, whilst elsewhere in the novel Conrad's insistent repetition of journalistic epithets (Ossipon is the 'doctor', Michaelis the 'ticket-of-leave apostle', Yundt the 'terrorist') apes the inelegant variations of newspaper prose. There is no question, then, that the text shares with many of its characters a contempt for newspapers – a contempt for their shoddy appearance ('"prophetic bosh in blunt type on this filthy paper"' (p. 26)) and their banal content ('written by fools for the reading of imbeciles' (p. 211)). Whereas Vladimir fantasizes about a terrorist strike on pure mathematics, one senses that, given the opportunity, Conrad would throw a bomb into the language of the popular press. David Trotter argues persuasively that the text's mood of disgust is ultimately *textual*: the novel is obliged to inhabit, however provisionally, a journalistic idiom it finds insufferable.[14] Nowhere is this more dramatically apparent than in the fates of Winnie and Ossipon. After murdering Verloc, Winnie's guilt takes the form of a panic-stricken obsession with the standard newspaper description of hangings: 'The drop given was fourteen feet' (p. 268), and in the closing pages of the novel a single sentence from a newspaper (*'An impenetrable mystery seems destined to hang for ever over this act of madness or despair'* (p. 307)) is repeated in whole or part some twenty times. Like a scratched gramophone record, the text seems infuriatingly stuck on a single snatch of language. Although the repetition of this facile postscript to the report of Winnie's suicide seems intended as a symptom of Ossipon's creeping insanity, in the end, Ossipon's breakdown is something of a red herring: it is the *novel* that is obsessed with the phrase, and with journalism in general, to the point of hysteria.

Not only does journalistic language infect Conrad's prose, and mould the most intimate fears of his charaters into its own lexicon of cliché, but it is also implicated in the Greenwich explosion, an event that is stage-managed for an audience of newspaper readers. Engineered by a foreign embassy to discredit the circle of expatriate anarchists in London, the attack on the observatory depends for its impact on widespread press coverage to shift the weight of public opinion behind draconian measures against the anarchists. As the discursive precondition of the Greenwich explosion, popular newspapers manufacture the very urban experience of which they seemed mere grubby by-products. A theatrical pseudo-event, the Greenwich explosion might have been conceived as an illustration of Jean Baudrillard's theories of the 'Simulacral': 'The media are always on the scene in advance of terrorist violence . . . We all collude in the anticipation of a fatal outcome, even if we are emotionally affected or shaken when it occurs.'[15] The detonation of the bomb is merely a pre-echo of the mass publicity in the aftermath of the event; and the inevitable frantic search for the perpetrators belies the sense that, for Baudrillard, the ultimate origin of terrorism is always in the public's own susceptibility to terror.

Mr Vladimir's appraisal of the relation between terrorism and the media displays an impressive grasp of the theatricality of terrorism:

'An attempt upon a crowned head or on a president is sensational enough in a way, but not so much as it used to be. It has entered into the general conception of the existence of all chiefs of state. *It's almost conventional* . . . A murderous attempt on a restaurant or a theatre would suffer in the same way from the suggestion of non-political passion; the exasperation of a hungry man, an act of social revenge. All this is used up; it is no longer instructive as an object lesson in revolutionary anarchism. Every newspaper has ready-made phrases to explain such manifestations away.' (pp. 31–2; my italics)

Spare a thought for the terrorist, Vladimir pleads: his every homicidal exploit is pre-empted by the popular press, which has a stockpile of 'ready-made' phrases at its disposal to make instant sense of the most senseless action. What ought to be terrifying through its sheer arbitrariness is explained in terms of whatever grievances are imputed to the suspects. Vladimir is troubled by the *belatedness* of terrorism, the sense that its claims to a scandalous originality are sabotaged in advance by a discourse that ascribes every act of wanton violence to a motivating political intelligence which the public can promptly recognize – and forget. Vladimir views the prospect of reality being thus subsumed by language as a victory for the despised forces of liberalism, which exercise a moderating editorial control over the fanatics for whom they provide such a comfortable haven. Accordingly, Vladimir hopes to disrupt the prevailing climate of tolerance towards anarchism by exposing the limitations of the discourse that makes such a liberal consensus possible. At times, Vladimir seems oddly to concur with the Professor, whose campaign for real terrorism is conducted in the teeth of public indifference. Needless to say his revolt against the tyranny of political and linguistic convention is a resounding failure: in the aftermath of the explosion we hear nothing but a deafening silence from the public. A public as excitable as Stevie would be the terrorist's ideal audience; to the dismay of the Professor, however, it is Stevie's impassive sister whom they more closely resemble. It would appear that the reports of the Greenwich explosion, described by Ossipon as '"mere newspaper gup"' (p. 71) have explained the manifestation away with their customary efficiency. '[T]his Verloc affair. Who thought of it now?' (p. 306): just ten days after the explosion, the outrage has been silently forgotten.

It is left to the Assistant Commissioner, Conrad's detective-hero, to rise above the collective inertia of this paralysed city. Conrad found detective fiction a highly amenable genre. Some of his earlier fiction bears a marked resemblance to this mode – Marlow is something of an amateur sleuth – but, on the whole, intellectual curiosity is not the strong suit of Conrad's characters. The novelist, like the detective, makes it his business to expose baffling phenomena to systematic scrutiny, to uncover the truths, however unsavoury, behind the lies and evasions beneath which most of us naively and complacently shelter. The 'ostrich-factor'[16] is Cedric Watts's facetious shorthand for our perverse capacity *not* to perceive the mysteries or horrors around us, a capacity that Winnie Verloc has made the cornerstone of her life. That life 'doesn't stand much looking into' is the very motto of her existence. The Verlocs' reluctance to probe to 'the bottom of facts and motives' (p. 245) provides abundant confirmation of Conrad's impression that man is 'not an investigating animal' (p. viii), but the detective (and the narrator) are exceptions to that rule. Pitting English irony against continental extremism, the narrator and the Assistant Commissioner pursue their respective investigations with incisive rigour. The narrator exhibits a detective-like inquisitive persistence, penetrating a fog of duplicity to expose the compromising facts and self-serving motives by which Conrad's Londoners live and work.

'"Here I am stuck in a litter of paper"' (p. 115): the Assistant Commissioner's lament is expressed in terms that echo Conrad's own plight. Both the detective and his creator have undergone a deeply problematic transition from active, outdoors work to paper-work. The Assistant Commissioner's instincts as a hunter were honed during a spell in a tropical colony where he enjoyed a more openly combative role in the war against crime; now a desk-bound bureaucrat, he chafes at his administrative role in a way that is typical of his breed. The hero of detective fiction has traditionally appeared as lone virtuoso, flouting official procedure to brilliant effect; the roll-call of detective-heroes from Sherlock Holmes onwards is a litany of maverick individualists whose idiosyncratic methods provoke a mixture of indignation and grudging respect from their more pedestrian colleagues. On the face of it, the Assistant Commissioner belongs to this very tradition. Having obtained temporary exemption from the labyrinthine bureaucracy of Scotland Yard, Conrad's investigator has free rein to perform his bravura epistemological feats. Certainly he appears to score a famous victory against Vladimir; although, on reflection, his investigation seems almost suspiciously straightforward. Whereas in the Sherlock Holmes stories we marvel at the hero's knack of drawing uncannily accurate inferences from the scantiest evidence, in Conrad's novel the process of detection could scarcely have been simpler. Once the Assistant Commissioner has obtained the label of Stevie's coat the investigation becomes a mere formality, and he is able to report triumphantly back to Sir Ethelred on the same evening. But the ramifications of this particular murder mystery extend beyond even the Assistant Commissioner's scrutiny. Far from offering a comprehensive solution to the Greenwich mystery, the Assistant Commissioner's investigation precipitates the murder of Verloc, the suicide of Winnie, and the madness of Ossipon – a chain of horrific events that cannot but make the detective's suave résumé of his little adventure seem egregiously complacent.

Moreover, on one crucial point – the Greenwich explosion itself – the novel's system of surveillance is as defective as that of the police:

in the close-woven stuff of relations between conspirator and police there occur unexpected solutions of continuity, sudden holes in space and time. A given anarchist may be watched inch by inch and minute by minute, but a moment always comes when somehow all sight and touch of him are lost for a few hours, during which something (generally an explosion) more or less deplorable does happen. (p. 85)

Although the unruffled tone of this extract (with the allusion to Greenwich dropped into nonchalant parentheses) might suggest otherwise, the explosion seriously damages the epistemological confidence the novel has invested in its detective-story framework. The Greenwich

explosion is a botched pseudo-event elicited – and then almost ignored –
by the mass media. Its unrepresentable virtuality exceeds the limits of
Conrad's mimetic framework, resisting historical recuperation and seriously challenging the foundationalist epistemology of detective fiction.
As a creature of a cause-and-effect world, the detective is ill-equipped
to unravel terroristic Simulacra, to trace their destructive effects back
to a single culpable origin. Traditional detective narratives gratify our
desire to inhabit a legible universe: the reader is always confident that
mysterious crimes – local areas of obscurity in an otherwise transparent social medium – can be cleared up through the rigorous application
of scientific intelligence; but no detective, however brilliant, can get to
the bottom of an event that is effectively bottomless. Detective fiction –
still in the first flush of youth when Conrad published *The Secret Agent* –
is shown to be *already* anachronistic. Stevie's tragic pratfall en route to
the observatory is a self-consuming pseudo-event, an act of involuntary
self-destruction that dramatizes the novel's self-deconstruction.

Aaron Fogel, a notable dissenter from the view of *The Secret Agent* as a
great novel of London life, has observed the effect of 'corridorization'[17]
in it – an image connoting not only the corridors of power, Soho backstreets, and side alleys of Conrad's metropolis, but also the tunnel-vision
afflicting even its most perspicacious characters. A sense of community-
in-separation, of conspiratorial interconnectedness, clings to Conrad's
London. Indeed conspiracy is fast becoming the only viable model of
collective experience in his fiction. What Frederic Jameson has shown
to be true of the contemporary conspiracy movie – that it grants a kind
of fictive compensation for the profound disjunction between first-hand
experience and the invisible totality – is also true of the same genre in
its (literary) infancy in Conrad's fiction. In a world where it is increasingly difficult to imagine, still less experience, the totality of which we
are part, the conspiracy thriller enjoys a new lease of life as a form of
what Jameson calls 'cognitive mapping': a means of orienting ourselves
in a world where ostentatious power has been replaced by hidden bureaucratic control. For Jameson, the 'promise of a deeper inside view is
the hermeneutic content of the conspiracy thriller';[18] or, rather, the conspiracy narrative purveys for those on the outside the comforting myth
that someone, somewhere (behind closed doors, or in the espionage underworld) is still 'inside' the system.

The conspiracy movie offers its audience the opportunity to navigate
the clandestine landscape of politics, and the same is true of *The Secret
Agent*: from Scotland Yard and the corridors of power to the salons of elite

London society, from Belgravia boarding houses to the backstreets and shady continental hotels of Soho, the novel's dramatic itinerary traces a network of power and political intelligence with ramifications of ungraspable complexity that extend into the most unlikely corners of the city. An invisible network of faceless individuals is glimpsed, and, as Jameson puts it, 'two incommensurable levels of being impossibly intersect and . . . the individual subject of the protagonist somehow manages to blunder into the collective web of the hidden social order'.[19] The individual subject in Conrad's novel is not the canny urban investigator but the hapless ingenu Stevie – an innocent at large in a conspiratorial community who becomes the sacrificial pawn in a game played to a stalemate by invisible bureaucratic powers.

In Conrad's London every unilateral initiative either backfires grotesquely or is subsumed into an eventless paralysis reminiscent of Joyce's Dublin. At least, that's the way it seems at a political level. In the aftermath of the Greenwich affair the political macrocosm, with its innocuous anarchists, efficient detectives, stolid constabulary, and reassuringly cumbersome legislative procedures, continues with business as usual; but the familial microcosm, the Verloc household, is torn apart by the very anarchic forces that leave no trace on the body politic. The Assistant Commissioner puts his finger on it when he refers to the Greenwhich incident and its consequences as essentially a '"domestic drama"' (p. 222): domestic, that is, in the sense of pertaining to a family household rather than a home nation. What the novel shows on a public level – that Britain is in no danger from extremists – is contradicted by its domestic drama, which presents an all too plausible accommodation between English propriety and continental extremism.

Lord Jim is not the only Conrad novel to mutate into its own antithesis; but whereas that tale's notorious volte-face – the dreams of imperial heroism which the first half debunks are spectacularly vindicated in the second – is plain for all to see, the 'turn' in *The Secret Agent*, from tale of international espionage to 'domestic drama', is altogether more subtle, and infinitely more subversive. Having established the banality of terrorism, the novel shifts its attention to the terror of the banal. As Jacques Berthoud has shown, what began as an urbane ironist's critique of squalid political and textual emanations from the continent has itself become a subversive, anarchistic assault on English normality.[20] Some critics have, quite properly, seen *The Secret Agent* as a kind of sequel to 'Heart of Darkness'.[21] But whereas in the earlier work the confrontation with 'The horror' is an experience of great existential drama, in

The Secret Agent the same confrontation is drained of any sense of risk, danger or philosophical exhilaration.

Violence, madness, and despair are ultimately seen to be attributes of Englishness, which lurk ominously below the placid surface of English culture but, in the closing chapters of *The Secret Agent*, irrupt with anarchic fury into the lives of the Verlocs. The novel subjects the whole lexicon of decency, propriety, and respectability to corrosive scrutiny. Chapter 11, which drew such extravagant praise from Leavis – he called it 'one of the most astonishing triumphs of genius in fiction'²² – contains the novel's most powerful deconstruction of propriety. Conrad's lacerating insights are reserved not for the Soho anarchists but for the reticence, propriety, and decency that have sustained the Verloc household through years of loveless, sterile co-existence. The Verlocs' pact of non-communication buys seven years' marital stability at the expense of the grisly demise of Stevie, Adolf, and Winnie. Laid bare in this chapter is the obscene discrepancy between the euphemistic language of decent normality with which the household is protectively swaddled, and the profound vacuity of their emotional relationships.

There is a grating dissonance between Verloc's matter-of-fact disavowal of responsibility for Stevie's death, and the ardent, inarticulate grief of Winnie. Verloc's breathtakingly crass expressions of sympathy ('"What you want is a good cry"'), and his view of Stevie's death as a minor hiccup (a '"nuisance"') compared to his own imminent prison sentence, are sharply counterpointed by the silent anguish of his wife. But, somehow, the 'reticent decencies of their home life' survive the death of Stevie and even the murder of Verloc:

Except for the fact that Mrs Verloc breathed these two would have been perfectly in accord: that accord of prudent reserve without superfluous words, and sparing of signs, which had been the foundation of their respectable home life. For it had been respectable, covering by a decent reticence the problems that may arise in the practice of a secret profession and the commerce of shady wares. To the last its decorum had remained undisturbed by unseemly shrieks and other misplaced sincerities of conduct. And after the striking of the blow, this respectability was continued in immobility and silence. (pp. 263–4)

Mr and Mrs Verloc cling to the artifice of propriety for as long as possible after Stevie's death has rendered it meaningless. Not that Conrad's revelation of their lies and evasions heralds a brave new world of plain speaking and bracing candour. Winnie has had no option but to *live* a euphemism: the essential goodness of Verloc is the indispensable fiction around which her life is constructed; grateful for the stability Verloc provides she has no choice but to suppress her curiosity – how else could she save her mother from the poor-house and her brother from the asylum?

Verloc's plea for sympathy ('"I stood the risk of having a knife stuck into me any time these seven years we've been married"', '"I have no mind to get a knock on the head or a stab in the back"' (pp. 238, 248)) becomes an involuntary prophecy of his own death; little does he suspect that Winnie will obligingly convert his melodramatic scenario into reality. Verloc's words betray him with a treachery worthy of the very assassins whom he fears – although it is, of course, the domestic carving knife, rather than the assassin's dagger, by which he dies. This scene of physical violence, in which a downtrodden housewife stabs the secret agent of a foreign power, recapitulates the novel's generic violence: the vengeance of banal 'domestic drama' on exotic melodrama. Not that the novel vindicates Englishness in the face of continental fanaticism; rather, the conventional attributes of English moderation and continental extremism have, by the end, been violently transposed. The novel, which begins by setting up clear demarcations between itself and the sleazy contents of Verloc's shop, subtly encroaches on that territory of squalid indecency. If the sordid excrescences of urban life catalogued on the novel's opening page seem to be decently concealed from the majority of Londoners by being confined to Verloc's sleazy backstreet store, they nevertheless ooze their way into the substance of Conrad's novel, contaminating its linguistic texture and generic strategies, and ultimately subverting the very norms of decency that it is the job of irony to police.

CHAPTER NINE

'Gossip, tales, suspicions': language and paranoia in Under Western Eyes

If the reports of recent critics are anything to go by, *Under Western Eyes* should carry a health warning: a novel about the duplicity of language, it is itself adroitly duplicitous; an 'aggressive text', it 'hates its readers' and 'routs the liberal subject'. This is evidently not a novel for the faint-hearted, yet rumours of its aggressive designs on the unsuspecting reader have, if anything, served only to enhance its reputation. In the wake of a series of scholarly reassessments, many of which lay powerful emphasis of the linguistic self-consciousness of the novel, the critical standing of *Under Western Eyes* has never been higher.[1]

Espionage and political violence are as central to *Under Western Eyes* as they were to *The Secret Agent*; the novels also share a decidedly edgy relationship with the 'general reader'. But in terms of its representation of language and human subjectivity, *Under Western Eyes* might be read as a brutally unsentimental rewriting of *Lord Jim*. Kirylo Sidorovitch Razumov, the novel's studiously innocuous hero, commits a grievous betrayal of trust and is pursued from St Petersburg to Geneva by compromising rumours and echoes of his guilt. The St Petersburg/Geneva dichotomy superficially resembles the *Patna*/Patusan split in *Lord Jim*; but for Razumov there is no Patusan, no compensatory linguistic utopia, no Jim-like martyrdom – only a final deafness that functions both as a sadistic 'remedy' for his fear of words and as a violent caricature of the general reader's own 'deafness' to the finer nuances of Conrad's prose.

Throughout Razumov's time in St Petersburg and Geneva, he is immersed in gruelling, dismally hollow, and potentially dangerous conversations; his journal is an eye-witness account of Conrad's 'systematic deidealization of dialogue'.[2] As a theoretical context for the presentation and subversion of dialogue in *Under Western Eyes*, I want to cite some of Hans-Georg Gadamer's comments on the hermeneutic of suspicion, the kind of interpretative effort that aims to 'unmask' the text, to reveal 'the meaningfulness of statements in a completely unexpected sense and against the meaning of the author'.³ Although this tradition is commonly associated with Marx, Freud and Nietzsche, Gadamer reminds us that suspicious interpretations are neither radical nor particularly modern: 'Is not *every* form of hermeneutics a form of overcoming an awareness of suspicion?'.⁴ For Gadamer, the most rigorous and constructive means of overcoming suspicion is through *dialogue*: 'In dialogue we are really interpreting . . . It is the function of the dialogue that in saying or stating something a challenging relation with the other evolves, a response is provoked, and the response provides the interpretation of the other's interpretation.'⁵ *Under Western Eyes* stands as a pre-emptive travesty of this ideal of dialogue as an interpersonal, reciprocal, and consensual form of intellectual exchange. Intense and extended intellectual dialogues occupy a great deal of the novel; but at no stage is a comfortable rapport established between speaker and listener. This text is, as Fogel suggests, a 'set of anti-conversations',⁶ a drama of dialogic interpretation in which language veers constantly away from the truth.

Under Western Eyes is deeply exercised by questions of speech and writing, language and textuality. Its student-hero, who dreams of writing a prize-winning essay, becomes the object of compromising rumours, and later finds himself writing spy reports for the czarist authorities. Our narrator and guide in this word-obsessed text is himself a man of words, a teacher whose expertise in matters of language and translation has an obvious bearing on the novel's central themes. Many readers have remarked that the teacher's pedestrian intellect and obtuse moral commentary are profoundly at odds with the structural ingenuity of the novel he narrates; he might even be seen as a counterpart of *Nostromo*'s Fussy Joe Mitchell, a contemptible fuddy-duddy whose commentary is chiefly useful as an indication of how *not* to interpret the matter in hand. Terence Cave argues that the use of a bland narrator is 'a bluff designed to make a spurious plot *vraisemblable* by pre-empting any protestation a conventional reader might potentially be inclined to make'.⁷ The teacher is, according to Tony Tanner, 'a complacent filter' for the nightmarish intensity of Razumov's experiences, a 'vague peripheral fatuous presence'.⁸ But for all his apparent blandness and complacency, the teacher is under no illusions as to the limitations of language; his narrative is characterized by a clear-eyed scepticism over the treacherous ways of words.

Authentic language seems to have been one of the primary casualties of czarist oppression: Haldin's naïve, irresponsible gossip about Razumov, the feminist–spiritualist cant of Peter Ivanovitch and Madame de S–, the intransigent authoritarian rhetoric of Mr de P– and General T–, and the clouds of rumour and misinformation trailed by Razumov – the entire novel is an efflorescence of diseased rhetoric and deracinated words, a tortuous labyrinth of rumour in which Razumov is condemned blindly to wander. The narrator prepares us for our encounter with this murky speech community by asserting at the outset that words 'are the great foes of reality' (p. 3). But the narrator does nevertheless retain a rational belief in our ability to separate truth from lies. His rational scepticism comes to the fore when Razumov disputes the veracity of newspaper reports of Haldin's arrest:

'How can you tell truth from lies?' he queried in his new, immovable manner.

'I don't know how you do it in Russia,' I began, rather nettled by his attitude. He interrupted me.

'In Russia, and in general everywhere – in a newspaper, for instance. The colour of the ink and the shapes of the letters are the same.'

'Well, there are other trifles one can go by. The character of the publication, the general verisimilitude of the news, the consideration of the motive, and so on'. (p. 188)

This exchange is not a confrontation between naïve and sophisticated models of signification, but rather between robust, 'commonsense' scepticism and something closer to paranoia. The teacher would like to believe that the breakdown in language he witnesses in Geneva is a peculiarly 'Russian' affair; Razumov, on the other hand, contends that the divorce between words and reality is a problem in *any* speech community. One way of reading *Under Western Eyes* is as a book-length attempt to adjudicate this debate between the teacher's gentle scepticism and Razumov's incipient paranoia.

The teacher is pointedly critical of the way in which Geneva's Russian émigrés squander verbal energy in baseless political fantasy. Even Natalia Haldin, whose sincerity is above suspicion, is treated with polite scepticism: '"I suppose," I addressed Miss Haldin, "that you will be shocked if I tell you that I haven't understood – I won't say a single word; I've understood all the words . . ."' (p. 106). The narrator seems oddly eager to persuade both Natalia and his readership that his fluency in the Russsian language is in inverse proportion to his understanding of the Russian mindset. The rendering of one tongue into another is for him nothing more than a technical accomplishment – it certainly doesn't entail any sort of profound rapport with the material under translation. But the teacher's own rather academic view of translation should not blind us to its complex function in the novel as a whole. Although it isn't always obvious, *Under Western Eyes* is the work of an Anglo-Polish novelist masquerading as a British (but Russian-born) professor of languages whose English narrative derives from a translation of a diary in Russian that records conversations in Russian, French, German, and English. Consider, for example, the five-point political credo penned by Razmov in his St Petersburg room. This key text would naturally have been written in Russian, in Cyrillic script. But both the Russian language and alphabet have been erased by the language teacher. Russian has been largely repressed by narrative into a kind of 'textual unconscious'[9] beneath the bland, rational, 'conscious' surface of his English prose. This unconscious is sampled by the narrator – but in the form of *transliteration* rather than full translation: technically polyglot, the teacher is ideologically unilingual, speaking the discourse of liberal empiricism with quiet, invincible confidence. But just as his bland reassurances are not enough to allay Razumov's scepticism, so the novel's readers have followed suit in treating the text itself as a suspicious artefact. Faced with this stark choice between 'Russian' paranoia and 'western' commonsense – 'nightmare and complacency', as Tony Tanner has it – Conrad's readers have declared almost unanimously on the 'Russian' side of the novel, scenting strains of dark linguistic pessimism in Conrad's conspiratorial text.

Nothing can be taken at face-value in *Under Western Eyes*; its structure is every bit as secretive as the culture it depicts. According to Kermode, in the course of the novel a 'story' is palmed off on the unsuspecting general reader by a text that harbours 'secrets' – 'invitations to interpretation rather than appeals to consensus' – accessible only to more perspicacious interpreters. In Kermode's view, the text takes a certain sadistic pleasure in the knowledge that most of its readers will be oblivious to its more arcane features: in short, the text 'hates its readers'. Taking his cue from Kermode, David Leon Higdon places *Under Western Eyes* in a class of novels that regard the reader 'as a potential victim'. A similar interpretation is proposed by Allan Hepburn, who reads *Under Western Eyes* as a novel that 'routs the liberal subject' even as he concedes that his interpretation may appear 'fantastically paranoid'.[10]

Jacques Berthoud maintains that no English writer can match Conrad's 'understanding of physical violence'.[11] No less powerful than Conrad's representation of violence is his understanding of the violence of representation. The three key scenes of violence in *Under Western Eyes* – the assassination of Mr de P–, the thrashing meted out to

Ziemianitch by Razumov, and the bursting of Razumov's eardrums – are all assimilated to the novel's overriding theme of linguistic violence. There is a certain symmetry between the murder of de P– and the murder-by-language of Razumov, just as Razumov's assault on the sledge-driver is an extension of his textual denial of Russian history. The deafening of Razumov, meanwhile, is the symbolic culmination of the 'aural trauma' he experiences throughout the novel.

The explosion that kills Mr de P– also injures a number of innocent bystanders. One of its 'secondary' victims is Razumov himself, whose commitment to the revolutionary cause has been widely and spuriously talked up in the gossip of St Petersburg's dissident students. The connection between the explosion and the reverberation of gossip is made by Razumov later in the novel:

> He smiled inwardly at the absolute wrong-headedness of the whole thing, the self-deception of a criminal idealist shattering his existence like a thunder-clap out of a clear sky, and re-echoing amongst the wreckage in the false assumptions of those other fools. (p. 258)

St Petersburg's circle of dissident students – Kostia, Haldin, the 'famine-stricken' student, and others – assume that Razumov is quietly but passionately dedicated to their cause. Razumov is the screen onto which these expendable footsoldiers of the revolution project their fantasies – he is seen as a one-man think tank, hatching in his hours of solitary study the intellectual corroboration for their impassioned political dreams. Haldin's decision to single out Razumov as his confidant brings to mind Doña Rita's observation in *The Arrow of Gold* that '"Certain confidences . . . are the bitterest kind of insult."'[12] Like his view of the drunkard Ziemianitch as a '"bright spirit!"' (p. 18), Haldin's view of Razumov is spectacularly wrong; but his misconception does conceal a grain of truth – Razumov's conservatism is indeed leavened with 'vague liberal principles' that, given more tactful encouragement, might have flourished in different circumstances.

Haldin has Razumov in mind when he praises 'Unstained, lofty, and solitary existences' (p. 135) in a letter to his sister. Natalia's loving repetition of this phrase (pp. 135, 137, 169, 172) serves to reinforce the irony that Haldin's very words 'stain' and contaminate Razumov. No one in *Under Western Eyes* is immune from misrepresentation: even that loyal servant of autocracy, Councillor Mikulin, is found guilty of an unspecified offence in a state trial. If *Victory* is about murder by calumny, *Under Western Eyes* is a tale of murder by eulogy: Razumov is condemned to be fêted by people he despises. The nature of his ordeal by language is captured in an exchange with Peter Ivanovitch:

'You don't suppose, Kirylo Sidorovitch, that I have not heard of you from various points where you made yourself known on your way here? I have had letters.'

'Oh, we are great in talking about each other,' interjected Razumov, who had listened with great attention. 'Gossip, tales, suspicions, and all that sort of thing, we know how to deal in to perfection. Calumny, even.' (p. 206)

Like Axel Heyst, Razumov finds that to live a life of blameless isolation is no defence against the unwarranted curiosity of the world at large. To be tested against language, to have cherished notions about one's own self grotesquely caricatured in the public arena, is the ordeal faced by Conrad's heroes. Many readers have remarked on the nice stroke of metafictional humour implicit in Razumov's ignorance of his own fictionality: '"I am not a young man in a novel"' (pp. 185–6); but this assertion in part stems from a recognition that he is *already* enmeshed in fictions, already 'rewritten' in the overheated, wish-fulfilling dialogues between Haldin and his St Petersburg comrades. The devastating irony for Razumov is that he is compelled for his own safety to identify with the very misrepresentations that have so damaged his life. In Geneva, he begins to flesh out the revolutionists' fantasies about his role in the assassination of Mr de P–. No longer the author of his own identity, he must follow the script laid down by Haldin, providing in his conduct active corroboration for the revolutionists' wild misconceptions, whilst secretly acting out the role assigned to him by Mikulin. The 'gossip, tales, suspicions' that were formerly parasitic on Razumov's private life have become his curriculum vitae. His fate in Geneva is to become a '"living, acting, speaking lie"' (p. 349).

Daily life in Geneva is almost surreally uneventful: social visits, strolls, excursions, and afternoon tea are the genteel rituals by which the Russians measure out their days. Passionate emotion is sublimated almost entirely into conversation, the sole focus of which is Russian politics. Proscribed in Russia, idle speculative conversation is the very lifeblood of the Russian colony in Switzerland. General T– expresses hostility to free speech when he asks Razumov if he often indulges in '"speculative conversation"' (p. 48). The General's question finds a kind of answer, some two-hundred pages later, when Sophia Antonovna asks: '"What's the use of talking . . . "' (p. 246). In Geneva, the abundance of idle talk is indicative of political impotence: the revolutionists can do nothing *but* talk, and the more they talk, the more they are conscious of their decadent inaction and envious of Razumov's dramatic debut on the revolutionary scene – itself a mere product of idle talk and wishful thinking.

To a great extent this is a novel in which 'meaning' has been displaced from language to gesture. Nowhere else does Conrad describe in such detail the *choreography* of conversation: the interplay of gesture, speech, and thought, and the manner in which they veil and reveal one another. As Jeremy Hawthorn observes, actions in the novel tend to speak truer than words.[13] One might speculate that the physical restlessness of the novel's conversationalists compensates for what Fogel calls the dialogical 'gridlock'[14] of the novel. Since conversation in Conrad tends to take place *in situ*, these peripatetic colloquies are a striking new form of dialogic encounter. On the face of it, Conrad's characters invite comparison with the Greek peripatetic thinkers, as they stroll around the university gardens and the aptly named *Boulevard des Philosophes*:[15] but these alfresco conversations are every bit as claustrophobic as the earlier 'Russian' cross-examinations. When Peter Ivanovitch invites Razumov for a '"stroll and a good open-hearted talk"' (p. 205) he unwittingly defines the very qualities that are conspicuously absent from conversation in the novel. Take, for example, the language teacher's account of his discussions with Natalia: 'I was but a Westerner, and it was clear that Miss Haldin would not, could not listen to my wisdom; and as to my desire of listening to her voice, it were better, I thought, not to indulge overmuch in that pleasure' (p. 141). His 'wisdom' falls on deaf ears in the course of their conversations: he is nothing more than a sounding-board for Natalia, who values his company more than his conversation. Similarly, he disregards the semantic content of her words to dwell on their aesthetic–erotic pleasures. It would be hard to find a better microcosm of the cultural 'stalemate' between east and west than these asymmetrical dialogues between teacher and pupil.

In the very long conversation between Razumov and Sophia Antonovna there is a similar preoccupation with forms of attention. Frequently in the grip of a mood of surly abstraction, Razumov is a reluctant and inattentive conversationalist: 'Razumov's attention had wandered away on a track of its own – outside the bars of the gate – but not out of earshot' (p. 250). Razumov listens as an overhearer rather than face-to-face interlocutor, eavesdropping on Sophia Antonovna as though from beyond the boundaries of the Château Borel. 'Razumov was not listening' (p. 254), 'Razumov listened without hearing' (p. 279) – for Razumov, genteel conversation is incalculably less real than his inner turmoil. Yet he is compelled to participate, both because of his job – as a spy, he is a professional listener – and because the dialogue circles ominously around the topic of Haldin. Inattentive to the point of rudeness, Razumov must also be paranoiacally vigilant: he has no time for pleasantries but every suspicion that innocuous small talk conceals darker motives. Take, for instance, the description of Sophia Antonovna: 'She had been looking at him all the time, not as a listener looks at one, but as if the words he chose to say were only of secondary interest' (p. 242). Still more disconcerting is Razumov's perception of 'the steady curiosity of the black eyes fastened on his face as if the woman revolutionist received the sound of his voice into her pupils instead of her ears' (p. 257). Razumov's overwrought imagination has become a fertile breedingground for delusion. Sophia Antonovna seems to be monitoring his every word with merciless vigilance, poised to seize on the one false move, the one careless word that will betray her tormented interlocutor.

What unfolds in Geneva is a collective inquest on the news from St Petersburg: the assassination of Mr de P–, the obscure fate of Haldin, and the enigma of Haldin's accomplice Razumov, all provoke impassioned discussion, not least because reliable information is so thin on the ground. The Genevan revolutionists have to sift their way through a welter of gossip, rumour, and conjecture: the Russian authorities' official version of events as reported in the French and Swiss press; the fresh details unearthed by an English journalist; the letters from a friend of Haldin in St Petersburg, from Haldin himself, from revolutionists with whom Razumov has had contact en route to Geneva, and from the 'famine-stricken' student who has been listening to 'the popular gossip' (p. 277) of the eating-house – this is the 'archive' of texts from which history must be extracted. The archive is supplemented by the testimony of Razumov, himself accredited in a letter from Father Zosim – about whom 'all sorts of rumours' are afloat (p. 137). Neither the living voice nor the written word seems to speak with any authority about Razumov; and *Under Western Eyes* is itself another misleading document on this matter. In effect, Parts II and III of the novel show the residents of *La Petite Russie* attempting to reconstruct the substance of Part I. A variety of perspectives are offered: the bereaved Haldins have a personal interest in Razumov as the only friend of Victor; the other Russians are veteran revolutionists keen to appraise their new recruit; whilst for the 'impartial' English narrator the whole affair is further confirmation of Russian barbarity. The Genevan interpretative community tries to piece the story together, making inferences, collating evidence, moving ever closer to the truth. The constant risk for

Razumov is that any new information may implicate him in Haldin's death. The reader is in a position of false privilege, aware that Razumov did indeed betray Haldin, but ignorant of Razumov's new role as czarist spy. Faced with this welter of rumour and conjecture, the Russian expatriates fail to notice the culprit under their very noses. In a culture of surveillance and suspicion, Razumov is a blind spot, misread by the Russian authorities, by his would-be comrades, and, inevitably, by the first-time reader of the novel. The Genevan colony's reconstruction of events in St Petersburg would be uncannily accurate, were it not for its misreading of Razumov. Paradoxically, the very fact that Razumov is miraculously exempt from suspicion places him in his singular predicament.

If the explosion that kills de P– reverberates in the gossip of Geneva, Razumov's attack on Ziemianitch oddly precipitates a mood of serene contemplation. The streak of supercilious cruelty in Razumov is evidenced when he thrashes the sledge-driver. It is as though Razumov is staging a tableau of czarist oppression: an already intoxicated, feckless peasantry is beaten mercilessly, and with imperious disdain, into comatose submission by a member of the intelligentsia whose noble blood is clearly boiling with rage. But what follows afterwards is equally compelling: Razumov's fit of violence functions as an overture to a reverie in which he justifies to himself his allegiance to autocracy and achieves a kind of communion with Russia:

Under the sumptuous immensity of the sky, the snow covered the endless forests, the frozen rivers, the plains of an immense country, obliterating the landmarks, the accidents of the ground, levelling everything under its uniform whiteness, like a monstrous blank page awaiting the record of an inconceivable history. It covered the passive land with its lives of countless people like Ziemianitch and its handful of agitators like this Haldin – murdering foolishly. (p. 33)

Even if this starlit reverie seems to be a spontaneous acquiescence in the 'sacred inertia' of Russia, it is provoked by Razumov's encounter with another side of Russian history: the low 'eating-house' in the 'quarter of the very poor'. It is 'an enormous slum, a hive of human vermin, a monumental abode of misery towering on the verge of starvation and despair' (p. 28). Razumov can barely suppress his disgust at its destitute clientele, who are perceived by him as vile and barely human. The general squalour – the rancid food, the 'reek of spirits', and the coarse jeering voices of its patrons – is equated by him with spiritual degradation. The true Russia is envisioned by Razumov as a boundless landscape frozen in a timeless stasis inhabited only by anonymous millions. His homeland is apprehended not as an 'historical fact' but as a timeless entity with which only the most presumptuous fool would tamper. The snow effaces local topographical differences; in effect, it obscures the contours of history, substituting in their place a vision of transcendental purity whose symbol is, crucially, the blank page.

The blank page connotes Razumov's voluntary amnesia, not only about his conduct at the eating-house, but also about what the eating-house represents historically – hunger and poverty as economic and political problems rather than as the trappings of spiritual degradation. Razumov's erasure of Russian history provides discursive confirmation of the fearsome thrashing of Ziemianitch. The abolition of history is a concomitant of autocracy's claim to divinely-ordained power. This scene shifts from squalid urban poverty to the tranquillity of nature; from the unseemly 'babble' of the eating-house – the laughter, jeers, and raucous interjections which disconcert Razumov – to the pristine, preverbal purity of the blank page, awaiting the inscription of the author, just as the destiny of Russia is determined by the autocrat. The blank page further connotes the unwritten prize essay – in which Razumov had invested so much hope as an instrument of obtaining distinction – and also his 'blank' identity. He is described as a '"perfect blank"' (p. 277) by Sophia Antonovna; and later feels himself to be a 'great cold blank' (p. 303). As Terence Cave puts it: 'Razumov's "personality" is a void to which an arbitrary chain of signifiers attaches itself, creating a fiction of such power that it absorbs every new detail that comes to light.'[16] The pristine *tabula rasa* offers a mirage of freedom from language, immunity from the contaminating influence of other people's words. But images of preverbal purity – silence and the blank page – are systematically discredited by this novel.

If Razumov attempts to deny Russian history, can the history of Russia be told with any confidence in this novel? There is a clear continuity between the interpretative problems faced by the Russian émigrés and the narrator's own position as self-appointed historian of the Russian psyche. Take, for example, his digression on the sources of his information about Madame de S–:

My informant was the Russian wife of a friend of mine already mentioned, the professor of Lausanne University. It was from her that I learned the last fact of Madame de S–'s history, with which I intend to trouble my readers. She told me, speaking positively, as a person who trusts her sources, of the cause of Madame de S–'s flight from Russia, some years before. It was neither more nor less than this: that she became suspect to the police in connexion with the assassination of the Emperor Alexander. The ground of this suspicion was either some unguarded expressions that escaped her in public, or some talk overheard in her *salon*. Overheard, we must believe, by some guest, perhaps a friend, who hastened to play the informer, I suppose. (pp. 162–3)

'History', in this passage, collapses into hearsay: fact is so diluted by rumour that no reputable historian would treat these tales as anything but colourful apocrypha. Is it pure naïveté that prompts the language teacher to draw attention to the flimsy foundation of his knowledge about Madame de S–'s shady past? His purpose here seems to be not factual precision but the evocation of a peculiarly Russian atmosphere of historical obscurity, of half-truths, and political conspiracies, that can no more be coaxed into the light of rational analysis than the Russian temperament itself. With reliable information such a scarce commodity, it would appear that the 'official' history of Russia remains as elusive as the history of Costaguana in *Nostromo*, a novel whose cast of failed historians stands as Conrad's strongest reproach to the pretensions of the discipline. In *Under Western Eyes* official communiqués and state papers are no more to be believed than the most evanescent rumour; indeed, there is a sense in which rumour becomes more plausible precisely because it does not bear the imprimatur of the 'authorities'. What is also remarkable about this passage is the extent to which Madame de S–'s revolutionary career foreshadows Razumov's: indeed, it is an unnoticed instance of the pervasive motif of 'doubling' in the novel.[17] Both Madame de S– and Razumov are falsely implicated in the assassination of a high-ranking dignitary; both fall under the suspicion of the police; both seem to inhabit a tenebrous borderland between political history and popular rumour; and both flee to Geneva – Madame de S– to peddle her freakish cocktail of spiritualist–feminist revolutionary politics, Razumov as a spy in the pay of the Russian authorities. They are both impostors, products of a culture that seems to preclude the possibility of transparent sincerity.

One of the central enigmas of this novel is the timing of Razumov's decision to reveal himself as an impostor: he does so only when lingering doubts about his political credentials have been dispelled: 'Nothing could touch him now; in the eyes of the revolutionists there was now no shadow on his past' (p. 340). Why does his position become intolerable only when he is no longer in danger? Razumov makes a triple confession: an oral confession to Natalia, a written confession in his diary, and a further oral confession to the revolutionists. By the end of *Under Western Eyes*, Razumov has, to paraphrase Foucault, become a confessing animal.[18] Some readers have suggested that with these confessions Razumov makes a triumphant exit from his prison of lies. My own view, not quite so optimistic, is partly influenced by Marlow's denunciation of confession in *Chance*, which offers a polemical sketch of its ethical and narratological problems: '"Never confess! Never, never! . . . a confession of whatever sort is always untimely . . . What a sell these confessions are! What a horrible sell! You seek sympathy, and all you get is the most evanescent sense of relief"' (p. 212). The vehemence of Marlow's hostility to confession is remarkable, given that his first-person narratives contain a strong confessional element, and that he acts as a lay confessor to Kurtz, Jim, and Flora. According to Marlow, the confessant obtains a short-lived relief from the pangs of conscience by offloading his or her guilty secrets onto a morally voyeuristic listener who is invested for the duration with quasi-clerical authority. One might argue that this tells us more about Marlow's cynicism than it does about the true nature of confession: certainly Marlow communicates a strong sense that confession is, above all, *embarrassing* – that gushing penitential candour does not sit easily with an ethic of masculine stoicism.

Marlow usefully identifies two key conflicting impulses at work in any confession: 'sympathy' and 'relief'. Confession elicits sympathy inasmuch as it overcomes the isolating effects of transgression; but it produces 'relief' inasmuch as it can be merely a self-serving effort to get something off one's chest. But the 'relief' sought by Razumov, as he intimates in the portion of his diary addressed to Natalia, is in the finality of death: 'I felt that I must tell you that I had ended by loving you. And to tell you that I must first confess. Confess, go out – and perish' (p. 361). Razumov's diary entry, composed after his confession to Natalia, supplies both the psychological motive for his confession and a disturbing interpretation of its existential implications. The last residue of his original self has been eliminated: he has colluded with the revolutionists in the process of transforming himself into a 'living, acting, speaking lie'. Shattered by Haldin, his identity is reconstructed into a seamless, consummately unimpeachable narrative. His triple confession disrupts that finality, demolishing the false persona he has been compelled to inhabit: it is a courageously 'suicidal' definitive affirmation of self-identity. However, Razumov's confessions to Peter Ivanovitch's revolutionary clique lead not to death but to deafness.

When Nikita shatters Razumov's eardrums, he inflicts physically the kind of aural trauma that Razumov has been experiencing linguistically throughout the novel. In his student days, Razumov shunned active participation in dialogue: 'With his younger compatriots he took the attitude of an inscrutable listener, a listener of the kind that hears you out intelligently and then – just changes the subject' (p. 5). But even the fact of his having listened to dissident speeches is itself potentially compromising; and his aural ordeal intensifies when he decides to betray Haldin:

> He was now in a more animated part of the town. He did not remark the crash of two colliding sledges close to the curb. The driver of one bellowed tearfully at his fellow –
> 'Oh, thou vile wretch!'
> This hoarse yell, let out nearly in his ear, disturbed Razumov. He shook his head impatiently and went on looking straight before him. Suddenly on the snow, stretched on his back right across his path, he saw Haldin, solid, distinct, real, with his inverted hands over his eyes, clad in a brown close-fitting coat and long boots. (pp. 36–7)

In this scene Razumov sees and hears both too little and too much. Although he fails to notice the crash, he can't help but hear an accusation in the words '"Oh, thou vile wretch!"' Here we have an unmistakeable echo of the 'wretched cur' incident in *Lord Jim*: a piece of background 'noise' that strikes a chance overhearer with accusatory force – sparking in this instance Razumov's first vision of Haldin. This perceptual sequence – the problem of visual failure leading to hypersensitive listening which itself yields a problematic visionary moment – should now be familiar to us as the very grammar of Conradian narrative.

Despatched to Geneva by Mikulin, Razumov endures agonizing uncertainty as rumours about the assassination of Mr de P– and the death of Haldin trickle ominously through from St Petersburg. He gives further rein to his capacity for *over*hearing in a bizarre interview with Madame de S– (perhaps a distant cousin of that other modernist supernatural charlatan, Madame Sosostris) – an encounter which, given the supernatural reputation of his hostess, has the air of a seance: '"There is a smouldering fire of scorn in you"', she says to Razumov. '"You are darkly self-sufficient, but I can see your very soul"' (p. 224). Madame de S–'s phraseology, which in any other context could be dismissed as mere mystical mumbo-jumbo, conjures up horribly familiar memories in Razumov. With uncanny linguistic serendipity, reminiscent of Gentleman Brown in *Lord Jim*, this fraudulent 'spiritualist' taps into a vein of experience private to Razumov: her words, which seem to imply knowledge of Razumov's brush with the supernatural, reinforce his position as the man fated to hear too much.

Razumov's 'acute sense of hearing' (291), far from being a God-given talent, connotes rather acute vulnerability to language:

[I]t occurred to him that this was about the only sound he could listen to innocently, and for his own pleasure, as it were. Yes, the sound of water, the voice of the wind – completely foreign to human passions. All the other sounds of this earth brought contamination to the solitude of a soul. (p. 291)

The loss of auditory innocence is a core theme in *Under Western Eyes*, one that culminates, of course, in the deafening of Razumov by Nikita. This brutal act functions as a climax to the novel's preoccupation with aurality, which, if it has hitherto been subordinated to vision, is now dramatically foregrounded. Some commentators have been struck by the irony that only after he has been deafened can Razumov enter into full human relations – a sentimental extension of this view would be that Razumov's physical deafness 'cures' his emotional deafness.[19] But a more convincing clue to the meaning of this motif of deafness is to be found in an intriguing historical footnote to the novel. As Jocelyn Baines has suggested, there is a very strong likelihood that Razumov is modelled, at least in part, on the Russian revolutionist S. M. Kravtchinsky, alias Sergey Stepniak.[20] An acquaintance of the Garnett family, Stepniak was a veteran revolutionist who had in his time been imprisoned in Italy, Bulgaria, and Turkey, but met his death in 1895 near his Shepherd's Bush home, run over by a train on a level-crossing. Because of the appalling noise in Turkish prisons, Stepniak had trained himself in the ability to shut out exterior sounds: 'In a state of concentrated thought he could, at will, make himself actually deaf.'[21] Oblivious to external distractions, Stepniak failed to hear the warning whistles of the train as it approached. This tragi-comic story might shed some light on the motif of deafness in *Under Western Eyes*: for Razumov, deafness holds out the tantalizing promise of freedom from the 'noise' of language and interpretation. Alone among Conrad's fugitives from language, Razumov has the mixed blessing of both surviving his ordeal and getting out of earshot forever. For this reluctant listener and professional eavesdropper, the loss of hearing is both poetic justice and a consummation devoutly to be wished.

The deafening of the hero coincides with a significant change in the reader's relationship with this text. Certain passages in *Under Western Eyes* become fully 'audible' to the reader only after Razumov's loss of hearing: namely, those sullen, cryptic asides in which Razumov gestures obliquely towards the fact that he is a police spy – a fact we could not know, but might have guessed, if our western ears were not so quite so dull. The 'miserable ingenuity in error' (p. 305) of the novel's characters extends to the reader, who is forced to misconstrue Razumov's presence in Geneva. Kermode, Higdon, and Hepburn construct a reader whose relationship to the text is precisely analogous to the way Razumov is 'constructed' in the gossip of his contemporaries. From being the helpless plaything of a sadistic text the reader graduates to a position of complicity in the very hermeneutic violence about which *Under Western Eyes* is such a potent cautionary tale. The real victim of the novel, it would appear, is that obtuse dullard, the occidental reader, a complacent empiricist with no appetite for secrets whose myopic western eyes scan the text in vain for anything resembling story, plot or life-like character. Error, in *Under Western Eyes*, is both destructive of truth and productive of interpretation: it signifies both sheer misapprehension – as when Haldin's circle co-opt Razumov without his knowledge – and the opportunities for creative 'misreading' that the text affords its readers. The use of Razumov as a source of error suggests that any blind-spot in a given text can be the fulcrum against which interpretative leverage is obtained. The greatness of *Under Western Eyes* lies precisely in its intermingling of these two versions (constructive and destructive) of error to produce what is a properly *de*constructive novel, where hermeneutic violence is the very precondition of interpretative insight. Of course, this bravura achievement is consequent on the betrayal of the ideal of transparent language expressed in Conrad's essays and maritime fiction; regardless of the presence of our kindly pedagogic chaperon, *Under Western Eyes* is Conrad's most sophisticated, least hospitable text.

Conclusion

My decision to use *Under Western Eyes* as the final case-study of this book has a twofold origin: first, in my sense that this singularly comfortless meditation on the dangers and limitations of language is the most 'typical' novel in Conrad's oeuvre – in much the same way that *Tristram Shandy* was, for Victor Shklovsky, 'the most typical novel in world literature'.[1] *Under Western Eyes* crystallizes the fear and distrust of language that is more definitively 'Conradian' than any of the more familiar trappings of his fiction: the world of ships and sailors and the sea, or the grafting of psychological drama onto exotic travelogue. In its obsession with its own textual ontology, *Under Western Eyes* directly confronts the issues of language, voice, and textuality that Conrad, elsewhere in his work, sought ever more resourcefully to evade; it is the novel he was trying *not* to write throughout his career. *Victory* and *Lord Jim* in particular might be seen as abortive drafts of *Under Western Eyes*, the former retreating into antiseptic omniscience, and the latter relocating to Patusan, in order to evade the deconstructive logic the text has set in motion.

My second reason for privileging *Under Western Eyes* is that it offers an excellent vantage-point from which to reflect on Conrad's problematic modernism. I have argued in this study that the generative paradox of Conrad's fiction is that it can be grasped both as an extremely belated rearguard action against print culture and as a precocious adumbration of high-modernist textuality. I have sought to construct a version of Conrad's career that lays maximum emphasis on the immense reluctance with which he arrives at the full-blown modernism of *The Secret Agent* and *Under Western Eyes*. What drains away in the course of Conrad's career is not his faith in language – *that* was fragile and tentative from the very start – but his confidence that such compensatory fictions as the storyteller and the speech community might hold out some possibility of damage-limitation. *Victory* shows how easily the speech community can turn maliciously against its most innocuous member; indeed, linguistic violence is shown to be fundamentally constitutive of the speech community. 'Sea-talk' is celebrated but also problematized in the nautical fiction; *The Arrow of Gold* preserves the integrity of maritime language only by pushing it to the very fringes of the text. The Marlow narratives, in which Conrad's storytelling surrogate endeavours to rescue Kurtz, Jim, and Flora from the quicksand of narrativity, themselves fail to rescue the traditional storyteller from modernist textuality. If *Nostromo* somehow manages to perform an impossible synthesis of phonocentric nostalgia and modernist *écriture*, *The Secret Agent* and *Under Western Eyes* are profoundly disillusioned visions of a world from which storytelling has vanished.

A major corollary of the transformations I have charted in Conrad's speech communities is a transformation in the way his fiction configures its own reception. In the journey from the carefree storytelling of 'Youth' to the austere textuality of *Under Western Eyes*, Conrad found himself demanding ever more strenuous interpretative efforts from his readers. By the time of *The Secret Agent* and *Under Western Eyes*, the reader is no longer constituted as a member of an audience of friends who listen in agreeable passivity. Indeed, the reader is pulled increasingly towards the 'scapegoat' position formerly occupied by Conrad's heroes. When Kermode says that *Under Western Eyes* hates its readers, he means of course that it hates the *general* reader. Kermode discerns and accepts that novel's division between general and specialist readers, with the latter group exempt from the novel's disdain because they have winkled out the clues secreted in its obscure textual folds. According to Kermode's strategy of reading, *Under Western Eyes* is to be valued for the textual idiosyncrasies that serve to undermine 'clearness and effect'; plot, character, and theme are revealed as mere structural hangovers from traditional storytelling – a system of empty decoys among which the general reader flounders. The textual pleasure of a privileged minority of 'successful' readers is in part contingent on the knowledge that a significant proportion of the novel's readers are guaranteed to fail. Whatever superficial generic incentives *Under Western Eyes* offers the general reader, its true pitch is for the attentions of the professional connoisseur of narrative secrecy.

In these respects *Under Western Eyes* connects with and illuminates the emergence of modernism and its attendant sense of Literature as a minority pursuit. The 'literary' in the early twentieth century was becoming the province of a shrinking coterie of highbrow cosmopolitans – Henry James, James Joyce, Ezra Pound, T. S. Eliot – each cultivating his own version of the new aesthetic of obscurity. '[I]t appears likely that poets in our civilization, as it exists at present, must be *difficult*.'² What T. S. Eliot felt to be necessary for modern poetry seems also to have been true of modernist art in general. Modernism is, definitively, difficult: it constitutes itself by banishing the general reader, the average sensibility, from its precincts. *The Waste Land*, the archetypal text of modernism, with its break from received ideas of linear narrative, its anti-mimetic formalism, its polyglot dialect, and its intimidating (and mischievous) erudition, could scarcely be more deterrent to the non-specialist reader. Some readers cannot forgive the modernists for closing ranks against popular culture; an especially pungent version of this argument, John Carey's *The Intellectuals and the Masses*, traces connections between the modernists' contempt for the masses and Hitler's final solution.³ Carey's book is, for obvious reasons, designed to be a crowd-pleasing performance; but it leaves us in no doubt that there is a case to answer. How can we reconcile democratic values with the anti-democratic bias of modernism? This wider question is clearly beyond the scope of the present discussion, but when we come to answer it, Conrad will surely figure as a decisive test-case – whilst the inadequacy of Carey's answers is partly suggested by the absence of Conrad from his study. Even a cursory examination of Conrad's fiction would have undermined Carey's neat dichotomy between supercilious aesthetes (Eliot, Pound, et al.) and champions of common humanity (Conan Doyle, Arnold Bennett). Caught between speaking for everyone and writing for no one, positioned at the interface between high art and popular culture, Conrad was given to proud affirmations of the universality of art but found in the end that he could in no sense *entertain* the general reader. It was never part of Conrad's master-plan to estrange himself from the mass of general readers: that would have been contrary to his artistic – not to mention financial – instincts. He was the most reluctant of modernists; and he will continue to be read seriously and valued highly because he exhibits all the breathtaking innovations of modernism without losing sight of everything that is sacrificed in the bid to make it new.

Notes

INTRODUCTION

1 Letter of 5 January 1907, *The Collected Letters of Joseph Conrad*, ed. Frederick R. Karl and Laurence Davies, 8 vols. (Cambridge University Press, 1983–), III, 401.

2 George Steiner, *Extraterritorial: Papers on Literature and the Language Revolution* (London: Faber and Faber, 1972), pp. 3–11.

3 Letter of 4 October 1907 to Edward Garnett, Conrad, *Collected Letters*, III, 488.

4 'It is possible', Martin Ray has argued, 'that Conrad's use of a foreign language is only quantitatively different from the language which all writers employ, a more extreme instance of those changes and distortions which every author inflicts upon his native tongue in the course of producing a literary text.' 'The Gift of Tongues: The Languages of Joseph Conrad', *Conradiana* 15 (1983), 86.

5 F. R. Leavis, *The Great Tradition* (London: Chatto and Windus, 1948; repr. Harmondsworth: Penguin, 1983), p. 28.

6 Letter of 14 August 1906 to Ada and John Ada Galsworthy, Conrad, *Collected Letters*, III, 350.

7 'Solitude overpowers me; it absorbs me. I see nothing, I read nothing. It is like a kind of tomb, at the same time a hell, where one has to write, write, write.' Letter of 22 August 1903, *Collected Letters*, III, 51. Throughout this study I have left errors in Conrad's French uncorrected.

8 Ford Madox Ford, *Joseph Conrad: A Personal Remembrance* (London: Duckworth, 1924), p. 113.

9 Joseph Conrad, *Almayer's Folly: A Story of an Eastern River* (London: Dent, 1923), pp. 199–200; *Nostromo: A Tale of the Seaboard* (London: Dent, 1923), p. 235; *The Secret Agent: A Simple Tale* (London: Dent, 1923), p. 210.

10 Joseph Conrad, *Notes on Life and Letters* (London: Dent, 1926), p. 83.

11 Raymond Williams, *The English Novel from Dickens to Lawrence* (London: Chatto and Windus, 1970), p. 141.

12 Mary Louise Pratt, 'Linguistic Utopias', in *The Linguistics of Writing: Arguments between Language and Literature*, ed. Nigel Fabb, Derek Attridge, Alan Durant, and Colin MacCabe (Manchester University Press, 1987), pp. 48–66.

13 Edward Said, 'Conrad: The Presentation of Narrative', in *The World, the Text and the Critic* (Cambridge, MA: Harvard University Press, 1983), p. 94.
14 Joseph Conrad, *The Arrow of Gold: A Story between Two Notes* (London: Dent, 1924), p. 3; 'The Inn of the Two Witches', in *Within the Tides* (London: Dent, 1923), p. 177.
15 Letter to William Blackwood, 13 December 1898, Conrad, *Collected Letters*, II, 130.
16 Jacques Derrida, *Of Grammatology*, tr. Gayatri Chakravorty Spivak (Baltimore: Johns Hopkins University Press, 1976), p. 301.
17 Ibid., p. 158.
18 Joseph Conrad, *Last Essays* (London: Dent, 1926), pp. 59–65.
19 Joseph Conrad, *A Personal Record* (London: Dent, 1923), p. 90.
20 Mikhail Bakhtin, *Speech Genres and Other Late Essays*, ed. Caryl Emerson and Michael Holquist, tr. Vern W. McGee (Austin: University of Texas Press, 1986), pp. 60–102.
21 Martin Ray sees Conrad as heir to two traditions: the first, stemming from Mallarmé and Rimbaud, regards silence as a 'cathartic release' from the inadequacy of language; the second, which originates with Pascal, regards silence as a terrifying negation of the writer's achievement: 'The suspicion and deep distrust of language which this preference for silent men would seem to indicate is, however, opposed by that almost neurotic addiction to language and to writing which is revealed in his letters and essays, and which several of his leading characters are made to share.' 'Language and Silence in the Novels of Joseph Conrad', in *Critical Essays on Joseph Conrad*, ed. Ted Billy (Boston, MA: G. K. Hall, 1987), pp. 46–57.
22 Joseph Conrad, *The Rover* (London: Dent, 1924), p. 3.
23 Joseph Conrad, 'Falk: A Reminiscence', in *Typhoon and other Tales* (London: Dent, 1923), pp. 145–6.
24 The impact of theory on Conrad studies might conveniently be measured by comparing the contents of a recent critical anthology, such as Andrew Michael Roberts (ed.), *Joseph Conrad: A Critical Reader*, Longman Critical Readers (London: Longman, 1998) with one published in the 1970s, such as Frederick R. Karl (ed.), *Joseph Conrad: A Collection of Criticism* (New York: McGraw-Hill, 1975).
25 Said, 'Conrad: The Presentation of Narrative', p. 90.
26 Eloise Knapp Hay, *The Political Novels of Joseph Conrad: A Critical Study* (University of Chicago Press, 1963; second edition, 1981), p. vii.

1. 'THE REALM OF LIVING SPEECH': CONRAD AND ORAL COMMUNITY

1 Joseph Conrad, *The Mirror of the Sea* (London: Dent, 1923), pp. 134, 151.
2 Jacques Berthoud, 'Introduction: Conrad and the Sea', *The Nigger of the 'Narcissus'* (Oxford University Press, 1984).

3 Joseph Conrad, 'Typhoon', in *Typhoon and Other Tales* (London: Dent, 1923), p. 28.
4 See Francis Mulhern's brief but incisive discussion of the return of the (sexual, linguistic, and political) repressed in 'Typhoon', in *Nation and Narration*, ed. Homi K. Bhabha (London: Routledge, 1990), pp. 255–6.
5 Joseph Conrad, *The Nigger of the 'Narcissus'* (London: Dent, 1923), p. 101.
6 Joseph Conrad, *An Outcast of the Islands* (London: Dent, 1923), pp. 95–6.
7 Derrida, *Of Grammatology*, pp. 136, 138, 137 (italics in original).
8 As Cedric Watts points out, Abdulla's betrayal of Dain to the Dutch authorities is the first of many 'covert plots' – sequences of action likely to escape the attention of the first-time reader – in Conrad's fiction. *The Deceptive Text: An Introduction to Covert Plots* (Sussex: Harvester Press, 1984), pp. 47–53.
9 See Mark Conroy, 'Ghostwriting (In) "Karain"', *The Conradian* 18 (1994), 1–16 for a subtle reading of the tale as a meditation on the problems of 'translation' across the frontiers of culture, language and time.
10 Joseph Conrad, 'Karain: A Memory', in *Tales of Unrest* (London, Dent, 1923), p. 26.
11 Joseph Conrad, 'The Partner', in *Within the Tides* (London: Dent, 1923), p. 172.
12 Walter Benjamin, 'The Storyteller: Reflections on the Works of Nikolai Leskov', *Illuminations*, ed. Hannah Arendt, tr. Harry Zohn (London: Fontana, 1973), pp. 83–107. Mark Conroy's chapter in *Modernism and Authority: Strategies of Legitimation in Flaubert and Conrad* (Baltimore: Johns Hopkins University Press, 1985), ch. 7, is the best discussion of the Conrad/Benjamin connection known to me.
13 Benjamin, 'The Storyteller', p. 83.
14 Ibid., p. 87.
15 Ibid., p. 87.
16 Raymond Williams, *The Country and the City* (London: Hogarth, 1985), ch. 2.
17 Benjamin, 'The Storyteller', p. 84.
18 See the following articles for useful observations on multilingualism in Conrad: Robert Hampson, '"Heart of Darkness" and "The Speech that Cannot be Silenced"', *English* 39 (1990), 15–32; Claude Maisonnat, '*Almayer's Folly*: A Voyage Through Many Tongues', *L'Epoque Conradienne* 16 (1990), 39–49; Gene M. Moore, 'Chronotopes and Voices in *Under Western Eyes*', *Conradiana* 18 (1986), 9–25.
19 Joseph Conrad, *Under Western Eyes* (London: Dent, 1923), p. 92.
20 Jan B. Gordon, *Gossip and Subversion in Nineteenth-Century British Fiction: Echo's Economies* (London: Macmillan, 1996), p. 81.
21 See Don Ihde, *Listening and Voice: A Phenomenology of Sound* (Athens: Ohio University Press, 1976), for an exploratory 'phenomenology' of auditory experience, particularly reminiscent of Conrad in its emphasis on the *'primacy of listening'* in discourse, and on sound and language as a *'penetrating,*

invading presence' (pp. 117–18 and 80–2; Ihde's italics); Gemma Corradi Fiumara, in *The Other Side of Language: A Philosophy of Listening*, tr. Charles Lambert (London: Routledge, 1990).

22 Useful material on hearing/listening in Conrad includes: Owen Knowles, '"To Make You Hear..."': Some Aspects of Conrad's Dialogue', *The Polish Review* 20 (1975), 164–80; Aaron Fogel, *Coercion to Speak: Conrad's Poetics of Dialogue* (Cambridge, MA: Harvard University Press, 1985), pp. 30–2, 48–58; Thomas Dilworth, 'Listeners and Lies in "Heart of Darkness"', *Review of English Studies* 38 (1987), 510–22; Michael S. Macovski, 'The Heartbeat of Darkness: Listening in(to) the Twentieth Century', in *Dialogue and Literature: Apostrophe, Auditors, and the Collapse of Romantic Discourse* (Oxford University Press, 1994), pp. 151–70.

23 Fogel, *Coercion to Speak*, pp. 49–50.

24 Joseph Conrad, 'Heart of Darkness', in *Youth: A Narrative; and Two Other Stories* (London: Dent, 1923), p. 155.

25 Joseph Conrad, *Typhoon and Other Tales* (London: Dent, 1923), p. 106.

26 Fogel, *Coercion to Speak*, p. 10; italics in original.

27 Ibid., p. 55.

28 Joseph Conrad, 'The Brute', in *A Set of Six* (London: Dent, 1923), p. 103.

29 'Tympan', in Jacques Derrida, *Margins of Philosophy*, tr. Alan Bass (Sussex: Harvester Press, 1982), pp. ix–xxix. In a different context, Joel Fineman has described the ear as an 'instrument of delay' which came in the Renaissance to stand for an emerging sense of the 'intermediating maze' of corrupt textuality in a lyric poetry hitherto centred on the pure immediacy of vision. 'I believe', contends Fineman, 'that this Shakespearean ear eventually determines Derrida's account of the reader's, any reader's, relation to a text, any text.' 'Shakespeare's Ear', in *The New Historicism Reader*, ed. H. Aram Veeser (London: Routledge, 1994), pp. 116–23.

30 Mikhail Bakhtin, *Rabelais and His World*, tr. Helene Iswolsky (Cambridge, MA: MIT Press, 1968), pp. 105–6.

2. 'MURDER BY LANGUAGE': 'FALK' AND *VICTORY*

1 See Gordon, *Gossip and Subversion*, pp. 367–71, for a brief discussion of *Victory*.

2 Martin Heidegger, *Being and Time*, tr. John Macquarrie and Edward Robinson (Oxford: Blackwell, 1962), p. 212.

3 See Max Gluckman, 'Gossip and Scandal', *Current Anthropology* 4 (1963), 307–16; Robert Paine, 'What Is Gossip About? An Alternative Hypothesis', *Man* 2 (1967), 278–85. Noting that gossip has long attracted the odium of moralists for fostering a 'speculative', attitude to morality, Patricia Meyer Spacks, *Gossip* (University of Chicago Press, 1985), attempts to salvage its reputation by drawing analogies between gossip and such reputable genres as biography, the diary, and the novel itself.

4 Gluckman, 'Gossip and Scandal', p. 313.

5 cf. D. A. Miller's discussion of gossip and parochial conservatism in *Middlemarch*, in *Narrative and Its Discontents: Problems of Closure in the Traditional Novel* (Princeton University Press, 1981), pp. 110–29.

6 Paine, 'What Is Gossip About?', pp. 280–1.

7 See Allon White, 'Godiva to the Gossips: Meredith and the Language of Shame', in *The Uses of Obscurity: The Fiction of Early Modernism* (London: Routledge and Kegan Paul, 1981), pp. 79–107.

8 A useful term coined by Cedric Watts to describe characters who crop up in two or more otherwise unrelated Conrad narratives. See *The Deceptive Text: An Introduction to Covert Plots*, pp. 149–50, for a full list of such characters.

9 Joseph Conrad, *Lord Jim: A Tale* (London: Dent, 1923), p. 198.

10 Roland Barthes, *Roland Barthes par Roland Barthes* (Paris: Editions du Seuil, 1975), p. 171.

11 Letter of 29? June 1906 to Alice Rothenstein, Conrad, *Collected Letters*, III, 338.

12 Tony Tanner, '"Gnawed Bones" and "Artless Tales" – Eating and Narrative in Conrad', in *Joseph Conrad: A Commemoration*, ed. Norman Sherry (London: Macmillan, 1976), pp. 17–36.

13 Søren Kierkegaard, *The Two Ages*, ed. and tr. Howard V. Hong and Edna H. Hong (Princeton University Press, 1978), p. 100.

14 M. H. Abrams, 'The Deconstructive Angel', and J. Hillis Miller, 'The Critic as Host', in *Modern Criticism and Theory: A Reader*, ed. David Lodge (London: Longman, 1988), pp. 265–76, 278–85. The two papers were give consecutively at a session of the MLA in December 1976.

15 Tanner, '"Gnawed Bones" and "Artless Tales"', p. 35.

16 *Victory* offers the most clear-cut corroboration of the Conradian world-view as distilled by Ian Watt in 'Joseph Conrad: Alienation and Commitment', in *The English Mind: Studies in the English Moralists Presented to Basil Wiley*, ed. Hugh Sykes Davies and George Watson (Cambridge University Press, 1964), pp. 257–78.

17 William W. Bonney, 'Narrative Perspectives in *Victory*: The Thematic Relevance', in *Critical Essays on Joseph Conrad*, ed. Billy, pp. 128–41.

18 Joseph Conrad, *Victory: An Island Tale* (London: Dent, 1923), p. 174.

19 Albert J. Guerard describes *Victory* as Conrad's 'easiest', novel, in *Conrad the Novelist* (Cambridge, MA: Harvard University Press, 1958), p. 255.

20 Tony Tanner, 'Joseph Conrad and the Last Gentleman', *Critical Quarterly* 28 (1986), 110–11.

21 Ibid., p. 118.

22 Roland Barthes, *A Lover's Discourse: Fragments*, tr. Richard Howard (London: Cape, 1979), p. 185. Italics in original.

23 Ibid., p. 183.

24 Joseph Conrad, *Suspense: A Napoleonic Novel* (London: Dent, 1925), pp. 93, 261.

25 'For where two or three are gathered together in my Name, there I am in the midst of them', Matthew, 18:20.

26 'Falk', p. 205.

27 The figure of the *flâneur* or urban stroller is famously evoked by Walter Benjamin in 'On Some Motifs in Baudelaire', in *Illuminations*, pp. 152–96.

28 John Batchelor (ed.), *Victory* (Oxford University Press, 1986), p. 420n.

29 For Robert Hampson, the split in narrative perspectives reflects the split between Heyst's obscure 'identity-for-self', and his 'shifting identity-for-others'. *Joseph Conrad: Betrayal and Identity* (New York: St Martin's Press, 1992), pp. 231–50; Daphna Erdinast-Vulcan similarly regards the narrative split as a projection of 'the protagonist's frame of mind, the fault-lines within his consciousness'. *Joseph Conrad and the Modern Temper* (Oxford: Clarendon Press, 1991), p. 182.

3. 'DRAWING-ROOM VOICES': LANGUAGE AND SPACE IN *THE ARROW OF GOLD*

1 Zdzisław Najder, *Joseph Conrad: A Chronicle*, tr. Halina Carroll-Najder (Cambridge University Press, 1983), p. 48. Most Conrad critics imply their verdict on *The Arrow of Gold* by ignoring it. There are disparaging discussions in Guerard, *Conrad the Novelist*, pp. 278–84, and Daniel R. Schwarz, *Conrad: The Later Fiction* (London: Macmillan, 1982), ch. 8, both of which attribute the novel's aesthetic flaws to its 'biographical' content. Erdinast-Vulcan takes a more circumspect view of the novel's 'failure' in *Joseph Conrad and the Modern Temper*, pp. 186–200.

2 Hampson, *Joseph Conrad: Betrayal and Identity*, ch. 8, and 'The Late Novels' in *The Cambridge Companion to Joseph Conrad*, ed. J. H. Stape (Cambridge University Press, 1996), pp. 140–59; Susan Jones, *Conrad and Women* (Oxford University Press, 1999), pp. 171–6, 185–7; Andrew Michael Roberts, 'The Gaze and the Dummy: Sexual Politics in *The Arrow of Gold*' in *Joseph Conrad: Critical Assessments*, ed. Keith Carabine, 4 vols. (Robertsbridge, East Sussex: Helm Information, 1992), III, 528–50.

3 Hampson, 'The Late Novels', p. 150.

4 Schwarz, *Conrad: The Later Fiction*, p. 127.

5 Ibid., p. 133.

6 Sandra M. Gilbert and Susan Gubar, *The Madwoman in the Attic: The Woman Writer and the Nineteenth Century Literary Imagination* (New Haven: Yale University Press, 1979), p. 17.

7 Roberts, 'The Gaze and the Dummy', is a valuable discussion of the objectification of women in this novel.

8 Frederic Jameson, *The Political Unconscious: Narrative as a Socially Symbolic Act* (London: Methuen, 1981), p. 213.

4. MODERNIST STORYTELLING: 'YOUTH' AND 'HEART OF DARKNESS'

1 Barbara Hardy, *Tellers and Listeners: The Narrative Imagination* (London: Athlone Press, 1975), p. 154.

2 Joseph Conrad, 'Author's Note', *Youth: A Narrative; and Two Other Stories* (London: Dent, 1923), p. x.

3 Ford, *Joseph Conrad: A Personal Remembrance*, pp. 160–1.

4 Letter of 3 December 1902 to Elsie Hueffer, Conrad, *Collected Letters*, II, 460.

5 Leavis, *The Great Tradition*, p. 204. As well as William York Tindall's 'Apology for Marlow', in *From Jane Austen to Joseph Conrad*, ed. Robert C. Rathburn and Martin Steinmann (Minneapolis: University of Minnesota Press, 1958), pp. 274–85, see Jan Verleun, 'The Changing Face of Charlie Marlow', *The Conradian* 8 (1983), 21–7 and 9 (1984), 15–24, which aims to rescue Marlow's reputation as a decent, trustworthy narrator from the suspicion of contemporary critics. Ian Watt, *Conrad in the Nineteenth Century* (London: Chatto and Windus, 1980), pp. 200–14 offers the standard contemporary interpretation/justification of Marlow.

6 Conrad, 'Author's Note', *Youth*, pp. ix–x.

7 See Hampson, *Joseph Conrad: Betrayal and Identity*, p. 310n.; Jakob Lothe, *Conrad's Narrative Method* (Oxford: Clarendon Press, 1989), p. 38; Watts, *The Deceptive Text*, pp. 138–9.

8 Letter of 10 June 1890, Conrad, *Collected Letters*, I, 54. In a letter of 5 December 1903 to Kazimierz Waliszewski, Conrad remarks: 'Homo duplex has in my case more than one meaning.' *Collected Letters*, III, 89.

9 Roland Barthes, 'The Death of the Author', in *Image/Music/Text*, tr. Stephen Heath (Glasgow: Fontana, 1977), pp. 142–8; Michel Foucault, 'What Is an Author?', in *Language, Counter-Memory, Practice*, tr. Donald F. Bouchard and Sherry Simon (Oxford: Blackwell, 1977), pp. 113–38.

10 John Batchelor, *The Life of Joseph Conrad* (Oxford: Blackwell, 1994), p. 34. Italics in original.

11 Letter of ?November 1911, Conrad, *Collected Letters*, IV, 506.

12 For a different view of the Conrad/James relationship, see Jameson, *The Political Unconscious*, pp. 219–224.

13 Conrad, 'Henry James: An Appreciation', in *Notes on Life and Letters*, p. 13.

14 Hampson, '"Heart of Darkness" and "The Speech that Cannot be Silenced"', p. 15.

15 Berthoud, 'Introduction: Conrad and the Sea', *The Nigger of the 'Narcissus'*, p. viii.

16 His work ethic is most succinctly expressed in a letter of 4 September 1892 to Marguerite Poradowska on the subject of the journey to emotional maturity: Conrad traces a path from youthful egotism, through a transitional phase of disillusion, to mature solidarity ('l'homme ne vaut ni plus ni moins que le travail qu'il accomplit'). *Collected Letters*, I, 112.

17 Miller, *Narrative and Its Discontents*, p. 110.

18 Edward Said, *Culture and Imperialism* (London: Chatto and Windus, 1993), p. 25.

19 Watt, *Conrad in the Nineteenth Century*, p. 245.

20 Owen Knowles, 'The Year's Work in Conrad Studies, 1985: A Survey of Periodical Literature', *The Conradian* 11 (1986), 58. The deconstructionists

Knowles has in his sights are Vincent Pecora and Charles Eric Reeves. Pecora's *'Heart of Darkness* and the Phenomenology of Voice', *ELH* 52 (1985), 993–1015, reads the novella as a classic modern record of the divorce between voice and intentionality; Reeves's 'A Voice of Unrest: Conrad's Rhetoric of the Unspeakable', *Texas Studies in Literature and Language* 27 (1985), 284–310, views 'Heart of Darkness' (and *Lord Jim*) as evidence of the collapse of Conrad's 'myth of telling'. The other key poststructuralist engagements with 'Heart of Darkness' are Peter Brooks, 'An Unreadable Report: Conrad's *Heart of Darkness*', in *Reading for the Plot: Design and Intention in Narrative* (Oxford: Clarendon Press, 1984), pp. 238–63; Tzvetan Todorov, 'Knowledge in the Void: *Heart of Darkness*', *Conradiana* 21 (1989), 161–72; and J. Hillis Miller, *'Heart of Darkness* Revisited', in *Conrad Revisited: Essays for the Eighties*, ed. Ross C. Murfin (Birmingham: University of Alabama Press, 1985), pp. 31–50.

21 See the chapter on 'Heart of Darkness' in Valentine Cunningham, *In the Reading Gaol: Postmodernity, Texts, and History* (Oxford: Blackwell, 1994).

22 Conrad, *The Secret Agent*, p. 21.

23 Bette London, *The Appropriated Voice: Narrative Authority in Conrad, Forster, and Woolf* (Ann Arbor: University of Michigan Press, 1990), p. 43.

24 John Vernon, 'Reading, Writing, and Eavesdropping: Some Thoughts on the Nature of Realistic Fiction', *Keynon Review* 4. 4 (1982), 44–54.

25 Cedric Watts, *Conrad's 'Heart of Darkness': A Critical and Contextual Discussion* (Milan: Mursia International, 1977), pp. 83–5.

26 For Derrida on the 'logic of the supplement', see *Of Grammatology*, pp. 144–57.

27 Benjamin, 'Theses on the Philosophy of History', in *Illuminations*, p. 248.

28 Chinua Achebe, 'An Image of Africa: Racism in Conrad's *Heart of Darkness*', in *Hopes and Impediments* (London: Heinemann, 1988), pp. 1–13 (a revised version of a lecture originally given in February 1975). A strong case for the defence is made by Cedric Watts in ' "A Bloody Racist": About Achebe's View of Conrad', *Yearbook of English Studies* 13 (1983), 196–209.

29 Two of the best (both attuned to the complexities of Conrad's narrative technique in a way that Achebe isn't) are Benita Parry, *Conrad and Imperialism: Ideological Boundaries and Visionary Frontiers* (London: Macmillan, 1983), ch. 2, and Patrick Brantlinger, *Rule of Darkness: British Literature and Imperialism, 1830–1914* (Ithaca: Cornell University Press, 1988), ch. 9.

30 Said, *Culture and Imperialism*, pp. 20–35, 197–200.

31 Hampson, ' "Heart of Darkness" and "The Speech that Cannot be Silenced" ', pp. 17–18.

32 Anthony Fothergill, *'Heart of Darkness'* (Milton Keynes: Open University Press, 1989), p. 95.

33 Letter of 22 March 1902 to Harriet Mary Capes, Conrad, *Collected Letters*, II, 394.

34 Nina Pelikan Straus, 'The Exclusion of the Intended from Secret Sharing in Conrad's *Heart of Darkness*', *Novel* 20 (1987), 123–37.

35 Lionel Trilling, *Beyond Culture: Essays on Literature and Learning* (Oxford University Press, 1980), p. 18; Watts, *Conrad's 'Heart of Darkness'*, p. 120.

36 Benjamin, 'The Storyteller', p. 93.

5. THE SCANDALS OF *LORD JIM*

1 W. H. Auden, 'The Joker in the Pack', in *The Dyer's Hand* (London: Faber and Faber, 1962), pp. 246–72.

2 For detailed information on the *Jeddah* scandal see Norman Sherry, *Conrad's Eastern World* (Cambridge University Press, 1966), ch. 3.

3 Conroy, *Modernism and Authority*, p. 99.

4 Watt, *Conrad in the Nineteenth Century*, p. 297.

5 Guerard, *Conrad the Novelist*, p. 130.

6 According to John Batchelor, 'the shift from spoken to written narrative accompanies a shift from moral relativity to moral "flatness" in the novel's dramatic organization, and the privileged man's simple moral outlook is an aesthetic necessity if this flatness is to be "smuggled" past the reader's natural requirement that the text should be reasonably consistent in the degree of moral complexity and moral sophistication that it displays'. *'Lord Jim'* (London: Unwin, 1988), p. 141.

7 Miller, *Narrative and Its Discontents*, p. 113.

8 See Heidegger, *Being and Time*, pp. 163–8.

9 Miller, *Narrative and Its Discontents*, pp. 123–4.

10 Letter of 13 December 1899, Conrad, *Collected Letters*, II, 226–7.

11 Jan Verleun, *'Patna' and Patusan Perspectives* (Groningen: Bouma's Boekhuis, 1979).

12 *Conrad: The Critical Heritage*, ed. Norman Sherry (London: Routledge, 1973), p. 118.

13 Leavis, *The Great Tradition*, p. 218.

14 cf. Fogel on filibustering dialogue and the structure of *Nostromo*, in *Coercion to Speak*, pp. 98–101.

15 Watt, *Conrad in the Nineteenth Century*, p. 305.

16 Frank Kermode, *The Genesis of Secrecy: On the Interpretation of Narrative* (Cambridge, MA: Harvard University Press, 1979), p. 13.

17 Letter of 17 October 1897, Conrad, *Collected Letters*, I, 399.

18 Jonathan Culler, *On Deconstruction: Theory and Criticism after Structuralism* (London: Routledge, 1983), p. 259.

19 'In the second part of *Lord Jim*, Conrad is not dealing with realities that can stand up to three-dimensional scrutiny; he is trapped in an intractable contradiction between the basic terms of his previous, and his present, narrative assumptions; it is somewhat as if, in the end, Almayer had found gold up the river.' Watt, *Conrad in the Nineteenth Century*, p. 308.

20 Ibid., p. 322.

21 For a useful survey of interpretations see ibid., pp. 325–31.

22 Guerard, *Conrad the Novelist*, p. 166.

23 E. M. Forster, 'Joseph Conrad: A Note' (1929), in *Abinger Harvest* (London: Arnold, 1940), pp. 134–8. 'What is so elusive about him is that he is always promising to make some general philosophic statement about the universe, and then refraining with a gruff disclaimer.'

24 Martin Ray, *Joseph Conrad* (London: Arnold, 1993), p. 44.

25 See Alexander Welsh, *George Eliot and Blackmail* (Cambridge, MA: Harvard University Press, 1985), for an important study of this subgenre.

26 Batchelor, *'Lord Jim'*, p. 131.

6. THE GENDER OF *CHANCE*

1 John Batchelor, *The Edwardian Novelists* (London: Duckworth, 1982), p. 43.

2 See especially Jones, *Conrad and Women*.

3 Joseph Conrad, *Within the Tides* (London: Dent, 1923), p. 175.

4 Letter of ? June 1913 to J. G. Huneker, Conrad, *Collected Letters*, v, 236.

5 Cited by Cedric Watts in *Joseph Conrad: A Literary Life* (London: Macmillan, 1989), p. 115.

6 In the serial version of *Chance*, Marlow's interlocutor was a professional novelist, and their exchanges included reflections on the nature of fiction. In his study of the revisions between serial and book-form, Robert Siegle argues that the deletion of these passages is evidence of the dwindling of aesthetic self-consciousness that blighted Conrad's late fiction. Susan Jones, however, interprets Conrad's revisions as the signs of a positive evolution from insular reflections on the male storyteller's craft to a self-conscious engagement with the relationship between romance conventions and female subjectivity. Siegle, 'The Two Texts of *Chance*', *Conradiana* 16 (1984), 83–101; Jones, *Conrad and Women*, ch. 5.

7 John Batchelor, 'Introduction' to *Lord Jim* (Oxford University Press, 1983), p. xix.

8 C. B. Cox, *Joseph Conrad: The Modern Imagination* (London: Dent, 1974), p. 124.

9 *Chance: A Tale in Two Parts* (London: Dent, 1923), p. 53.

10 Andrew Michael Roberts, 'Secret Agents and Secret Objects: Action, Passivity, and Gender in *Chance*', in *Conrad and Gender*, ed. Andrew Michael Roberts (Amsterdam: Rodopi, 1993), p. 91.

11 See, for example, Ruth Nadelhaft, *Joseph Conrad* (Hemel Hempstead: Harvester Wheatsheaf, 1991), pp. 109–17, which accepts that there is a clear ironic distance between Conrad and Marlow; Gail Fraser, 'Mediating Between the Sexes: Conrad's *Chance*', *Review of English Studies* 43 (1992), 81–8, also regards *Chance* as a serious attempt to accommodate both male and female experience. More sceptical of the novel's feminist credentials is Paul Armstrong, who argues that its clumsy handling of irony ('the text botches the generic signals it gives about how to classify Marlow's tone') leaves no room for alternatives to Marlow's sexism: 'Misogyny and the Ethics of Reading: The Problem of Conrad's *Chance*', in *Contexts for Conrad*, ed. Keith

Carabine, Owen Knowles, and Wiesław Krajka (Lublin: Maria Curie-Skłodowska Press, 1993), pp. 151–74.

12 Lothe, *Conrad's Narrative Method*, ch. 2.

13 Thomas C. Moser, *Joseph Conrad: Achievement and Decline* (Hamden, CT: Archon Books, 1966), pp. 172.

14 Schwarz, *Conrad: The Later Fiction*, p. 46.

15 Robert Siegle, *The Politics of Reflexivity* (Baltimore: Johns Hopkins University Press, 1986), pp. 66–121; Erdinast-Vulcan, *Joseph Conrad and the Modern Temper*, pp. 156–72.

16 Erdinast-Vulcan, *Joseph Conrad and the Modern Temper*, pp. 159–60.

17 Henry James, 'The New Novel' (1914), in *Henry James: Selected Literary Criticism*, ed. Morris Shapira (Cambridge University Press, 1981), pp. 311–42.

18 Ibid., p. 320.

19 Ibid., p. 331.

20 Ibid., p. 333.

21 E. E. Duncan-Jones, 'Some Sources of *Chance*', *Review of English Studies* 20 (1969), 468–71; Jones, *Conrad and Women*, pp. 123–33. Useful biographical perspectives on the Conrad/James relationship are given by Ian Watt, 'Conrad, James and *Chance*', in *Imagined Worlds: Essays on some English Novels and Novelists in Honour of John Butt*, ed. Maynard Mack and Ian Gregor (London: Methuen, 1968), pp. 301–22; and Leon Edel, 'A Master Mariner', in *Henry James: The Master, 1901–1916* (London: Hart-Davis, 1972), pp. 46–55.

22 Jameson, *The Political Unconscious*, p. 222.

23 The note of condescension is more strongly evident in a letter to Edith Wharton on the subject of efforts by admirers of 'poor dear J. C.' to compile a *Festschrift* to raise Conrad's profile in the United States. James offers to send Wharton a copy of *Chance*, describing it as 'really rather *yieldingly* difficult and charming'. Letter of 27 February 1914, in *A Portrait in Letters: Correspondence to and about Conrad*, ed. J. H. Stape and Owen Knowles (Amsterdam: Rodopi, 1996), p. 97.

24 Letter of 24 May 1916, Conrad, *Collected Letters*, V, 595.

25 Mikhail Bakhtin, *The Dialogic Imagination: Four Essays*, ed. Michael Holquist, tr. Caryl Emerson and Michael Holquist (Austin: University of Texas Press, 1981), p. 232.

26 For a different (and more positive) view of the pattern of surrogacy in *Chance*, see *Joseph Conrad and the Modern Temper*, pp. 166–72, where Daphna Erdinast-Vulcan notes that 'every male character in the novel is mistaken for or substituted by another at some point in the novel' – a process that draws passive male onlookers (including Powell and Marlow) into the role of champion/protector of Flora.

27 George Steiner, *After Babel: Aspects of Language and Translation* (London: Oxford University Press, 1975), p. 41.

28 Spacks, *Gossip*, pp. 38–42.
29 Gordon, *Gossip and Subversion*, p. 62.

7. *NOSTROMO* AND ANECDOTAL HISTORY

1 Guerard, *Conrad the Novelist*, p. 180.
2 Jameson, *The Political Unconscious*, p. 279.
3 Conroy, *Modernism and Authority*, pp. 95–6.
4 Joseph Conrad, *A Set of Six* (London: Dent, 1923), p. 10.
5 Robert Hampson, 'Conrad and the Formation of Legends', in *Conrad's Literary Career*, ed. Keith Carabine, Owen Knowles, and Wiesław Krajka (Lublin: Maria Curie-Skłodowska University, 1992), p. 177.
6 Joseph Conrad, *Tales of Hearsay* (London: Dent, 1928), p. 15.
7 John Crompton, 'Conrad and Colloquialism', in Carabine, Knowles, and Krajka (eds.), *Conrad's Literary Career*, p. 221.
8 Joel Fineman, 'The History of the Anecdote: Fiction and Fiction', in *The New Historicism*, ed. H. Aram Veeser (London: Routledge, 1989), pp. 49–76; John Lee, 'The Man who Mistook his Hat: Stephen Greenblatt and the Anecdote', *Essays in Criticism* 45 (1995), 285–300.
9 Hampson, 'Conrad and the Formation of Legends', p. 173.
10 Robert Holton, *Jarring Witnesses: Modern Fiction and the Representation of History* (New York: Harvester Wheatsheaf, 1994), p. 62.
11 Holton, *Jarring Witnesses*, p. 92.
12 Gordon, *Gossip and Subversion*, p. 7.
13 Hugh Epstein, 'Trusting in Words of Some Sort: Aspects of the Use of Language in *Nostromo*', *The Conradian* 12 (1987), 20.
14 Bakhtin, 'Discourse in the Novel', in *The Dialogic Imagination*, p. 293.
15 Edward Said, *Beginnings: Intention and Method* (New York: Basic Books, 1975), p. 106.
16 Fogel, *Coercion to Speak*, p. 96.
17 The term is introduced and defined by Bakhtin in 'Forms of Time and of the Chronotope in the Novel', in *The Dialogic Imagination*, pp. 84–5. See Bruce Henricksen, *Nomadic Voices: Conrad and the Subject of Narrative* (Urbana: University of Illinois Press, 1992), ch. 4, for a different view of the 'chronotopes' of *Nostromo*.

8. LINGUISTIC DYSTOPIA: *THE SECRET AGENT*

1 Geoffrey Galt Harpham, 'Abroad Only by a Fiction: Creation, Irony, and Necessity in Conrad's *The Secret Agent*', *Representations* 37 (1992), 97.
2 Andrew Michael Roberts, '"What Else Could I Tell Him": Confessing to Men and Lying to Women in Conrad's Fiction', *L'Epoque Conradienne* 19 (1993), 7–23.
3 Straus, 'The Exclusion of the Intended from Secret Sharing in Conrad's *Heart of Darkness*', p. 126.

4 John Hagan Jr, 'The Design of Conrad's *The Secret Agent*', *ELH* 22 (1955), 148–64.

5 In *Conrad: The Critical Heritage*, pp. 186–9.

6 Letter to Methuen of 7 November 1906, in Conrad,*Collected Letters*, III, 370–1.

7 Brian W. Schaffer, '"The Commerce of Shady Wares": Politics and Pornography in Conrad's *The Secret Agent*', *ELH* 62 (1995), 443–66.

8 Paul Armstrong, 'The Politics of Irony in Reading Conrad', *Conradiana* 26 (1994), 85–101; Jacques Berthoud in *The Cambridge Companion to Joseph Conrad*, ch. 6. For Armstrong, the novel draws the reader into a series of hermeneutic dilemmas: suspicion (exemplified by the narrator's 'sarcastic disdain' for Verloc) is inadequate because it undermines solidarity and fellow-feeling, whereas trust, sympathy, and compassion (exemplified by Stevie) can betray the individual into a vulnerable and debilitating naïveté. Berthoud's focus on the liberal reader is more historically specific. Conrad's circle of left-leaning friends and correspondents – Galsworthy, Garnett, Cunninghame Graham – are taken to be the novel's implied readers; and their 'Edwardian liberal ideology' is subverted by a text whose 'presentation of suffering … constitutes a rebuttal of the sentimentalism and patronage that characterizes well-bred sympathy'.

9 Letter of 13 February 1897 to Edward Garnett, Conrad, *Collected Letters*, II, 339.

10 Erdinast-Vulcan, *Joseph Conrad and the Modern Temper*, p. 5n.

11 Ibid., p. 5n; Daniel R. Schwarz, *Conrad: 'Almayer's Folly' to 'Under Western Eyes'* (Ithaca, NY: Cornell University Press, 1980), p. 160; Muriel Bradbrook, *Joseph Conrad: Poland's English Genius* (Cambridge University Press, 1941; repr. New York: Russell and Russell, 1965), p. 50.

12 Walter Bagehot, *Literary Studies*, 2 vols. (London: Dent, 1911), II, 176.

13 For further remarks on the affinity between novels and newspapers, see Conroy, *Modernism and Authority*, pp. 152–5.

14 'The treatment [of Ossipon and fellow delinquents] oozes disgust: disgust, in part, at its own failure to be fully, uniquely ironic … [D]isgust becomes a matter of form rather than content, because it is directed at vulgar techniques of representation which the ironist had thought to expel from his writing, but in the end must rely on.' David Trotter, *The English Novel in History, 1895–1920* (London: Routledge, 1993), pp. 256–7.

15 Jean Baudrillard, *The Transparency of Evil: Essays on Extreme Phenomena*, tr. James Benedict (London: Verso, 1993), pp. 75–6.

16 Watts, *Conrad's 'Heart of Darkness'*, p. 79.

17 Fogel, *Coercion to Speak*, pp. 155–6.

18 Frederic Jameson, *The Geopolitical Aesthetic: Cinema and Space in the World System* (London: BFI Publishing, 1992), p. 15.

19 Jameson, *The Geopolitical Aesthetic*, p. 33.

20 Jacques Berthoud, *Joseph Conrad: The Major Phase* (Cambridge University Press, 1978), ch. 6.

21 'In *The Secret Agent*, writes J. Hillis Miller, 'Conrad's voice and the voice of the darkness most nearly become one.' *Poets of Reality: Six Twentieth-Century Writers* (Cambridge, MA: Harvard University Press, 1966), p. 39.

22 Leavis, *The Great Tradition*, p. 244.

9. 'GOSSIP, TALES, SUSPICIONS': LANGUAGE AND PARANOIA IN *UNDER WESTERN EYES*

1 Key re-evaluations of the novel include Avrom Fleishman, 'Speech and Writing in *Under Western Eyes*', in *Joseph Conrad: A Commemoration*, ed. Sherry, pp. 119–29; Frank Kermode, 'Secrets and Narrative Sequence', in *Essays on Fiction, 1971–1982* (London: Routledge and Kegan Paul, 1983), pp. 133–55; Penn R. Szittya, 'Metafiction: The Double Narration in *Under Western Eyes*', *ELH* 48 (1981), 817–40.

2 Fogel, *Coercion to Speak*, p. 207.

3 Hans-Georg Gadamer, 'The Hermeneutics of Suspicion', in *Hermeneutics: Questions and Prospects*, ed. Gary Shapiro and Alan Sica (Amherst: University of Massachusetts Press, 1984), p. 58.

4 Ibid., p. 54.

5 Ibid., p. 63.

6 Fogel, *Coercion to Speak*, p. 184.

7 Terence Cave, *Recognitions: A Study in Poetics* (Oxford: Clarendon Press, 1988), p. 472.

8 'Nightmare and Complacency – Razumov and the Western Eye', in *Conrad: 'Heart of Darkness', 'Nostromo' and 'Under Western Eyes'*, Macmillan Casebooks, ed. C. B. Cox (London: Macmillan, 1981), pp. 163–85. One of the few critics to credit the professor with any intelligence is Jacques Berthoud: '[W]hat he represents in the novel is the power of rationality. His reiterated confessions of incompetence or bafflement when confronted by the effusions of the Russian mind are not without some overtone of Socratic irony.' *Joseph Conrad: The Major Phase*, p. 163. Keith Carabine argues that the disagreements over the professor stem from ignorance of the way he *accumulated* different functions through successive revisions: *The Life and the Art: A Study of Conrad's 'Under Western Eyes'* (Amsterdam: Rodopi, 1996), pp. 209–22.

9 I have derived the concept of a 'textual unconscious' from Claude Maisonnat's remarks on multilingualism in *Almayer's Folly*: 'If in the end, the English text appears to be the translation of discourses held in Dutch, Malay, Arab or Chinese, then the narrative must unavoidably be described as a palimpsest, the English version being the visible part and the previous texts in the other languages being imperfectly erased as if they were repressed into the unconscious, struggling all the while to return to the conscious.' *'Almayer's Folly*: A Voyage Through Many Tongues', p. 46.

10 Kermode, 'Secrets and Narrative Sequence', p. 140; David Leon Higdon, '"His Helpless Prey": Conrad and the Aggressive Text', *The Conradian* 12

(1987), 108–21; Allan Hepburn, 'Above Suspicion: Audience and Deception in *Under Western Eyes*', *Studies in the Novel* 24 (1992), 282–97, p. 295.

11 Berthoud, *Joseph Conrad: The Major Phase*, p. 183.

12 Conrad, *The Arrow of Gold*, p. 100.

13 Jeremy Hawthorn, *Joseph Conrad: Narrative Technique and Ideological Commitment* (London: Arnold, 1990), ch. 9, contains a detailed analysis of the 'expressive body' in the novel.

14 Fogel, *Coercion to Speak*, p. 181.

15 Paul Kirschner, in a valuable discussion of dialogue and space in the novel, argues that 'the decisive compositional elements are not love-interest and plot but conflicting ideas and places for discussing and debating them: the narrative is, in a word, *topodialogic* . . . If we look at the various itineraries followed by the novel . . . we cannot help seeing that after the first one, from the Russian church to the Haldins' apartment, they are all on foot and progressively longer, "taking in" more and more of the town in greater and greater detail.' 'Topodialogic Narrative in *Under Western Eyes* and the Rasoumoffs of "La Petite Russie"', in *Conrad's Cities: Essays for Hans van Marle*, ed. Gene M. Moore (Amsterdam: Rodopi, 1992), pp. 223–54.

16 Cave, *Recognitions*, p. 479.

17 See Szittya, 'Metafiction', pp. 818–19.

18 In *The History of Sexuality*, 3 vols., tr. Robert Hurley (London: Allen Lane, 1979), I, 59, Foucault claims that 'Western man has become a confessing animal.'

19 '[H]is final deafness', writes Owen Knowles, 'is a symbol of both his free-dom from the toils of a poisonously corrupted language and his ability to commune with inner silences.' '"To Make You Hear . . . ": Some Aspects of Conrad's Dialogue', p. 174.

20 Jocelyn Baines, *Joseph Conrad: A Critical Biography* (London: Weidenfeld and Nicolson, 1960), pp. 370–1.

21 David Garnett, *The Golden Echo* (London: Chatto and Windus, 1954), pp. 19–20.

CONCLUSION

1 Victor Shklovsky, 'Sterne's *Tristram Shandy*: Stylistic Commentary', in *Russian Formalist Criticism: Four Essays*, ed. and tr. Lee T. Lemon and Marion J. Reis (Lincoln: University of Nebraska Press, 1965), p. 57.

2 T. S. Eliot, 'The Metaphysical Poets', in *Selected Essays* (London: Faber and Faber, 1951), p. 289.

3 *The Intellectuals and the Masses: Pride and Prejudice Among the Literary Intelligentsia, 1880–1939* (London: Faber and Faber, 1992).

Bibliography

All references to Conrad's fiction and essays are to the Uniform Edition (London: Dent, 1923–8). Other editions that I have consulted are included in the bibliography of secondary texts under the names of their respective editors.

Achebe, Chinua, 'An Image of Africa: Racism in Conrad's *Heart of Darkness*', in *Hopes and Impediments* (London: Heinemann, 1988), pp. 1–13.

Armstrong, Paul, *The Challenge of Bewilderment: Understanding and Representation in James, Conrad, and Ford* (Ithaca: Cornell University Press, 1987).

'Conrad's Contradictory Politics: The Ontology of Society in *Nostromo*', *Twentieth Century Literature* 31 (1985), 1–21.

'The Politics of Irony in Reading Conrad', *Conradiana* 26 (1994), 85–101.

Auden, W. H. 'The Joker in the Pack', in *The Dyer's Hand* (London: Faber and Faber, 1962), pp. 246–72.

Bagehot, Walter, *Literary Studies*, 2 vols. (London: Dent, 1911).

Baines, Jocelyn, *Joseph Conrad: A Critical Biography* (London: Weidenfeld and Nicolson, 1960).

Bakhtin, Mikhail, *The Dialogic Imagination: Four Essays*, ed. Michael Holquist, tr. Caryl Emerson and Michael Holquist (Austin: University of Texas Press, 1981).

Problems of Dostoevsky's Poetics, tr. R. W. Rotsel (Ann Arbor, MI: Ardis, 1973).

Rabelais and His World, tr. Helene Iswolsky (Cambridge, MA: MIT Press, 1968).

Speech Genres and Other Late Essays, ed. Caryl Emerson and Michael Holquist, tr. Vern W. McGee (Austin: University of Texas Press, 1986).

Barthes, Roland, *Image/Music/Text*, tr. Stephen Heath (Glasgow: Fontana, 1977).

A Lover's Discourse: Fragments, tr. Richard Howard (London: Cape, 1979).

The Pleasure of the Text, tr. Richard Miller (London: Cape, 1976).

Roland Barthes par Roland Barthes (Paris: Editions du Seuil, 1975).

Batchelor, John, *The Edwardian Novelists* (London: Duckworth, 1982).

The Life of Joseph Conrad (Oxford: Blackwell, 1994).

'Lord Jim' (London: Unwin, 1988).

(ed.), *Lord Jim* (Oxford University Press, 1983).

(ed.), *Victory* (Oxford University Press, 1986).

Baudrillard, Jean, *The Transparency of Evil: Essays on Extreme Phenomena*, tr. James Benedict (London: Verso, 1993).

Beer, Gillian, 'Circulatory Systems: Money, Gossip, and Blood in *Middlemarch*', in *Arguing with the Past: Essays in Narrative from Woolf to Sidney* (London: Routledge, 1989), pp. 99–116.

Benjamin, Walter, *Illuminations*, ed. Hannah Arendt, tr. Harry Zohn (London: Fontana, 1973).

Berthoud, Jacques, *Joseph Conrad: The Major Phase* (Cambridge University Press, 1978).

'Narrative and Ideology: A Critique of Frederic Jameson's *The Political Unconscious*', in *Narrative: From Malory to Motion Pictures*, ed. Jeremy Hawthorn (London: Edward Arnold, 1985), pp. 101–15.

(ed.), *The Nigger of the 'Narcissus'* (Oxford University Press, 1984).

Bhabha, Homi K. (ed.), *Nation and Narration* (London: Routledge, 1990).

Billy, Ted (ed.), *Critical Essays on Joseph Conrad* (Boston, MA: G. K. Hall, 1987).

Bonney, William W., 'Joseph Conrad and the Betrayal of Language', *Nineteenth-Century Fiction* 34 (1979), 127–53.

Bradbrook, Muriel, *Joseph Conrad: Poland's English Genius* (Cambridge University Press, 1941; repr. New York: Russell and Russell, 1965).

Brantlinger, Patrick, *Rule of Darkness: British Literature and Imperialism, 1830–1914* (Ithaca: Cornell University Press, 1988).

Brooks, Peter, 'An Unreadable Report: Conrad's *Heart of Darkness*', in *Reading for the Plot: Design and Intention in Narrative* (Oxford: Clarendon Press, 1984), pp. 238–63.

Busza, Andrzej, 'Conrad's Polish Literary Background and some Illustrations of the Influence of Polish Literature on his Work', *Antemurale* 10 (1966), 109–255.

Carabine, Keith, *The Life and the Art: A Study of Conrad's 'Under Western Eyes'* (Amsterdam: Rodopi, 1996).

Carabine, Keith, Owen Knowles, and Wiesław Krajka (eds.), *Conrad's Literary Career* (Lublin: Maria Curie-Skłodowska University, 1992).

(eds.), *Contexts for Conrad* (Lublin: Maria Curie-Skłodowska University, 1993).

Carey, John, *The Intellectuals and the Masses: Pride and Prejudice Among the Literary Intelligentsia, 1880–1939* (London: Faber and Faber 1992).

Cave, Terence, *Recognitions: A Study in Poetics* (Oxford: Clarendon Press, 1988).

Conrad, Joseph, *The Collected Letters of Joseph Conrad*, ed. Frederick R. Karl and Laurence Davies, 8 vols. (Cambridge University Press, 1983–).

Joseph Conrad's Letters to R. B. Cunninghame Graham, ed. Cedric Watts (Cambridge University Press, 1969).

Joseph Conrad: Letters to William Blackwood and David S. Meldrum, ed. William Blackburn (Durham, NC: Duke University Press, 1958).

Letters from Joseph Conrad, 1895–1924, ed. Edward Garnett (London: Nonesuch, 1928).

Conroy, Mark, 'Ghostwriting (In) "Karain"', *The Conradian* 18 (1994), 1–16.

Modernism and Authority: Strategies of Legitimation in Flaubert and Conrad (Baltimore: Johns Hopkins University Press, 1985).

Cox, C. B. (ed.), *Conrad: 'Heart of Darkness', 'Nostromo' and 'Under Western Eyes'*, Macmillan Casebooks (London: Macmillan, 1981).

Joseph Conrad: The Modern Imagination (London: Dent, 1974).

Culler, Jonathan, *On Deconstruction: Theory and Criticism after Structuralism* (London: Routledge, 1983).

Cunningham, Valentine, *In the Reading Gaol: Postmodernity, Texts, and History* (Oxford: Blackwell, 1994).

Derrida, Jacques, *Dissemination*, tr. Barbara Johnson (London: Athlone Press, 1981).

Margins of Philosophy, tr. Alan Bass (Sussex: Harvester Press, 1982).

Of Grammatology, tr. Gayatri Chakravorty Spivak (Baltimore: Johns Hopkins University Press, 1976).

Speech and Phenomena, tr. David B. Allison (Evanston: Northwestern University Press, 1973).

Dilworth, Thomas, 'Listeners and Lies in "Heart of Darkness"', *Review of English Studies* 38 (1987), 510–22.

Duncan-Jones, E. E., 'Some Sources of *Chance*', *Review of English Studies* 20 (1969), 468–71.

Eagleton, Terry, *Criticism and Ideology* (London: Verso, 1978).

Exiles and Emigrés (London: Chatto and Windus, 1970).

Edel, Leon, 'A Master Mariner', in *Henry James: The Master, 1901–1916* (London: Hart-Davis, 1972), pp. 46–55.

Eliot, T. S., *Selected Essays* (London: Faber and Faber, 1951).

Epstein, Hugh, 'Trusting in Words of Some Sort: Aspects of the Use of Language in *Nostromo*', *The Conradian* 12 (1987), 17–31.

Erdinast-Vulcan, Daphna, *Joseph Conrad and the Modern Temper* (Oxford: Clarendon Press, 1991).

Fineman, Joel, 'The History of the Anecdote: Fiction and Fiction', in *The New Historicism*, ed. H. Aram Veeser (London: Routledge, 1989), pp. 49–76.

'Shakespeare's Ear', in *The New Historicism Reader*, ed. H. Aram Veeser. (London: Routledge, 1994), pp. 116–23.

Fiumara, Gemma Corradi, *The Other Side of Language: A Philosophy of Listening*, tr. Charles Lambert (London: Routledge, 1990).

Fogel, Aaron, *Coercion to Speak: Conrad's Poetics of Dialogue* (Cambridge, MA: Harvard University Press, 1985).

Ford, Ford Madox, *Joseph Conrad: A Personal Remembrance* (London: Duckworth, 1924).

Forster, E. M., 'Joseph Conrad: A Note' (1929), in *Abinger Harvest* (London: Arnold, 1940), pp. 134–8.

Fothergill, Anthony, *'Heart of Darkness'* (Milton Keynes: Open University Press, 1989).

Foucault, Michel, *The History of Sexuality*, vol. I, tr. Robert Hurley (London: Allen Lane, 1979).

'What Is an Author?', in *Language, Counter-Memory, Practice*, tr. Donald F. Bouchard and Sherry Simon (Oxford: Blackwell, 1977), pp. 113–38.

Fraser, Gail, 'Mediating Between the Sexes: Conrad's *Chance*', *Review of English Studies* 43 (1992), 81–8.

Gadamer, Hans-Georg, 'The Hermeneutics of Suspicion', in *Hermeneutics: Questions and Prospects*, ed. Gary Shapiro and Alan Sica (Amherst: University of Massachusetts Press, 1984), pp. 54–65.

Garnett, David, *The Golden Echo* (London: Chatto and Windus, 1954).

Gilbert, Sandra M. and Susan Gubar, *The Madwoman in the Attic: The Woman Writer in the Nineteenth Century Literary Imagination* (New Haven: Yale University Press, 1979).

Gluckman, Max, 'Gossip and Scandal', *Current Anthropology* 4 (1963), 307–16.

Gordon, Jan B., *Gossip and Subversion in Nineteenth-Century British Fiction: Echo's Economies* (London: Macmillan, 1996).

Guerard, Albert J., *Conrad the Novelist* (Cambridge, MA: Harvard University Press, 1958).

Hagan Jr, John, 'The Design of Conrad's *The Secret Agent*', *ELH* 22 (1955), 148–64.

Hampson, Robert, '*Chance*: The Affair of the Purloined Brother', *The Conradian* 6 (1980), 5–15.

(ed.), *Heart of Darkness* (Harmondsworth: Penguin, 1995).

'"Heart of Darkness" and "The Speech that Cannot be Silenced"', *English* 39 (Spring 1990), 15–32.

Joseph Conrad: Betrayal and Identity (New York: St Martin's Press, 1992).

Hardy, Barbara, *Tellers and Listeners: The Narrative Imagination* (London: Athlone Press, 1975).

Harpham, Geoffrey Galt, 'Abroad Only by a Fiction: Creation, Irony, and Necessity in Conrad's *The Secret Agent*', *Representations* 37 (Winter 1992), 79–103.

One of Us: The Mastery of Joseph Conrad (University of Chicago Press, 1996).

Hawthorn, Jeremy, *Joseph Conrad: Language and Fictional Self-Consciousness* (London: Arnold, 1979).

Joseph Conrad: Narrative Technique and Ideological Commitment (London: Arnold, 1990).

Hay, Eloise Knapp, *The Political Novels of Joseph Conrad: A Critical Study* (University of Chicago Press, 1963; second edition, 1981).

Heidegger, Martin, *Being and Time*, tr. John Macquarrie and Edward Robinson (Oxford: Blackwell, 1962).

Henricksen, Bruce, *Nomadic Voices: Conrad and the Subject of Narrative* (Urbana: University of Illinois Press, 1992).

Hepburn, Allan, 'Above Suspicion: Audience and Deception in *Under Western Eyes*', *Studies in the Novel* 24 (1992), 282–97.

Hervouet, Yves, 'Conrad and the French Language', *Conradiana* 11 (1979), 229–51 and 14 (1982), 23–49.

Hewitt, Douglas, *Conrad: A Reassessment* (Cambridge: Bowes and Bowes, 1952).

Higdon, David Leon, '"His Helpless Prey": Conrad and the Aggressive Text', *The Conradian* 12 (1987), 108–21.

Holton, Robert, *Jarring Witnesses: Modern Fiction and the Representation of History* (New York: Harvester Wheatsheaf, 1994).

Ihde, Don, *Listening and Voice: A Phenomenology of Sound* (Ohio University Press, 1976).

Illich, Ivan and Barry Sanders, *ABC: The Alphabetization of the Popular Mind* (San Francisco: North Point Press, 1988).

James, Henry, *Selected Literary Criticism*, ed. Morris Shapira (Cambridge University Press, 1981).

Jameson, Frederic, *The Geopolitical Aesthetic: Cinema and Space in the World System* (London: BFI Publishing, 1992).

The Political Unconscious: Narrative as a Socially Symbolic Act (London: Methuen, 1981).

Jean-Aubry, G. (ed.), *Joseph Conrad: Life and Letters*, 2 vols. (London: Heinemann, 1927).

Johnson, Bruce, *Conrad's Models of Mind* (Minneapolis: University of Minnesota Press, 1971).

Jones, Susan, *Conrad and Women* (Oxford University Press, 1999).

Jordan, Elaine (ed.), *Joseph Conrad*, New Casebooks (London: Macmillan, 1996).

Karl, Frederick R. (ed.), *Joseph Conrad: A Collection of Criticism* (New York: McGraw-Hill, 1975).

Joseph Conrad: The Three Lives (London: Faber and Faber, 1979).

Kermode, Frank, *Essays on Fiction, 1971–82* (London: Routledge and Kegan Paul, 1983).

The Genesis of Secrecy: On the Interpretation of Narrative (Cambridge, MA: Harvard University Press, 1979).

Kierkegaard, Søren, *The Two Ages*, ed. and tr. Howard V. Hong and Edna H. Hong (Princeton University Press, 1978).

Kirschner, Paul, *Joseph Conrad: The Psychologist as Artist* (Edinburgh: Oliver and Boyd, 1968).

Knowles, Owen, *An Annotated Critical Bibliography of Joseph Conrad* (Hemel Hempstead: Harvester Press, 1992).

'"To Make You Hear . . .": Some Aspects of Conrad's Dialogue', *The Polish Review* 20 (1975), 164–80.

'The Year's Work in Conrad Studies, 1985: A Survey of Periodical Literature', *The Conradian* 11 (1986), 57–71.

Leavis, F. R., *The Great Tradition* (London: Chatto and Windus, 1948; repr. Harmondsworth: Penguin, 1983).

Lee, John, 'The Man who Mistook his Hat: Stephen Greenblatt and the Anecdote', *Essays in Criticism* 45 (1995), 285–300.

Lemon, Lee T. and Marion J. Reis (eds.), *Russian Formalist Criticism: Four Essays* (Lincoln: University of Nebraska Press, 1965).

Levenson, Michael, 'The Value of Facts in the *Heart of Darkness*', *Nineteenth-Century Fiction* 40 (1985), 261–280.

Lodge, David (ed.), *Modern Criticism and Theory: A Reader* (London: Longman, 1988).

London, Bette, *The Appropriated Voice: Narrative Authority in Conrad, Forster, and Woolf* (Ann Arbor: University of Michigan Press, 1990).

Lothe, Jakob, *Conrad's Narrative Method* (Oxford: Clarendon Press, 1989).

Macovski, Michael S., *Dialogue and Literature: Apostrophe, Auditors, and the Collapse of Romantic Discourse* (Oxford University Press, 1994).

Maissonat, Claude, '*Almayer's Folly*: A Voyage Through Many Tongues', *L'Epoque Conradienne* 16 (1990), 39–49.

McLauchlan, Juliet, *Conrad: 'Nostromo'* (London: Edward Arnold, 1969).

Miller, D. A., *Narrative and Its Discontents: Problems of Closure in the Traditional Novel* (Princeton University Press, 1981).

Miller, J. Hillis, *Fiction and Repetition: Seven English Novels* (Oxford: Blackwell, 1982).

　Poets of Reality: Six Twentieth-Century Writers (Cambridge, MA: Harvard University Press, 1966).

Moore, Gene M., 'Chronotopes and Voices in *Under Western Eyes*', *Conradiana* 18 (1986), 9–25.

　(ed.), *Conrad's Cities: Essays for Hans van Marle* (Amsterdam: Rodopi, 1992).

Moser, Thomas C., *Joseph Conrad: Achievement and Decline* (Hamden, CT: Archon Books, 1966).

Mudrick, Marvin (ed.), *Conrad: A Collection of Critical Essays* (New Jersey: Prentice-Hall, 1966).

Murfin, Ross C. (ed.), *Conrad Revisited: Essays for the Eighties* (Birmingham: University of Alabama Press, 1985).

Nadelhaft, Ruth, *Joseph Conrad* (Hemel Hempstead: Harvester Wheatsheaf, 1991).

Najder, Zdzisław, *Joseph Conrad: A Chronicle*, tr. Halina Carroll-Najder (Cambridge University Press, 1983).

　(ed.), *Conrad's Polish Background: Letters to and from Polish Friends*, tr. Halina Carroll (London: Oxford University Press, 1964).

Paine, Robert, 'What Is Gossip About? An Alternative Hypothesis', *Man* 2 (1967), 278–85.

Parry, Benita, *Conrad and Imperialism: Ideological Boundaries and Visionary Frontiers* (London: Macmillan, 1983).

Pecora, Vincent, '*Heart of Darkness* and the Phenomenology of Voice', *ELH* 52 (1985), 993–1015.

Pousada, Alicia, 'Joseph Conrad's Multilingualism: A Case Study of Language Planning in Literature', *English Studies* 75 (1994), 335–49.

Pratt, Mary Louise, 'Linguistic Utopias', in *The Linguistics of Writing: Arguments between Language and Literature*, ed. Nigel Fabb, Derek Attridge, Alan Durant, and Colin MacCabe (Manchester University Press, 1987), pp. 48–66.

Ray, Martin (ed.), *Chance* (Oxford University Press, 1988).

　'The Gift of Tongues: The Languages of Joseph Conrad', *Conradiana* 15 (1983), 83–109.

　Joseph Conrad (London: Arnold, 1993).

　(ed.), *Joseph Conrad: Interviews and Recollections* (London: Macmillan, 1990).

Reeves, Charles Eric, 'A Voice of Unrest: Conrad's Rhetoric of the Unspeakable', *Texas Studies in Literature and Language* 27 (1985), 284–310.

Roberts, Andrew Michael (ed.), *Conrad and Gender* (Amsterdam: Rodopi, 1993).

'The Gaze and the Dummy: Sexual Politics in *The Arrow of Gold*', in *Joseph Conrad: Critical Assessments*, ed. Keith Carabine, 4 vols. (Robertsbridge, East Sussex: Helm Information, 1992), III, 528–50.

(ed.), *Joseph Conrad: A Critical Reader*, Longman Critical Readers (London: Longman, 1998).

'"What Else Could I Tell Him?": Confessing to Men and Lying to Women in Conrad's Fiction', *L'Epoque Conradienne* 19 (1993), 7–23.

Said, Edward, *Beginnings: Intention and Method* (New York: Basic Books, 1975).

Culture and Imperialism (London: Chatto and Windus, 1993).

The World, the Text, and the Critic (Cambridge, MA: Harvard University Press, 1983).

Schleifer, Ronald, 'Public and Private Narrative in *Under Western Eyes*', *Conradiana* 9 (1977), 237–54.

Schwarz, Daniel R., *Conrad: 'Almayer's Folly' to 'Under Western Eyes'* (Ithaca, NY: Cornell University Press, 1980).

Conrad: The Later Fiction (London: Macmillan, 1982).

Sedgwick, Eve Kosofsky, *Between Men: English Literature and Male Homosocial Desire* (New York: Columbia University Press, 1985).

Shaffer, Brian W., '"The Commerce of Shady Wares": Politics and Pornography in Conrad's *The Secret Agent*', *ELH* 62 (1995), 443–66.

Sherry, Norman (ed.), *Conrad: The Critical Heritage* (London: Routledge, 1973).

Conrad's Eastern World (Cambridge University Press, 1966).

Conrad's Western World (Cambridge University Press, 1971).

(ed.), *Joseph Conrad: A Commemoration* (London: Macmillan, 1976).

Siegle, Robert, 'The Two Texts of *Chance*', *Conradiana* 16 (1984), 83–101.

The Politics of Reflexivity (Baltimore: Johns Hopkins University Press, 1986).

Simmons, Allan H., '*Under Western Eyes*: The Ludic Text', *The Conradian* 16 (1992), 18–37.

Spacks, Patricia Meyer, *Gossip* (University of Chicago Press, 1985).

Stape, J. H. (ed.), *The Cambridge Companion to Joseph Conrad* (Cambridge University Press, 1996).

Stape, J. H. and Owen Knowles (eds.), *A Portrait in Letters: Correspondence to and about Conrad* (Amsterdam: Rodopi, 1996).

Steiner, George, *After Babel: Aspects of Language and Translation* (London: Oxford University Press, 1975).

Extraterritorial: Papers on Literature and the Language Revolution (London: Faber and Faber, 1972).

Language and Silence (London: Faber and Faber, 1967).

Straus, Nina Pelikan, 'The Exclusion of the Intended from Secret Sharing in Conrad's *Heart of Darkness*', *Novel* 20 (1987), 123–37.

Szittya, Penn R., 'Metafiction: The Double Narration in *Under Western Eyes*', *ELH* 48 (1981), 817–40.

Tanner, Tony, 'Gentlemen and Gossip: Aspects of Evolution and Language in Conrad's *Victory*', *L'Epoque Conradienne* 7 (1981), 1–56.

    'Joseph Conrad and the Last Gentleman', *Critical Quarterly* 28 (1986), 109–42.

    'Lord Jim' (London: Edward Arnold, 1963).

    'Paper Boats and Casual Cradles', *Critical Quarterly* 37 (1995), 42–56.

Tindall, William York, 'Apology for Marlow', in *From Jane Austen to Joseph Conrad*, ed. Robert C. Rathburn and Martin Steinmann (Minneapolis: University of Minnesota Press, 1958), pp. 274–85.

Todorov, Tzvetan, 'Knowledge in the Void: *Heart of Darkness*', *Conradiana* 21 (1989), 161–72.

Trilling, Lionel, *Beyond Culture: Essays on Literature and Learning* (Oxford University Press, 1980).

Trotter, David, *The English Novel in History, 1895–1920* (London: Routledge, 1993).

Verleun, Jan, 'The Changing Face of Charlie Marlow', *The Conradian* 8 (1983), 21–7 and 9 (1984), 15–24.

    'Patna' and Patusan Perspectives (Groningen: Bouma's Boekhuis, 1979).

    The Stone Horse (Groningen: Bouma's Boekhuis, 1978).

Vernon, John, 'Reading, Writing, and Eavesdropping: Some Thoughts on the Nature of Realistic Fiction', *Kenyon Review* 4. 4 (1982), 44–54.

Watt, Ian, *Conrad in the Nineteenth Century* (London: Chatto and Windus, 1980).

    'Conrad, James and *Chance*', in *Imagined Worlds: Essays on Some English Novels and Novelists in Honour of John Butt*, ed. Maynard Mack and Ian Gregor (London: Methuen, 1968), pp. 301–22.

    'Joseph Conrad: Alienation and Commitment', in *The English Mind: Studies in the English Moralists Presented to Basil Wiley*, ed. Hugh Sykes Davies and George Watson (Cambridge University Press, 1964), 257–78.

    'Nostromo' (Cambridge University Press, 1988).

    (ed.) *'The Secret Agent': A Casebook* (London: Macmillan, 1973).

Watts, Cedric, '"A Bloody Racist": About Achebe's View of Conrad', *Yearbook of English Studies* 13 (1983), 196–209.

    Conrad's 'Heart of Darkness': A Critical and Contextual Discussion (Milan: Mursia International, 1977).

    The Deceptive Text: An Introduction to Covert Plots (Sussex: Harvester Press, 1984).

    Joseph Conrad: A Literary Life (London: Macmillan, 1989).

    A Preface to Conrad (London: Longman, 1993).

Welsh, Alexander, *George Eliot and Blackmail* (Cambridge, MA: Harvard University Press, 1985).

White, Allon, *The Uses of Obscurity: The Fiction of Early Modernism* (London: Routledge and Kegan Paul, 1981).

Wilding, Michael, 'The Politics of *Nostromo*', *Essays in Criticism* 16 (1966), 441–56.

Williams, Raymond, *The Country and the City* (London: Hogarth, 1985).

    The English Novel from Dickens to Lawrence (London: Chatto and Windus, 1970).

Index